In the early 1910s, my mother, Alice Irene Dibert (the second of three girls dressed in white), attended the Dibert Family Reunion. I'm fascinated by this scene. The men, seated at the long middle table, have been served by the women, standing by their wicker food baskets. In my mother's family, this custom of women not eating with the rest of the family continued into the 1960s. At dinners with her brother's and sister's families, Aunt Gladys or Aunt Mary, always attentive to others, ate their dinners after we left.

preserving memories

# preserving memories:

## recollections and recipes
## from family and friends

joanne fletcher slaughter

*preserving memories: recollections and recipes from family and friends* reflects the author's present recollections of her life. In this book, the author has done her best to impart accurate facts.

Copyright © 2019 by Gary Slaughter Corporation. All rights reserved. No part of this publication may be reproduced, stored in a retrieval system, or transmitted in any form or by any means, electronic, mechanical, photocopying, recording, or otherwise, without prior written permission of Gary Slaughter Corporation.

Layout and design: Publish & Launch
Cover design: Damonza
Publicity: JKS Communications


Publisher's Cataloging-in-Publication Data

Names: Slaughter, Joanne Fletcher, author.
Title: Preserving memories: recollections and recipes from
   family and friends / Joanne Fletcher Slaughter.
Description: Nashville, TN : Fletcher House, 2019. | Includes
   index. | Illustrated; 31 b&w photos. | Summary:
   Recollections and recipes of the author, friends, and
   family.
Identifiers: LCCN 2019909719 | ISBN 9781733802123
   (softcover)
Subjects: LCSH: Slaughter, Joanne Fletcher -- Biography. |
   Cooking, American. | BISAC: BIOGRAPHY &
   AUTOBIOGRAPHY / Culinary. | BIOGRAPHY &
   AUTOBIOGRAPHY / Personal Memoirs. | BIOGRAPHY &
   AUTOBIOGRAPHY / Women. | COOKING / General.
Classification: LCC TX649.A1 S63 2019 | DDC 641.509 S6--dc23
LC record available at https://lccn.loc.gov/2019909719

Published by Fletcher House
Nashville, TN 37205

I have compiled these vignettes and recipes
to recognize the special people
who have helped me preserve my memories.


I am particularly grateful for those of you
with whom I have shared
close friendships through the decades.


My special thanks to Gary.
Without his encouragement to record my life,
this story would only have been a pleasant memory.

My parents, Alice Irene Dibert and Harry Robert Fletcher, were married on May 3, 1931. They set-up housekeeping in an apartment on Richard Street in Bedford, Pennsylvania. Mother was secretary to Ms. Jesse Barclay, Director of the Bedford County Child Welfare Office. Daddy had recently acquired the Bedford County franchise for the distribution of Sinclair Oil Company products.

# contents

| | | |
|---|---|---|
| a bite of family history | | 2 |
| a slice of my past | | 8 |
| | | |
| category 1 | aperitifs | 14 |
| category 2 | savories | 30 |
| category 3 | breads | 56 |
| category 4 | soups | 76 |
| category 5 | salads | 88 |
| category 6 | sides | 110 |
| category 7 | brunch | 126 |
| category 8 | entrees | |
| | pheasant and chicken | 142 |
| | meat | 154 |
| | seafood | 168 |
| category 9 | preserves | 184 |
| christmas morsels | | 198 |
| category 10 | sweets | |
| | cookies | 212 |
| | desserts | 238 |
| epilogue | | 266 |
| | | |
| index: recipes in alphabetical order | | 269 |
| index: recipes by category | | 273 |
| index: recipes by contributor | | 279 |
| Index: recipes by major ingredient | | 287 |
| index: cookbooks and recipe booklets | | 295 |

Love the curls and hair ribbon! Mother sprayed my sister, Harriet's and my hair with Wave-Set and wound thick strands of hair around her finger. When she pulled her finger out, long, shoulder length curls appeared. During my first grade, my sister, Sharon, was born. While Mother was in the hospital, Daddy had great difficulty creating those curls every morning.

*To ▮... Enjoy!*

# preserving memories:

## recollections and recipes from family and friends

by
joanne fletcher slaughter

*Joanne Fletcher Slaughter*

Indian Eve, Eve Imler, was born in 1740. She was the sister of George Imler, a Revolutionary War patriot and my ancestor, whom I researched for membership in the National Society of the Daughters of the American Revolution.

# a bite of family history

Our ancestors are totally essential to our every waking
moment, although most of us don't even have
the faintest idea about their lives, their trials,
their hardships, or their challenges.
-Anne Lenox

It is indeed a desirable thing to be well-descended,
but the glory belongs to our ancestors.
-Plutarch

Our ancestors lived out of doors. They were as familiar
with the night sky as most of us are
with our favorite television programs.
-Carl Sagan

joanne fletcher slaughter

## A BITE OF FAMILY HISTORY

On June 5, 2019, my application for membership in the National Society of the Daughters of the American Revolution (DAR) was approved. Then, I became a member of the General James Robinson Chapter in Nashville.

As a child, I was familiar with the story of Indian Eve. But I was unsure how I was related to her until I researched my Revolutionary War Patriot, George Michael (Immel) Imler. I discovered that George Imler and Eve Imler were brother and sister. My father (Harry Robert Fletcher) was the great, great-great-great grandson of Eve.

### George Michael (Immel) (Imler)

George Michael (Immel) Imler, was born in 1739 in York County, Pennsylvania. His father, Errich Mens Immel, was born in Bavaria, Germany, in 1705. He came to America on the ship, *Mary*, from Rotterdam, Holland, and landed in Philadelphia, Pennsylvania on September 22, 1732. Later, he changed his name to Isach Marcus Imler.

In 1763, his son, George Michael Imler, a farmer, moved to Bedford County and married Catharina Walter. During the Revolutionary War, Private Imler served in Captain Hermann's Company of the York County Militia.

According to George's will, when he died, he owned a "plantation" of 300 acres, 50 acres of mountain timber land, and a "mansion" that went to his two sons, John and Jacob. He also owned 300 acres in Greenfield Township that went to his son, Peter, and a tract of land in Ohio went to his son, Henry.

George died on February 23, 1816, in Dutch Corner, Bedford County, Pennsylvania, and is buried in the George Michael Imler Family Cemetery on Imlertown Road, Bedford Township, Bedford, Pennsylvania.

### Eve Imler Earnest (Indian Eve)

Eve Imler was born in 1740. She married Adam Henry Earnest. During the Revolutionary War, Adam and Eve Earnest built a cabin north of old Fort Bedford along Dunnings Creek, nine miles north of Bedford. They had six children: Johannas, George, Mary, Jacob, Henry, and Michael. They cleared

## A BITE OF FAMILY HISTORY

the land, grew grain for food and flax for clothing, and split rails for fences.

One autumn morning in 1777, several neighbors came to the Earnest home to help split rails. While they were at work, Indians arrived and attacked the group. Unable to reach their guns in time, the men were killed and scalped by the Indians. Young George managed to escape from the cabin and flee. Fearing that the Indians would burn the cabin, Eve went to the loft and put her children, Mary and Jacob, out on the roof. Mary ran away and escaped while Jacob hid in the tall weeds. Johannas also managed to escape.

Eve had been weaving a coverlet on her loom. The Indians took a fancy to it and cut it out of the loom. While the Indians were arguing about who should get the coverlet, Eve hid her husband's scalp and one of the others. When the Indians realized that the scalps were missing, they took this as a bad omen and left abruptly. They took the remaining scalp, cutting it into several pieces so it would look as though they had killed many men. Eve along with her children, Henry and Michael, were forced to go with the Indians.

People from Fort Bedford followed the Indian group. The Indians eluded the searchers by hiding in hollow trees. They traveled through Indian Path Valley and on through Blair County over an old Indian trail through the gorge at Kittanning Point. Eve carried the children on her back most of the way. They were treated well by the Indians, and, if the Indians had plenty, Eve and the other captives shared their food.

During the Revolutionary War, the British forces at Fort Detroit in Michigan encouraged the Indians to harass the white settlements in Pennsylvania, Ohio, and Virginia, and to capture settlers and take them to Detroit where they were sold to the British. The Indians headed to Fort Detroit with Eve and her sons. The Indians liked Henry whom they referred to as the dark one, but didn't care for Michael who was fair. During the journey to the fort, the Indians taught Henry to ride and shoot with a bow and arrow. They also dressed him in Indian clothing. Upon arrival at the fort, the Indians began negotiations with the British for the sale of their captives. Although the Indians wanted to keep Henry, the British tricked them into selling all three, the mother and her two sons. The Indians stayed

**A BITE OF FAMILY HISTORY**

around the fort and tried to get Henry back. He actually preferred the excitement of the Indian life to the dullness of the fort. Eve had to keep a close watch on Henry so he wouldn't run off with the Indians. Eventually, the Indians gave up and demanded that Henry return his Indian clothing and the bow and arrow.

Eve worked industriously at the fort to pay her ransom. Because she earned more than her daily allowance, she was able to save money.

When she worked harvesting in the fields, Henry kept the crows and black birds off the corn. She made clothes from the cast-off officers' uniforms.

Nine years after Eve and the two boys were taken from their home in Pennsylvania, Eve had earned enough money to pay their ransom. After being released from the British, Eve bought a pony so they could ride back home. At this point, Henry was in his teens, possibly eighteen, and Michael was about eleven. They probably traveled during the summer as the forests would have been marshy and the streams would have been nearly impassable in the winter. They crossed the Allegheny Mountains on the Forbes Road. Eve, eventually, was able to find the home of George, her oldest son.

After Eve returned to Pennsylvania, she was given the name of *Indian Eve.* Her son, George, had married Elizabeth Samuels, daughter of Conrad Samuels. Eve later married Conrad who owned a great deal of land, and they lived in one of the better houses. When Conrad died, he left Eve the house and fifty acres of land.

Messiah Lutheran Church in Bedford Township was a log building, built in 1790. Eve's house was in sight of the church. When the church was being erected, she cooked for the workers and would run a red flag up a pole when the meals were ready.

Eve died in 1815 and was buried at Messiah Lutheran Church.

*This story is summarized from* Indian Eve and Her Descendants, *written by Mrs. Emma Replogle. The book was printed in 1911 by Messiah Lutheran Church.*

In 1941 at our home on Watson Street. Left to Right: Besse Lysinger (our next-door neighbor), me, Aunt Lillian (Daddy's sister) and my sister, Harriet. Our family spent several summer vacations with Aunt Lillian who lived in Atlantic City, a few blocks from the beach. Daddy told us that the waves were not turned on until 10am. We were always relieved to arrive at the Boardwalk and see them crashing onto the sand.

Miss Ross, my first-grade class teacher, always hung our artwork in the classroom. I'm standing to the left of the Mother Goose board. Marjorie Claar is on the right. Norma Lee Gloor has a broken right arm. Alice Carol Foy is next to Fred Heath, reading a book. Jean Diehl is seated in front of Alice Carol.

# a slice of my past

**Life is all memory, except for the one present moment
that goes by you so quickly you hardly catch it going.**
-Tennessee Williams

**Photography was a way for me to freeze time and
to capture the moments that were happy and healthy.
I saw a photo as a way to go back to a memory
if I ever needed to.**
-Rachel Morrison

**Happiness is good health and a bad memory.**
-Ingrid Bergman

## A SLICE OF MY PAST

Certain foods evoke memories of special times with family and friends. I'm sure that you have had similar recollections.

My heritage was Pennsylvania German (colloquially referred to as Pennsylvania Dutch). Intimate thoughts and family interactions were not discussed. Family recipes were also closely guarded, handed down from generation to generation. Sometimes these were purposely shared with an essential ingredient omitted or an inaccurate cup, tablespoon, or teaspoon measure included.

During the 1940s, I was growing up in southwestern Pennsylvania in Bedford County which was both agricultural and historical. My mother found Indian arrowheads on the ground her father had overturned when doing his spring plowing. The bakery in Bedford was headquarters for President George Washington during his move westward to end the Whiskey Rebellion, a tax protest, in the late 1700s. During World War II, the sprawling and elegant Bedford Springs Hotel became a Navy communications school and later the heavily guarded quarters for Japanese diplomats. During the summers, the Bedford Lions Club offered children free swimming lessons at Red Oaks Lake, located on the Springs property.

As a small child in the 1940s, early spring days were spent making mud or sand pies in the back yard under a sprawling apple tree. Early evenings were spent sifting earth through a window-screen that rested on four cinder blocks. This process provided the fine soil for a kitchen garden of lettuce, asparagus, rhubarb, onions, peas, and radishes.

Our large garden, north of Bedford, provided vegetables for canning, freezing, and preserving. During the summer on Saturday afternoons, my sister, Harriet, and I rode in the back of our father's pick-up truck with Daddy, Mother, and my youngest sister, Sharon, in the cab. The entire family was on its way to the garden for the weekly weeding, hoeing, and picking. By July, our truck was constantly filled with bushel baskets of peas to be shelled, beans to be snapped, tomatoes to be canned, corn to be husked, and cucumbers to be processed into pickles.

During this era, if you wanted to buy fruits or vegetables, it was necessary to "engage" (order) them from growers for a specific day and

## A SLICE OF MY PAST

time. We engaged raspberries from Essie Imler. Because I was extremely fond of red raspberries, I was always eager to drive into the country with my mother. On our arrival, Essie, garbed in her bonnet and long dress with apron, entered the gate of her garden and began picking the ordered berries. I always hoped that I would be invited to join her there. Everywhere else, the engaged produce was always ready when you arrived.

The Fourth of July was our annual cherry-picking day in the orchards of nearby Osterburg. Daddy hooked a bucket to his belt and climbed a ladder into the highest part of the trees to find the largest rosy-white Queen Anne or deep-red Bing cherries. Upon returning home, cherry pitting involved the whole family, as cherries were prepared for canning.

The arrival of several crates of blueberries from the Maryland eastern shore always created quite a stir at the post office. These berries were immediately frozen for winter pies. And, an August Sunday might mean a trip east to Chambersburg for peaches and plums. Late summer, found the five of us headed for the blackberry thickets. Daddy always preceded us, beating the bushes with a stick (to flush out the snakes I later discovered). Drives on a country road furnished currents for jelly, essential for jellyrolls. Uncle Ralph, Mother's brother, provided strawberries in spring and grapes in fall for jams and jellies. Fruits and vegetables were always processed immediately upon picking.

Many Sunday dinners were shared an enjoyed with one of Daddy's sisters and their families. On other Sundays, we would drive into the country around Imlertown to visit with Mother's brother, Ralph, or her sister, Mary. A ritual of these trips was visiting their gardens, each with its profusion of flowers and abundance of vegetables. Much conversation centered on the newest seeds, varieties of flowers, techniques of growing, and the latest recipes. Later, trips to my sisters' homes included a visit to their gardens where many flowers were grown from former cuttings of a family member or friend.

An invitation to Sunday dinner at Uncle Ralph's meant chicken and ham along with numerous, tasty side dishes. On summer afternoons, the men gathered in the shed to chat while they hand-cranked fresh peach or

## A SLICE OF MY PAST

strawberry ice cream. To entertain ourselves in this pre-TV era, my sisters and I would retreat to the front porch where we were transported to the church that my father had helped build. We played "church" or wandered through the cemetery where our grandparents were buried. Eventually, everyone gathered around the kitchen table for dishes of smooth, soft ice cream, while Uncle Ralph spooned his from the flyers from inside the ice-cream churn. I thought that eventually my turn for the flyers would come. But it never did.

Before we left, Uncle Ralph cut bouquets of flowers and picked fruit or vegetables for us to take home. Sometimes there would be a visit to his smoke house for ham or bacon that hung from the ceiling. Or, a trip to his hen house to search for fresh eggs.

Each summer, Mother took us to Aunt Mary's for the haying or threshing. The area farmers shared both labor and machinery as they moved from farm to farm. While my mother helped her sister and her nieces prepare the enormous midday meals, we three spent the day outside. With my cousins, we would explore the barns, search through the hay for new litters of kittens, retreat to the coolness of the springhouse for ice-cold water from the pipe, follow the stream through the meadow, or climb trees on the apple orchard on the hill behind the house. After the men had eaten, we took our places for the "second sitting." Desserts were always the highlight at Aunt Mary's. A cool room, behind the dining room, was always filled with a variety of cakes, cookies, and pies.

Late summer Saturday afternoons meant Ice-Cream Socials at the country churches. Long wooden tables punctuated with vases of garden flowers were placed in the churchyard. Each church family provided its special sandwiches, cakes, and freezers of ice cream. Trays, laden with an assortment of each, were passed. On the honor system, ten cents each bought a sandwich, a slice of cake, or a dish of homemade ice cream.

In the fall, Mother went to Aunt Mary's for apple-butter making. The morning was spent preparing applesauce. Cider was added, and the mixture slowly boiled in a huge copper kettle suspended over a wood fire in the side yard.

In the early winter, Mother returned for the butchering. At home in the evening, she and Daddy stuffed the sausage links and canned the

## A SLICE OF MY PAST

links. These jars of sausage, along with canned fruits and vegetables, were stored in the cellar pantry. In this room, the floor-to-ceiling shelves displayed food preserved for winter use. In addition, a root cellar had been dug into the earth under the side porch. Entered from the garage, the room contained bins for apples, potatoes, and nuts. Here we three girls spent long hours in late winter sprouting potatoes or cracking and shelling walnuts. Then, spring arrived and the tradition unfolded once again.

These were the beginnings of familiar foods and recipes collected, destined to be read or prepared and shared with family and friends!

In March 1947, my elementary school presented the operetta, *In the Land of Dreams Come True,* in the Bedford High School Auditorium. In the front row, Lois Hammer, Jim Smith, and I played the part of the children who fell asleep and awakened in *The Land of Dreams Come True*. There, we visited with Mother Goose (Norma Gloor in the center back row), and story-book characters, including Jack and Jill (James Young and Sara Ann Koontz), the Queen of Hearts (Judith Orvatz), Little Boy Blue (John Wright), and Bo Peep (Jane Koozer).

# aperitifs

Their beer was strong; their wine was port;
Their meat was large; their grace was short.
-Matthew Prior

A fruit is a vegetable with looks and money.
Plus, if you let fruit rot, it turns to wine,
Something Brussel sprouts never do.
-P. J. O'Rourke

## APERITIFS

### cranberry cordial.

*In 2003, I was invited to join the Sew 'n Sow Garden Club in Nashville. Our club is structured so that members divide into groups of four or five, select a month (September through May), plan the program, and provide the lunch for that month.*

*When this group was formed in 1976, members' children were in pre-school. In alternate months, the members met to **sew** clothing for their children or to talk about seeds to **sow** in their gardens.*

*In November 2003, Dori Howard's demonstrated "How to Make and Package Cranberry Cordial." Dori's early December tradition was to invite friends to her home to write their personal Christmas cards ... while sipping her Cranberry Cordial.*

| | |
|---|---|
| 1 pkg (12 oz) cranberries | 2 C vodka |
| 1 C sugar | 1 C water |
| 2 C light corn syrup | 1 C brandy (Not fruit flavor.) |

Coarsely chop (pulse) cranberries in a food processor or chop with a knife. Stir the cranberries and sugar in a large bowl until the berries are well coated. Stir in corn syrup, vodka, water, and brandy until blended. Put the mixture into a large glass jar, cover, and store in a cool, dark place for at least a month, stirring and shaking the jar every few days.

Before serving, strain the liquid from the cranberries through a fine strainer or dampened, double cheesecloth. The cordial may be tightly covered and stored at room temperature for up to 3 months. Refrigerate for a longer life and taste. Yield: 4 cups.

*****

*In 1980, Gary and I had purchased townhouses in Chevy Chase, Maryland. We met at a Christmas tree-trimming party for new townhouse owners. Instantly, we enjoyed one another's company and drove to dinner in Gary's car, Rosa (Result of Separation Agreement). As they say in French "tout le monde connait la suite."*

## APERITIFS

### dandelion wine.

*In the early 1900s during May, my mother's brothers, Ralph and Edgar, gathered dandelions to make dandelion wine. This wine fermented in the springhouse until August. After hot afternoons working in the fields, the men popped the cork for a very relaxing end of the day. While this practice was popular on farms in southwestern Pennsylvania, it was definitely frowned upon by the Women's Christian Temperance Union (WCTU) at the time.*

*In the early 1970s, I lived in the Washington, D.C. Maryland suburbs. I put my son, Billy, in his car seat and drove to the area across from Gilbert Grosvenor's (founder of* National Geographic Magazine*) estate, where dandelions grew in profusion. I quickly gathered enough flowers for a batch of dandelion wine. Not a great wine, but in keeping with the family tradition.*

1 gallon boiling water
1 quart dandelion blossoms and stems
3 oranges with rind
3 lemons with rind
3 pounds sugar
1/2 yeast cake

Pour boiling water over dandelions, oranges, and lemons. Allow to stand 3 days. Strain. Add sugar and yeast. Allow to stand 4 to 5 days.

Bottle and cork loosely until fermentation stops. Then, cork tightly and store in a cool place.

joanne fletcher slaughter

**APERITIFS**

**gin cool.**

*Celeste and Ken Lester, our Howell Place neighbors here in Nashville, discovered gin cool during a trip to Sonoma Valley in California. Celeste says, "Besides being tasty, it brings back fond memories."*

*Each spring, she specifically plants basil in her garden for creating this cool treat – to the delight of her friends who enormously enjoy this refreshing summer drink!*

2 oz Hendricks gin
3/4 oz simple syrup
1/2 oz fresh lemon juice
3 blackberries
3 cucumber slices
4 basil leaves

Muddle blackberries, cucumber, and basil. Add to gin, syrup, and lemon juice. Shake ingredients together. Strain over ice.

*****

*The only time I ever enjoyed ironing was the day
I accidentally put gin in the steam iron.
-Phyllis Diller*

**APERITIFS**

### hot mulled cider.

*In 2005, Marguerite Peterseim sponsored me for membership in the Herb Society of Nashville (HSN). HSN members maintain two gardens, one at the Cheekwood Estate and Gardens and the other in Nashville's Centennial Park. HSN's annual April plant sale funds the maintenance of the gardens and provides attendees with information on the culture, harvesting, and use of plants that are sold. The society's annual September Herb Day informs the public on the use of herbs. Sybil Long adapted this recipe, included in the* 2009 HSN Herb Gifts Booklet.

1 gallon unfiltered apple juice
2 apples, sliced thinly
2 oranges, sliced thinly
2 Tbsp Mulled Spice Mix
1-2 bay leaves
1 dash vanilla
Dark rum or brandy
Cinnamon sticks

Pour apple juice into large stainless steel or enamel pan. Add apples, oranges, spice mix, and bay leaves. Bring to a boil and reduce heat. Simmer 30 minutes. Add a dash of vanilla. Strain into cups with a splash of rum or brandy. Stir with cinnamon sticks.

**APERITIFS**

### hot mulled spice mix.

2 C whole coriander seeds
2 C whole Allspice
1 C whole cloves
1/2 C whole Anise seeds
1 C dried mint or Mexican Mint Marigold (optional)
2 C 3-inch cinnamon sticks
1 C dried lemon grass leaves and stalks (optional)
1 C dried orange peel
1 C whole star Anise (optional)

Mix all ingredients together. Package for gift-giving. Keep tightly sealed.

*****

### hot tea toddy.

*From 2008-2010, I chaired the HSN Culinary Committee and planned nine workshops for the members. At* Tea for the Season Workshop *in November 2009, Sarah Scarborough prepared a traditional hot toddy with a twist of spice.*

1 thin slice fresh ginger         1 Tbsp honey
1 cinnamon stick                  1-2 shots brandy
1 sachet of green tea             Slice lemon
6 oz boiling water

Put on a kettle. In a toddy glass, place ginger, cinnamon stick, and tea sachet. Pour boiling water in a glass and steep for 3 minutes. Remove sachet and stir in honey. Add brandy. Serve with a slice of lemon.

# APERITIFS

### infused water.

*In the fall of 2008,* Autumn Sonata, *an HSN culinary workshop, featured savories and sweets, enhanced with herbs from the garden. Arlene Haan created this recipe for infused water to accompany the tasting.*

12 C water
1 medium cucumber
3 thin orange slices
3 thin lemon slices
3 fresh, thin ginger slices
3 fresh sprigs of mint, parsley, rosemary, or cilantro
6 fresh or frozen cranberries

Cut two thin lengthwise slices from cucumber. Stir together cucumber slices with water and remaining ingredients in a pitcher. Cover and chill 1 hour.

*****

### janet's raspberry cordial.

*During* Preserving Summer, *an August 2009 HSN culinary workshop, Janet Exton shared her raspberry cordial recipe. Terrific holiday gift!*

1 pound fresh raspberries          Rind of 1 orange (No pith.)
1 1/2 C sugar                      3 C vodka
1 C brandy

Mash raspberries with sugar and add brandy. Let sit in a cool place 2 or 3 days. Then, add orange rind and vodka. Let stand about 2 weeks before straining and filtering. Store in a cool place.

**APERITIFS**

### kalua.

*In 1979, the Women's Suburban Democratic Club (WSDC), located in Montgomery County, Maryland, launched a cookbook,* Democratic Delectables, *as a fundraiser. I collected the recipes and edited the book. Today, of course, the internet provides many different recipes for home-made Kahlua. Adele Derman provided her Kahlua recipe for the book.*

2 C boiling water
1 jar (2 oz) instant coffee
4 C sugar
1 1/2 pints brandy
1 vanilla bean

Mix 8/10 jar of instant coffee into boiling water. While boiling, add sugar. Cool for 3/4 hours. Pour into 1/2 gallon bottle or jug. Add brandy and vanilla bean. Cap mixture and refrigerate for two weeks. Remove vanilla bean. Enjoy sipping over ice.

*****

*For a delicious spin on the Banana Bread recipe (See Breads Category.), consider a Kahlua glaze. While the loaf is cooling in the pan, whisk 1 1/4 C powdered sugar and 1/2 C Kahlua coffee liqueur until very smooth. Flip the loaf out of the pan and use a wooden skewer to poke holes in the top of the bread. Pour glaze over the loaf.*

**APERITIFS**

### lavender iced-tea sangria.

*On July 9, 2009, the HSN Morning Study Group met for a Ladies in Lavender Luncheon. We began with this aperitif, prepared by Sara Gillum. The secret of this refreshing, fruity iced tea is lavender black tea.*

4 C water
4 lavender black tea bags
4 to 5 Tbsp sugar
1 peach or apple, peeled, pitted or seeded, and chopped
4 large strawberries, hulled and cut in half
1 orange, peeled and chopped into 3/4-inch pieces
1 C dry red wine

Bring the water to a boil. Remove from the heat and add the tea bags. Steep for 3 minutes, then remove the tea bags. Pour the tea into a pitcher. Add the sugar. Stir until the sugar is dissolved. Cool. Cover and refrigerate. Can be made 1 day ahead.

In a bowl, mix the peach or apple, strawberries, and orange. Divide among four 16-ounce glasses and add ice. Add the wine to the pitcher and pour into the glasses. Serve icy cold at afternoon parties or at the cocktail hour.

*****

*There are a few things I've learned in life:*
*always throw salt over your left shoulder,*
*keep rosemary by your garden gate,*
*plant lavender for good luck,*
*and fall in love whenever you can.*
     -Alice Hoffman

**APERITIFS**

### lemon-balm iced tea.

*The Herb Garden at Cheekwood features an annual display bed of the* Herb of the Year, *selected by The Herb Society of America. A wide variety of herbs, that were formerly unknown, stimulated interest in gaining more information about them. So, a morning study group was formed to explore The Herb of the Year.*

*HSN Study Groups meet from September through May to delve into the herb's history, literary references, cultivation, medicinal uses, chemistry, and culinary uses. In the 2000s, the study group findings were presented at general membership meetings, followed by a recipe tasting.*

*In August 2007, Sandra Frank prepared this tea for the HSN Lemon-Balm Study Group Presentation. The tasting of lemon-balm recipes also included Chicken Salad with Creamy Lemony Herb Dressing. (See* Salads Category.)

10 Earl Grey tea bags
5 sprigs lemon balm
2 sticks lemon grass
3 Tbsp dried lemon verbena
1 Tbsp lavender flowers
Honey

Combine the above, chill, and serve over ice with mint. Add honey to taste.

**APERITIFS**

### lemoncello.

*Carol Duncan perfected her recipe that we savored at many HSN culinary gatherings in her home. Some at 10am! Carol prepared her lemoncello for the Tea for the Season, a workshop that featured teas and other beverage recipes for the holidays. Today, Carol is living in southwest Florida with easy access to fresh lemons!*

*This liqueur is delicious when served with tiramisu (See Desserts Category.), fresh fruit, or a chocolate dessert. Drizzled over ice cream is another delightful option.*

Zest of 18 lemons (Use a micro plane for zesting to avoid the pith.)
1.75-liter bottle 100 proof vodka
5 C sugar
5 C water

Combine lemon zest and vodka in a glass container and place in a dark spot for 4 to 6 weeks. Prepare a simple syrup with sugar and water, simmering for 5 to 10 minutes. Strain the vodka-zest mixture and combine with simple syrup. Place in decorative bottles and store in a cool place. A perfect gift!

*****

*Limoncello is a strong, bright yellow after-dinner liqueur from Southern Italy. The full-flavored lemons found all along the Amalfi coast are ideal for making this potent drink. On the isle of Capri in the late 19$^{th}$ century, an innkeeper, Vincenza Canale, served her guests a homemade liqueur after dinner. Travelers spread the word and her family began producing her lemon liqueur commercially. Today, the family's company, Limoncello di Capri, is run by her grandchildren.*

## APERITIFS

### may wine punch.

*In shady spots, during late-April and early-May, sweet woodruff, a ground cover, starts to bloom with delicate, star-shaped white flowers. May Wine is made with sweet woodruff and a young Riesling wine, ideally from the Mosel region of Germany. This wine is often enjoyed on May Day, along with the German tradition of dancing around giant May Poles, decorated with ribbons and flowers.*

*In the 2000s, the culminating activity for new members of the Nashville Herb Society was an annual May Wine Party for new members and their sponsors. Here, we Provisionals, as we were called then, officially became members of HSN.*

*At Carol Duncan's home in May 2005, members of my class toasted one another with glasses of May Wine to celebrate the culmination of our year's work and study.*

15 sweet woodruff sprigs
2 pints strawberries
1/2 C sugar
1 1/2 quarts Rhine or Mosel wine
Edible flowers, optional

Heat 4 woodruff sprigs in a 200-degree oven for 5 minutes. Rinse and hull 1 pint strawberries and place in a large pitcher or crock. Mash berries with the sugar. Add heated woodruff sprigs and 8 more sprigs. Add wine and stir well. Cover tightly and refrigerate overnight or up to 24 hours.

Strain wine into punch bowl. Add rest of the berries and remaining woodruff. Garnish with edible flowers, if desired.

**APERITIFS**

### tea punches.

*In the spring of 1999, I became involved with several organizations in Nashville, including Cheekwood Friends of Art, the Nashville Symphony Guild, and Friends of the Nashville Ballet. At almost every meeting, a sweet tea punch was served. Very Southern, very traditional!*

*In September 2006, our Sew 'n Sow Garden Club celebrated its 30$^{th}$ Anniversary with a luncheon at Cheekwood. I compiled* Recipe Favorites*, a recipe book that included a recipe from each member. For the luncheon menu, the committee selected and then prepared dishes from the cookbook. These two tea punches are from that book.*

### kathy berry's tea punch.

5 C hot water
10 whole cloves
1 family-size tea bag

3/4 C sugar
1 can (6 oz) lemonade
3 cans water

Simmer water with the cloves until water is colored. Add tea bags and steep until dark. Add sugar, lemonade, and 3 cans of water. Strain. Serve hot or cold. Yield: 1 gallon.

*****

### robanne legan's tea punch.

5 family-size tea bags
1 gallon fresh orange juice
1 C sugar

1 C lemon juice
1 quart apple cider

Steep tea bags in 6 cups of water until strong. Add remaining ingredients. Divide between 2 gallon size containers (milk or juice cartons) and fill to top with water. Serve over ice.

## APERITIFS

### the sagittarius.

*For the culinary aspect in their study of dill, the HSN Study Group held A Dilly of a Luncheon on February 8, 2010. Kathy Wright prepared this drink, with a Swedish ambiance, dedicated to Sagittarius! Ideally the base would be a vodka with an earthy flavor.*

| | |
|---|---|
| 1 1/2 oz vodka | Freshly ground pepper |
| 2 tsp fresh lime juice | Ice cubes |
| 3 dill sprigs, plus more for garnish | 1 1/2 oz tonic water |

Combine vodka, lime juice, dill, and a pinch of pepper in a cocktail shaker. Crush dill using a muddler or the handle of a wooden spoon. Strain into an ice-filled glass. Top off with tonic water, stir to combine. Serve with a dill sprig and an additional pinch of pepper.

*****

### vanilla lemonade.

*In April 2019, the Horticultural Society of Middle Tennessee (HSMT) held its annual Spring Fashion Show and Luncheon where this refreshing vanilla lemonade was served.*

| | |
|---|---|
| 4 C water | 3 C fresh lemon juice |
| 2 C sugar | Lemon slices to garnish |
| 1 vanilla bean, split lengthwise with seeds reserved | |

Bring 2 cups of water, sugar, and vanilla bean and seeds to boil over medium-high heat. Cook 2 minutes. Remove from the heat and cool completely. Remove vanilla bean. In a large pitcher, stir together sugar mixture, lemon juice, and remaining water. Refrigerate until cold. Garnish with lemon.

In 1954, Mother and I rode burros to explore the Sierra Madre Oriental Mountain Range near Monterey, Mexico. The visit to Mexico, followed our trip to San Antonio, Texas, for the Supreme Assembly of the Order of Rainbow for Girls.

**WILSON COLLEGE CHOIR ENJOYS A BEDFORD LUNCH**—The touring Wilson College Choir paused briefly for refreshment in Bedford Sunday night on its way by bus back to Chambersburg after a concert series in Pittsburgh. The choir was entertained at the home of Mr. and Mrs. Harry Fletcher, Meadowbrook Terrace. Their daughter, Joan, is a member of the group. Shown in the photo, reading clockwise from foreground, are: Ellen Hagenou; Janice St. Clair; Caroline Smith; Anne Thomas; Gay Holthaus; Miss Fletcher; the director, Albert Van Ackere; Mrs. Van Ackere, the accompanist; and James Thompson, chairman of the music department at Wilson.

# savories

**"Nearly eleven o'clock," said Pooh happily.
"You're just in time for a little smackerel of something."**
-A. A. Milne

**The way to a man's heart is through his stomach.**
-Fanny Fern

**Anybody who believes that the way
to a man's heart is through his stomach
flunked geography.**
-Robert Byrne

## SAVORIES

### arancini – rose murdocca's.

*Michelle Murdocca and I became friends in 1988 when she and my son, Billy, were working at Videocraft in Boston. This recipe for Arancini originated with Michelle's great, great grandmother, who was Sicilian. Arancini originated in Sicily in the 10$^{th}$ century. The name is derived from their shape and color, reminiscent of an orange (arancia in Italian).*

1/2 C white rice
2 eggs
1/2 stick butter, softened
1/4 C Romano or Parmesan cheese
Dense red sauce, like Bolognese
Green peas
1 beaten egg
Bread crumbs
Canola oil

Heat red sauce. Cook peas. Cook rice and cool it. Mix the eggs, butter, and cheese into the rice. Salt and pepper to taste. Put some rice in one hand. Put a small amount of sauce and peas in the center of the rice. Add more rice to make a ball, about 3-inches in diameter. Dip the rice ball in beaten egg. Coat in bread crumbs. Refrigerate Arancini at least 2 hours or overnight. Deep fry in Canola oil (almost cover the ball in oil). Turn over to cook evenly to a golden brown, about 4 minutes. Drain on paper towel-lined plate. Serve at room temperature.

*Michelle has been with Sony Pictures in LA since 2002. Her film career has evolved from visual-effects line producer of* Air Force One *in 1997 to (just announced) producer of Hotel Transylvania 4 in 2021. The films she has produced, include* Stuart Little 1 *and* 2, Open Season 1 *and* 2, *and* Hotel Transylvania 1 *through* 3. *What a legacy for her twin daughters, Chloe and Bella. Living in Manhattan Beach offers Michelle the opportunity to pursue her avocation, paddle boarding among the whales in the Pacific Ocean.*

**SAVORIES**

### asparagus rolls.

*In 2011, Helen Hooper and Betty Ward sponsored me for membership in Nashville's Centennial Club. This club was organized in 1905 as the first women's civic club in Tennessee. In 1961, ground was broken at 2805 Abbott Martin Road for a clubhouse, and the elegant building was opened in May 1962. I enjoy luncheon programs planned by the Art, Garden, Literary, and Music committees, as well as monthly club luncheons, special events, and tours. Delicious luncheons are prepared by the staff. A club specialty is Asparagus Rolls. Susan James, a club member, recreated the recipe for these savory treats!*

2 jars long asparagus spears
Loaf of thin-sliced bread, crusts removed
Mayonnaise and grated onion mixture
Softened butter

Cut crust from bread and roll thin with a rolling pin. Spread bread with butter on one side and mayo/onion mixture on the other. Place asparagus spear diagonally on mayo-onion side. Fold over triangles and secure with a toothpick. Freeze on waxed paper. Store in a freezer bag.

Preheat oven to 350 degrees. Place frozen rolls on a cookie sheet. Bake for 15 minutes or until golden brown. Remove the toothpicks prior to serving.

## SAVORIES

### bacon crackers.

*Between 2015 and 2019, I served on the HSN Membership Committee during Lisa Ramsey's term of office. Lisa and her Board streamlined the HSN organizational structure. And Lisa worked tirelessly on the annual Herb Sale, procuring plants with Sandra Frank and managing the sale's logistics. Lisa's mother-in-law provided this savory recipe for bacon crackers that have been enjoyed at many Herb Society events.*

Nabisco Waverly wafer crackers
Thin sliced bacon, cut in half
Parmesan cheese

Preheat oven to 200 degrees. Separate crackers. Hold each cracker over a bowl and sprinkle with Parmesan cheese. Wrap half a strip of bacon lengthwise along the cracker, tucking ends under. Place on a wire rack over a baking sheet with sides. Place in middle of the oven and bake for 2 hours. Serve hot or cold. Store in cookie tins or freeze.

*To vary the recipe, place 1 teaspoon of Parmesan cheese on the cracker before wrapping it in bacon. After baking crackers, roll each warm cracker in Parmesan cheese. Serve immediately. Or cool and store in an air-tight container.*

## SAVORIES

### bacon-wrapped stuffed dates.

Ralph Henley and I met in 2016 when Julie Schoerke suggested that he lay-out the design for Gary's book, Sea Stories. Since then, he and I have established an extremely productive working relationship. But we both are certain we'll gain weight if I don't complete this book soon! We're inhaling calories right off of each page.

Ralph discovered these sweet and savory treats at his niece's wedding in Austin, Texas, several years ago. In classic Texas spirit, the bride and her attendants were dressed in flowing pastel gowns - and cowboy boots!

The outdoor wedding was held in the early evening. As guests gathered on the lawn, drinks and hors d'oeuvres were served. These bacon-wrapped stuffed dates were among the offerings. Ralph enjoyed them so much he asked for the recipe.

1 pound uncooked bacon slices, cut in half
1 pound Medjool dates
4 ounces gorgonzola cheese or blue cheese

Preheat oven to 375 degrees. Butterfly the dates open lengthwise. Pinch off pieces of cheese, and stuff them into the center of the dates. Close each date and wrap a half-slice of bacon around the outside. Secure each with a toothpick. Arrange on a foil-wrapped baking sheet with sides to catch any grease.

Bake for 30 to 40 minutes in the preheated oven, or until the bacon is crisp. For even cooking, turn dates over after the first 20 minutes. Serve warm or at room-temperature. The dates are delightful either way!

**SAVORIES**

**border guacamole.**

*In 1990, my son, Billy, moved from Boston to Los Angeles. In 1995, he directed* Real World, *MTV's popular television show. In 2000, Billy became Executive Producer of* Making the Video, Making the Super Bowl Half-Time, *and* Making the Movie. *And in 2003, he was named Executive Producer for Ashton Kutcher's* Punk'd. *Today, Billy is Executive Producer for major ad campaigns.*

*Visiting him was always a gourmet treat because the restaurants in LA were so outstanding, unlike Naples, Florida, at that time. I especially enjoyed Spago, the Beverly Hills Hotel, and The Border Grill in Santa Monica. Mary Sue Milliken and Susan Feniger, the chefs and Border owners, offered exciting and flavorful dishes. I especially enjoyed their guacamole. Perhaps the hint of lime makes the difference!*

2 ripe avocados, cut
1/3 medium onion, diced
2 jalapeno chilies, seeded and finely diced
1 Tbsp lime juice, freshly squeezed
1/4 tsp freshly ground black pepper
Shredded lettuce and sliced tomatoes

Mash avocados until chunky, and combine them with the next 5 ingredients. Serve as a dip or mound on a bed of shredded lettuce and garnish with sliced tomatoes drizzled with basil olive oil.

## SAVORIES

### cheese holiday party pops.

*In December 2013, Gary and I hosted an afternoon Christmas party for the neighborhood children, ranging in age from two to seven. The highlight of the gathering was the arrival of Santa Claus, our friend Steve Gregory.*

*Holland Strang facilitated a game of I Spy Ornaments on the Christmas Trees, craft activities, and stories. These activities kept the younger Strang, Hundley, and Schwartz children busy until Santa's arrival, following his stint as Cheekwood's Santa.*

*I had been warned that snacks for children in the 2010s differed considerably from those I served at parties for Billy and his friends in the 1970s. So, our party treats included fruit juice, gold fish, cut apples, tiny Christmas cookies, and cheese pops. Adults agreed that these cheese pops could be cocktail-party nibbles as well.*

8 oz cream cheese, softened
1/4 C (3 oz) crumbled blue cheese
3/4 C dried cranberries, finely chopped
1 1/2 C pecans
Thin pretzel sticks

Stir together cream cheese, blue cheese, and cranberries. Separate the mixture into large teaspoon-size balls and place on wax paper. Cover balls and chill in refrigerator for a few hours. Toast pecans until lightly brown, cool completely, and chop. Roll each ball in the pecans and insert a pretzel stick. Chill until ready to serve.

*****

*When I was in elementary school, every girl had an autograph book in which classmates, using their best Palmer method of penmanship, would write a poem, like the following:*
>*As sure as grass grows around the stump,*
>*I want you for my sugar lump.*

## SAVORIES

### cheese wafers - ambolyn's.

*In the late 1970s and early 1980s, Ambolyn Hervey came from Texarkana, Texas, to spend the holidays with her son, Homer, and his family in Chevy Chase, Maryland. Billy and HV (Homer Vaughn Jr.) were friends from nursery school days until 1984 when HV graduated from Georgetown Prep and Billy from Georgetown Day School.*

*My friend, Nancy Hervey's preparations for their family's annual New Year's Day Brunch were never complete until Ambolyn had baked her famous cheese wafers! We always looked forward to this gathering of Washington friends and a day of football, conversation, and delicious food!*

2 sticks butter, softened
2 jars Old English sharp cheese, softened
2 C flour
1 tsp salt
Dash of cayenne pepper
2 C chopped nuts

Preheat oven to 350 degrees. Cream softened butter and cheese. Combine with sifted flour, salt, and pepper. Mix with nuts. Form into rolls, and wrap in wax paper. Freeze. Cut into thin slices and bake 10 minutes. Store in an airtight container.

*****

*Age is of no importance, unless you are a cheese.*
*-Billie Burke*

# SAVORIES

## cheese wafers.

*Jack Daniel's* The Spirit of Tennessee Cookbook *was authored by Lynne Tolley and Pat Mitchamore. In 2004, Pat invited Gary to speak about his novel,* Cottonwood Summer, *at a Brentwood Baptist Church Dinner. Our friends attending the event included Helen and Jerry Hooper and Betty and Tom Ward.*

*Soon after arriving in Nashville, I discovered that cheese wafers or cheese straws are a staple for every Southern hostess! Each person has a special version. Mine is adapted from the Jack Daniels recipe.*

| | |
|---|---|
| 2 C flour | 1 C butter |
| 1/2 tsp ground red pepper | I tsp Worcestershire sauce |
| 1 tsp salt | 2 C Rice Krispies |
| 2 C shredded, sharp Cheddar cheese | |

Sift together the flour, salt, and pepper. Combine the cheese, butter, and Worcestershire sauce. Blend in flour mixture. Stir in the cereal. Chill dough for several hours. Preheat oven to 400 degrees. Shape into 1-inch balls. Arrange on baking sheets. Flatten each ball with a fork, making a crisscross pattern. Bake 10 minutes or until the wafers are lightly browned. Cool on a wire rack. Store in an airtight container. Yield: 6 dozen.

*****

*In 2002, Sally Wechsler of Wecksler-Incomo agreed to be our literary agent and introduced us to a New York book-publishing company. Midway through the publishing of* Cottonwood Summer, *two tragic events occurred. First, Sally died suddenly of a heart attack. Second, hard times hit the book industry and forced our publisher into bankruptcy. We were in shock. Our first book, ready to be printed and distributed. What to do?*

*An easy fix immediately came to mind. Gary and I would launch a new business. We acquired the current agency agreements and renamed the company - Fletcher House. And, I became a book publisher!*

## SAVORIES

### cream cheese-olive spread.

*Founded in 1869, Wilson College is a private, Presbyterian-related, liberal arts college, located in Chambersburg, Pennsylvania. The campus, with the Conococheague Creek running through its 300 acres of gracious lawns, mature trees, and rolling hills, is on the National Register of Historic Places.*

*My major was English Literature with a minor in Spanish and Education. Term papers, workshops, and studying, my Monday to Friday ritual netted me a Phi Beta Kappa membership and Cum Lauda on my diploma. On week-ends, we dated students from Dickinson, Franklin and Marshall, and Gettysburg. In our freshman year, there were mixers with the boys from the forestry school at Mont Alto, whom we affectionately referred to as the Chop Chop Boys. Choir rehearsals and field hockey filled in my free time.*

*Today, there are several venues for athletics and equestrian competitions, tennis courts, and a gymnasium. A dance studio is housed in Lenfest Commons where students also have access to the fitness center. In addition, Wilson College has an organic farm, that allows students to learn about approaches to sustainable living.*

*As a Wilson College student, my comfort food was a cream-cheese olive sandwich. In the 1950s, the ladies in the Snack Bar lovingly prepared these sandwiches on soft, white bread. Since moving to Nashville, I've learned that this sandwich is often served at Southern Ladies' Teas.*

8 oz cream cheese, softened
1/2 C pimento-stuffed Spanish olives, finely chopped
1/4 tsp garlic powder

Mix well and chill for 2 hours or overnight. Serve on crackers or as finger sandwiches.

*To vary the recipe, add chopped pecans, black olives, blue cheese, or fresh herbs. This is also terrific as a dip for celery or carrot sticks.*

## SAVORIES

### cucumber tea sandwiches.

*The Education Department at Cheekwood frequently hosted wedding and baby showers for fellow staff members. In September 2011, Chris Gregory prepared these tea sandwiches for Karen Kwarciak's baby shower.*

*This sandwich can be eaten - with or without tea. The tea version is dainty and cut into shapes, while the tea-less version is stacked with cucumbers. My father prepared the tea-less one for himself. He enjoyed just-picked, warm slices of cucumber, sprinkled with salt and pepper, on a slice of buttered bread.*

*Today, these cucumber tea sandwiches are usually prepared for wedding and baby showers. When roses are blooming, garnish the platter or sandwiches with fresh rose petals for a stunning presentation.*

1 loaf white sandwich bread
Fresh dill for garnishing sandwiches
1/2 C creme fraiche
1/4 tsp garlic powder
1/4 tsp salt or to taste
1/4 tsp white pepper
1 Tbsp finely chopped fresh dill
1 medium seedless cucumber, sliced thinly

Remove crust from bread with a sharp knife and cut into shapes, including triangles, squares, rectangles, hearts, or circles with cookie cutters. Place creme fraiche, garlic powder, salt, pepper and 1 tablespoon of dill in a small bowl. Stir to combine. Spread lightly on bread, top with cucumbers and garnish with fresh dill sprigs. (Can be made up to 1 week ahead and stored in the refrigerator). Cover with a damp paper towel until ready to serve to keep the sandwiches from drying out.

**SAVORIES**

### fourth of july salsa.

*Each week-day morning, I look forward to* Style Blueprint, *a Nashville on-line daily newsletter. In addition to articles about women, fashion, events, and area activities, recipes are often included. I've adapted this recipe for a salsa that could also be used as a side salad.*

1 1/2 C blueberries
2 1/2 C watermelon chunks, drained
1 small jicama, peeled and diced
Juice of 1 medium lime
1 small jalapeno, diced

Cut watermelon pieces to the size of the blueberries. Peel Jicama and dice into small pieces. Place blueberries, watermelon, and jicama in a bowl. Add jalapeno and lime juice. Stir to combine. Serve with thick tortilla chips or in *Scoops*. Or serve on Boston lettuce as a salad.

*****

*During our 20 years living in the Washington area, we spent many leisurely Fourth of Julys with Bob and Jan Alnutt and their sons. Jan always prepared a delicious cold soup to begin our picnic supper on the lawn near the Washington Monument. Billy, David, and Tommy hurried through dinner so they could attend the annual Beach Boys Concert. Later, the National Symphony Orchestra played a concert on the Capitol grounds. The finale was a fireworks display, accompanied by the playing of the 1812 Overture.*

*Other Fourth of Julys were spent in my hometown of Bedford, Pennsylvania. Our tradition was to drive to Osterburg to pick cherries. Of course, a picnic supper of fried chicken, potato salad, Mother's baked beans, and cake was also traditional. Usually, Mother's neighbors, the Whitmores, and their son, John Lynn, joined us.*

*In Naples, Florida, our July Fourths were spent with friends at the Port Royal Club's Celebration of the Fourth, followed by fireworks at the Naples City Pier.*

**SAVORIES**

### fresh spinach dip.

*In 2000, I joined the Nashville Chapter of the Women's National Book Association (WNBA). For several years. I served on the Board as Secretary. Our board meetings were held in the Board Room of Beaman Library on the Lipscomb University campus. Carolyn Wilson, Director of the Library, arranged for our meetings there, and she always had a delicious dinner waiting for us.*

*WNBA established the Carolyn Wilson Award, presented annually to a member for her outstanding contribution. In 2005, I was honored to receive this award. In 2009, I was selected as WNBA's ATHENA Award Nominee for an annual event sponsored by Nashville CABLE. I was thrilled to have WNBAs' members join me at the Athena Awards Ceremony at the Schermerhorn Symphony Center.*

*In 1982, WNBA had published* The Literary Allusions Cookbook. *Profits were used to fund scholarships for women interested in careers in the book world. Carolyn Wilson's recipe for fresh spinach dip, from that book, is delicious.*

1 C mayonnaise
1 C fresh spinach, finely chopped
1/4 C onion, chopped
1 tsp pepper
1 C sour cream
1/2 C parsley, chopped
1 tsp salt

Puree all ingredients in a blender. Chill until ready to serve with fresh vegetables or crackers.

## SAVORIES

### ham biscuits.

*At the 2006 February Sew 'n Sow business meeting, held at Lynn Parson's home, the President's gavel passed from me to Sue Smith. For the luncheon that followed, Anne Lane prepared these ham biscuits. Sometimes, Anne serves these with cheese grits and curried fruit for a* Do-Ahead Brunch.

*Don't over-stuff the biscuit! A great ham biscuit is as much about the biscuit as it is about the ham. Two or three slices of thick-cut ham are just right. And, you might offer various toppings such as honey butter, peach preserves, or pimento cheese.*

Marshall's or Pillsbury frozen biscuits or (*Gasp!*) homemade ones
Brown sugar glazed deli ham
Butter, softened
Spring onions, chopped (Anne says you can't have too many!)
Dijon mustard (1 Tbsp for each stick of butter)
Poppy seeds

Soften butter and add mustard, onions, and poppy seeds. Cover and refrigerate overnight to let the flavors blend.

Bake the biscuits according to the package instructions, but remove them from the oven before they're browned. Slice the biscuits open and spread the butter mixture on both sides. Add sliced ham. Reassemble biscuits and heat at 350 degrees until hot.

**SAVORIES**

### hot artichoke dip.

*Since the early 2000s, Gary and I frequently travel to Owosso, Michigan, his hometown. There, each of the five novels of the* Cottonwood Series *were reviewed by Dick Campbell, Publisher of the* Owosso Argus-Press. *Dick referred to Gary's writing as a "thinly-veiled autobiography." Each book was launched at the Shiawassee Arts Center. And, Gary presented "Behind the Book" talks to various organizations, including the county Rotary and Kiwanis Clubs, five libraries, church groups, and the Current Events Club.*

*Gary's family and friends are always extremely welcoming. Our stay in Owosso includes dinners with family or friends. Judy Bingaman prepared this dip for us during the 2004* Cottonwood Summer *book tour in Michigan. This savory is very similar to one that Betty Albrecht served us in Naples, Florida.*

*This could be a spontaneous dish, because you probably have all the ingredients in your pantry. If caught short, just substitute garlic powder, onion powder or canned pimentos.*

| | |
|---|---|
| 1 pkg (8 oz) light cream cheese | 3 cloves garlic, pressed |
| 1 Tbsp butter, melted | 3 green onions, chopped |
| 1 Tbsp mayonnaise | 4 artichokes, cut |
| 1/4 C red pepper, finely diced | Freshly ground Parmesan |

Preheat oven to 325 degrees. Grease a shallow baking dish. Combine all ingredients, except Parmesan cheese, and place in the dish. Sprinkle with Parmesan cheese. Bake 20-25 minutes or until hot in the center.

Serve as a spread with sliced French bread or pita bread, or as a dip with substantial crackers or chips.

## SAVORIES

### laurel's cheese ball.

*In 1979, I collected members' recipes and edited* Democratic Delectables, *a fund-raising recipe book for WSDC. Laurel Barron contributed this recipe for her cheese ball that had become a welcomed staple at Club functions.*

1 pkg (4 oz) crumbled blue cheese
1 stick butter
1 pkg (8 oz) cream cheese
1 can (3 oz) chopped ripe olives, well drained
1 bunch green onion tops, chopped

Cream butter and cheeses. Mix with ripe olives and onion tops. Form a ball and chill. Serve with bland crackers.

*****

### meng cheese.

*In the early 1960s, Addice and Peter Thomas moved to Washington D.C. from New Orleans. Peter, an artist, had been invited to join the faculty at the Corcoran School of Art. Addice's Meng Cheese was always served at the Thomas' cocktail parties. Men, especially, can become addicted to this savory!*

| | |
|---|---|
| 1 pound Velveeta cheese | 1 tsp red pepper |
| 1 bulb garlic | Splash of vermouth |
| 1 C chopped pecans | Chili powder |
| 3 oz cream cheese | |

Process Velveeta, garlic, and pecans. Mix with cream cheese, red pepper, and vermouth. Form into a log and roll in chili powder. Chill well. Slice thinly and serve on crackers.

**SAVORIES**

### mini prosciutto and cheese quiche.

*Each spring and fall, my friends and I look forward to Judi Smith and Liz Weller's presentation of the new cabi (Carol Anderson by Design) clothing line. For years, I have hosted a Saturday morning event, including coffee and conversation, a preview of the new line, and my friends trying on and selecting clothing for the next season.*

*Usually, I serve fresh fruit, sweets, and savories with coffee or peach tea. In the fall of 2018, Liz Weller shared this recipe for my cabi coffee. A definite winner for a brunch or a cocktail party!*

1 pkg (4 oz) prosciutto
4 eggs
1 Tbsp sour cream
4-5 green onions, sliced and slightly sautéed in a little olive oil
1 tsp fresh thyme or basil
1 oz cheese (Your choice.)
1/2 tsp pepper

Preheat oven to 400 degrees. Spray tins of two 12-cup mini muffin pans with cooking spray. Cut each slice of prosciutto into 3 pieces and press each piece into a muffin cup.

In a small bowl, beat eggs. Add sour cream, cheese, onions, thyme, and pepper. Pour into prosciutto-lined cups. Bake 10 minutes. Cool slightly before removing from the tin.

**SAVORIES**

**mushrooms escargot.**

*When Billy was four years old, he sampled an escargot and couldn't eat enough of them! Perhaps his fascination was using the little fork to pull the snail from the shell and then draining the garlic-butter onto a piece of French bread. A rather pricy appetizer for a child with a voracious appetite.*
	*Needless to say, I was excited to find this recipe. Quickly, it became one of my best hot appetizers. A vegetarian's delight - escargot without the snails! Be prepared for rave reviews!*


10 oz butter
2 large cloves garlic, mashed
2 scallions, finely chopped
1 Tbsp parsley, finely chopped
Mushroom caps
Bread squares
Fine bread crumbs

Mix butter, herbs, and seasonings into a fine paste, smooth and creamy. Choose mushroom caps that are just large enough for one big bite.  Stuff them with the garlic butter.  Refrigerate overnight.
	Preheat oven to 350 degrees. Toast little squares of bread on one side, one to a mushroom.  Place on a baking sheet, toasted side down, and top with a mushroom cap.  Sprinkle with a few bread crumbs.  Bake 15 minutes. Then, place under the broiler to brown.

**SAVORIES**

**pimento-cheese spread.**

*When I was growing up in southern Pennsylvania, pimento-cheese spread was a standard filling for sandwiches. My Aunt Mary Dively always prepared this spread during haying season. In Nashville, I was quite surprised to learn that this spread is revered as a Southern creation, a staple on buffet tables, as well as at football tailgating parties.*

*When Gary and I arrived in Nashville in the summer of 1998, we were excited to learn that the Houston Oilers football team would be making its home in Nashville and that we could become season ticket holders. For 20 years, we had lived in the Washington D.C. area, where Redskin tickets were handed down from generation to generation and impossible to secure. How exciting to become Titans ticket-holders and tailgate before games!*

*Rick Regen's mother, Tiger, always brought her pimento-cheese spread to the Titans' pre-game parties.*

2 (8 oz) blocks sharp Cheddar cheese, shredded
2 (4 oz) jar diced pimentos, un-drained
1 C homemade mayonnaise
3/4 C chopped pecans, toasted
1/4 to 1/2 tsp hot sauce

Stir all ingredients together. Cover and chill at least two hours. Serve with crackers. Or use the spread as a sandwich filling or to stuff celery.

**SAVORIES**

### ricotta and walnut stuffed endive.

*Suzanne Regen and I enjoy trips to Olivia Olive Oil in Cool Springs. It's always a treat to sample the latest flavor of oil or vinegar. A few years ago, the shop's owner, Christie Lassen, conducted an olive oil and balsamic vinegar workshop for PEO Chapter E.*

*Sometimes, she invites chefs to present cooking classes in her store, accompanied by Christie's olive oil and vinegar tastings.*

*Suzanne, Gary, and I have attended several classes and have enjoyed the recipes. A few years ago, Sherry and John Covington arrived early for Gary's birthday dinner. While I put the finishing touches on the dishes, they assembled Christie's stuffed endive as an appetizer.*

1/2 C walnuts
1/2 C golden raisins
2 Tbsp chives
3 Tbsp orange olive oil
1/8 tsp pepper
4 endives, trimmed and leaves separated
1 1/2 C ricotta

In a small bowl, combine walnuts, raisins, chives, oil, and pepper. Arrange endive leaves on a plate and top each with a dollop of fresh ricotta and a spoonful of the walnut mixture.

## SAVORIES

### rosemary pecans.

*Jana Talbot and Joan Pinkley, two HSN members, partner in selling residential real estate for Parks Real Estate in Green Hills. I look forward to their monthly newsletter,* What's Cooking in Real Estate with Jana and Joan. *These two friends are innovative cooks and enjoy sharing their recipes.*

*Rosemary pecans are a staple in our home during the holidays. Becky Talbot's recipe first appeared in the Herb Society of Nashville's* Hors Oeuvres *cookbook, ©1978. In July 2008, Becky's daughter, Jana Talbot, prepared these pecans to share during* Gifts from Your Garden, *an HSN culinary workshop.*

2 Tbsp butter
1 Tbsp dried rosemary, crumbled or 2 Tbsp fresh
2 C pecan halves
1 1/2 tsp salt
1/2 tsp cayenne red pepper

Preheat oven to 325 degrees. Melt butter in jellyroll pan. Add remaining ingredients, and mix well. Bake 10-15 minutes, stirring and shaking occasionally, until nicely browned. Be careful not to burn. Remove from the pan and spread on brown paper. Store in airtight container. Yield: 2 cups.

*Rosemary, a fragrant evergreen herb, is native to the Mediterranean. Fresh or dried leaves are used in traditional Mediterranean cuisine. When roasted with meats or vegetables, the leaves impart a mustard-like aroma with an additional fragrance of charred wood that goes especially well with barbecued foods. (See Seafood Category for the Rosemary Shrimp Scampi Skewers.)*

**SAVORIES**

**scotch eggs**

*This savory is typically served in pubs, and I have been serving them at holiday parties since the 1970's. These eggs were extremely popular at the Howell Place Christmas Gatherings at Celeste and Ken Lester's home here in Belle Meade.*

6 hard-boiled eggs, shelled
1 pound pork sausage meat
1 beaten egg mixed with 1 Tbsp of water
1/4 C fine dry bread crumbs
Deep fat for frying

With moistened hands, wrap each egg in sausage meat. Dip into egg-water mixture and then into crumbs, coating sausage meat completely. Deep fry eggs at 360-degrees for 5 to 6 minutes, or until brown on all sides. Drain well. Cut into quarters lengthwise. May be refrigerated before serving.

perfect hard-boiled eggs:

Place eggs in a heavy pot and cover with 1½ inches cold water. Partially cover pot and bring to a vigorous rolling boil. Reduce heat to low and cook eggs, completely covered, for 30 seconds. Remove pot from heat and let eggs stand in hot water, still covered, for 15 minutes. Run eggs under cold water for 5 minutes. This prevents the yolk from discoloring and makes eggs easier to peel, as does using eggs that are at least a few days old.

**SAVORIES**

### shrimp-corn salsa - ed marcoe's

*I look forward to Susan James' Facebook page. Usually, it is filled with multiple color photos of gourmet dishes that she recently enjoyed at new Nashville restaurants. My reaction is always the same. I want to head out to try the dishes. NOW! Susan, a fellow garden club member, added this tasty salsa recipe to the Sew 'n Sow's Favorite Recipes Cookbook.*

3/4 pound shrimp, cut into small pieces
1 C chopped red bell pepper
1 C chopped green bell pepper
1/3 C chopped green onions
3 jalapeno peppers, seeded, cored, and chopped
6 Tbsp lime juice
1 tsp kosher salt
1 tsp sugar
1 avocado, chopped
1 tsp minced garlic
1 tsp olive oil
Kernels from 3-4 ears of corn
1-2 tomatoes, chopped

Mix and allow to marinate. Serve as an appetizer with corn chips.

*****

*Corn is an efficient way to get energy calories off the land and soybeans are an efficient way of getting protein off the land, so we've designed a food system that produces a lot of cheap corn and soybeans resulting in a lot of cheap fast food.*
*-Michael Pollan*

**SAVORIES**

### shrimp cream dipping sauce.

*In July 1998, Gary was asked by Bob Chaput, his former Johnson & Johnson consulting client, to come to Nashville to establish an IT Consulting Business for J&J. Since Bob and his wife, Mary, had recently moved here from New Jersey, we four spent many week-ends becoming acquainted with our new hometown, Nashville. We frequented new restaurants, attended concerts or Oilers games, toured gardens, and visited historic homes. And Gary and I enjoyed dinners at Chaputs' Brentwood home, especially when Bob grilled on their tree-house deck. Mary shared her Aurora, New York's family recipe for this dipping sauce for shrimp.*

| | |
|---|---|
| 1/2 C mayonnaise | 1 Tbsp cocktail sauce |
| 1 small onion, finely chopped | 2 tsp Worcestershire sauce |
| Dash Tabasco | 1/2 C whipping cream |

Mix all ingredients except cream. Whip cream until it forms peaks. Fold cream into mixture. Chill before serving.

*****

### dijon dipping sauce.

*This sauce pairs well with Mary Chaput's Shrimp Cream Sauce.*

1 C reduced-fat sour cream
1/4 C Dijon mustard
3 Tbsp fresh parsley leaves, chopped
1/4 tsp freshly grated lemon peel

Combine ingredients and chill before serving.

**SAVORIES**

### shrimp louisiana.

*During the 1960s, June Jackson and I became fast friends when we taught at Springbrook High School in Silver Spring, Maryland. Over the years, June shared many of her Southern dishes from Monroe, Louisiana. This appetizer is delicious and spectacular when served in an ice bowl!!*

| | |
|---|---|
| 6 C water | 1 1/2 C vegetable oil |
| 3 pounds unpeeled medium shrimp | 3/4 C white vinegar |
| 1 Tbsp pickling spice | 2 Tbsp capers, undrained |
| 1 Tbsp salt | 2 tsp celery seed |
| 4 celery ribs with leaves | 1 tsp salt |
| 1 large purple onion, thinly sliced | 2 tsp hot sauce |
| 10 lemon geranium leaves | |

Bring water to a boil. Add shrimp and the next three ingredients. Cook 3 to 5 minutes or just until shrimp turn pink. Drain shrimp and rinse with cold water. Peel shrimp and devein. Layer shrimp with onions and geranium leaves.
     Stir the next 6 ingredients together. Pour this mix over the shrimp-onion mixture. Cover and chill 4 to 8 hours. Stir occasionally. Remove bay leaves before serving. Yield: 8 to 10 servings.

<u>ice bowl for shrimp</u>:

*Stack two metal bowls. Fill the larger outer bowl with water and geranium leaves. Add smaller bowl and weigh down the center with a can. Freeze. Remove can and bowls. Place ice bowl on a large platter covered with greens and fill the bowl with shrimp.*

In 1969, Billy and me with his companion, Enu. We lived on Post Oak Road in Potomac, Maryland, from 1965 until 1970. Then, we moved to Ascott Lane in Olney, Maryland. Our colonial home was located on three acres of land with a swimming pool, fed by spring water. Annually, we hosted an end-of-school swimming party For Billy's Georgetown Day School class.

# breads

**Her passion for bread-and-butter, covered with apple sauce and powdered sugar, was getting to be a serious matter.**
-Booth Tarkington

**Deliberation, n.: The act of examining one's bread to determine which side it is buttered on."**
-Ambrose Bierce

**How can a nation be great, if their bread tastes like Kleenex?**
-Julia Child

## BREADS

### banana bread.

*Following my sister, Harriet's graduation from Margaret Morrison Carnegie College, she landed a position with Pittsburgh Gas & Electric Company. Her work consisted of testing recipes or conducting food demonstrations. This moist bread keeps in the refrigerator and freezes extremely well. Save your ripe bananas and bake two small loaves. Gift one!*

| | |
|---|---|
| 3/4 C margarine | 2 C sifted flour |
| 1 1/2 C sugar | 1 tsp baking soda |
| 1 1/2 C mashed bananas | 3/4 tsp salt |
| 2 eggs, beaten | 1/2 C buttermilk |
| 1 tsp vanilla | 3/4 C chopped nuts |

Preheat oven to 325 degrees. Cream together the shortening and sugar. Blend in bananas, eggs, and vanilla. Sift flour, soda, and salt. To the banana base, add flour alternately with buttermilk. Mix thoroughly after each addition. Pour into a greased and floured 9x5x3-inch loaf pan or into two small loaf pans. Bake large loaf for 1 1/4 hours and the smaller loaves for 45-50 minutes. Bake until straw inserted in center comes out clean.

*No buttermilk? Substitute 1 1/2 teaspoon vinegar in 1/2 C milk. Allow the mixture to stand for 5 minutes before using.*
    *Often, I replace the nuts with white raisins or Rice Krispies.*
    *To enhance the banana bread, while the loaf is cooling in the pan, whisk 1 1/4 C powdered sugar and 1/2 C Kahlua for a very smooth glaze. Flip the loaf out of the pan and use a wooden skewer to poke holes in the top of the bread. Pour the glaze over the loaf. Cool.*

**BREADS**

### banana-wheat quick bread.

*A few years ago, Harriet created this recipe for her grandchildren, who literally beg her to bake it for them. Her granddaughter, Carolyn, asked for the recipe so she could bake the bread for her friends at NC State.*
   *Last Christmas, Harriet packaged all the dry ingredients and placed them in a loaf pan. Tied with a red ribbon, a most welcome gift.*

| | |
|---|---|
| 1 1/4 C unbleached flour | 2 Tbsp orange juice |
| 1/2 C whole wheat flour | 1 egg |
| 2/3 C sugar | 1/2 C raisins |
| 1 tsp baking soda | 1/2 C rolled oats |
| 1/4 tsp salt | 3 C (3 large) sliced bananas |
| 1/4 C canola oil | |

Preheat oven to 325 degrees. Combine all ingredients, and blend at low speed. Beat 2 minutes at medium speed. Pour into greased and floured 9x5x3-inch pan or 2 smaller pans. Bake large pan for one hour or two smaller pans for 45-50 minutes. Cool in pans for 5 minutes. Remove from pans and cool thoroughly.

*Quick breads evolved after the introduction of baking powder in 1850, because this substance allowed bread to rise quickly. Before that, breads and cakes were leavened with yeast. Baking powder has replaced yeast as a leavening agent for cakes but not yeast bread doughs. Quick breads made with a leavening agent, such as baking powder or baking soda, allow immediate baking of the dough or batter mixture. They are quick to make!*

## BREADS

### blueberry hill muffins.

*During the late 1960s, Joan Cole was my next-door neighbor in Potomac, Maryland, and our sons, Andrew and Billy, were a year apart in age. In the afternoons, Andrew played "big brother" and pushed Billy, in his stroller, down Post Oak Road.*

*In the early 1990s, I visited with Joan at The Elms, her summer home on Keuka Lake, one of New York's Finger Lakes. There the Mennonite markets offer produce and flowers from spring through autumn. How lucky can one be – Winters in Venice, Florida, and summers on Keuka Lake.*

*One day, after we had motor-boated across the lake to pick blueberries, we decided to use Joan's recipe to bake blueberry muffins for dinner. Obviously, we were chatting too much and became distracted, because the next morning we discovered the melted butter in the microwave. Since the texture and taste were not affected, we decided that butter could be an optional ingredient.*

| | |
|---|---|
| 1 C sugar | 1 C milk |
| 1/4 C melted butter | 1 egg |
| 1 1/3 C flour | 2 tsp baking powder |
| 1 tsp cinnamon | 1/2 tsp vanilla |
| 1 tsp nutmeg | 3/4 C blueberries |

Preheat oven to 375 degrees. Mix together all the ingredients except blueberries. Gently fold in blueberries lightly dusted with flour. Spoon into muffin cups. Bake 25 to 35 minutes. Yields: 12 muffins.

**BREADS**

### boston brown bread.

*During the summers between my sophomore and senior years in high school, I worked as a waitress at a Howard Johnson's restaurant. It was conveniently located near Bedford at the Midway Rest Area on the Pennsylvania Turnpike, half way between Pittsburgh and Harrisburg.*

*At one time, there were over 900 HoJo restaurants, each with its iconic orange roof, turquoise trim, and Simon the Pieman logo. Sadly, the HoJo restaurant chain is now closed. Back then, travelers stopped for frankfurters grilled in butter or fried clam strips in a butter-soaked roll. Another menu item was Boston baked beans with brown bread.*

*Well over 150 years ago, the Burnham & Morrill Company was founded in Portland, Maine. Today, if you need a HoJo fix, B&M baked beans and B&M brown bread, each packaged in cans, can be found in grocery stores. Or you can bake your own brown bread.*

| | |
|---|---|
| 1 C unsifted whole wheat flour | 1 1/2 tsp salt |
| 1 C unsifted rye flour | 3/4 C molasses |
| 1 C yellow corn meal | 2 C buttermilk |
| 1 1/2 tsp baking soda | |

Grease and flour a 2 quart mold. Combine flours, corn meal, soda, and salt. Stir in molasses and buttermilk. Pour into mold, and cover tightly. Place on a trivet in a deep kettle. Add enough boiling water to kettle to come half way up the sides of mold; cover. Steam 3 1/2 hours or until done. Remove bread from mold to a cake rack. Serve hot with baked beans. Makes 1 loaf.

## BREADS

### breakfast blintzes.

*In the early 2000s, Hillary Steinwinder became the Director of Educational Programs at Cheekwood. In 2003, she asked me to chair the logistics for the Scholastic Art Competition (SAC). This annual competition of two- and three-dimensional art is a Middle Tennessee event, open to 7th to 12th grade-students. Each year, it draws over a thousand entries.*

*Every year, I recruited a volunteer team of friends to check-in the art, organize and number each piece by category, present each piece to the judges for assessment, and organize the art by schools for pick-up.*

*I chaired this Competition until 2011 when art was submitted digitally for judging. Our mornings began with a Continental breakfast for the judges and volunteers. Hillary often prepared these sweets for us.*

1 C sugar
4 tsp cinnamon
1 pkg (8 oz) soft cream cheese
2 large loaves white bread, sliced and crusts trimmed
1/2 C sugar
2 egg yolks
1 C margarine, melted

Mix 1 cup sugar and cinnamon in a shallow dish. Combine cream cheese, 1/2 cup sugar, and egg yolks in a mixing bowl. Beat until creamy, scraping the side of the bowl as needed.

Flatten each slice of bread with a rolling pin. Spread one side of each slice of bread thinly with the cream cheese mixture. Roll each lengthwise to enclose the filling. Dip in margarine and roll in cinnamon-sugar. Arrange on a baking sheet and freeze until firm. Place in re-sealable plastic freezer bags. Freeze until baking time. Do not thaw before baking Preheat oven to 400 degrees. Bake for 15 minutes.

*****

*Between 2010 and 2012, I chaired the Cheekwood Volunteer Committee, organizing the committee members as liaisons to share programming with volunteers and to bring volunteer concerns for discussion with staff. I also served on the Cheekwood Board of Trustees in 2011 and in 2012.*

**BREADS**

### brown sugar muffins.

*In the mid-1980s, my friend, Susan Edwards, was instrumental in founding the Arts Council in Naples, Florida. In 1986, as Vice President of this organization, I chaired the first Cultural Wave, a February two-week celebration of the arts in Naples and on Marco Island. Each day featured a different art organization, either performing or displaying their work.*

*At our early morning, planning meetings, we enjoyed Susan's warm brown-sugar muffins.*

2 C all-purpose flour
1 tsp baking soda
1/4 tsp salt
1 C light brown sugar, packed
1 large egg
1 C milk
1/2 C butter

Preheat oven to 350 degrees. Mix flour, baking soda, salt, and sugar in medium-size bowl. In separate bowl, beat the egg, milk, and butter. Add to flour mixture, and beat well to mix. Spoon into muffin cups. Bake for 20 minutes or until lightly browned. Yields: 12 muffins. If there are any leftover, the muffins do freeze well.

## BREADS

### buttermilk pancake balls (Kærnemælks Æbleskiver).

*I met Judi Legerton when she joined PEO Chapter E. Judi's Mom and Mo-Mo (grandmother) made Æbleskiver at Christmas and for special Sunday occasions. The Danish way (at least Judi's family's way) is to pick up the Æbleskiver with your fingers. Dip it in the sugar, eat, and enjoy!*

2 C buttermilk (light buttermilk works well also)
1/2 tsp salt
2 C flour
1 tsp baking soda
3 eggs, separated
2 Tbsp granulated sugar
1 tsp baking powder
Apple sauce (optional)

Separate the eggs. Beat the whites, using an electric mixer, until they are stiff. Set them aside. Beat the yolks and stir in the sugar, salt, and buttermilk. Sift the flour, baking soda, and baking powder together and slowly add these to the mixture. Stir in one direction so the batter doesn't become tough. Fold in the stiffly beaten egg whites.
    Add a small amount of oil in each part of the Monk's Pan and heat until it bubbles when tested with a small piece of bread. Add dough, filling each part to about 1/2 full. Bake on medium heat (each stove-top is different). When the dough bubbles, it is half baked. Put a teaspoon of apple sauce on top of the dough. Turn it over with a knitting needle, skewer, or fork and finish baking. Test if done by sticking a toothpick in the center. If it comes out clean, put the balls on the serving platter or plates. If not, give them more time and check again. Serve with powdered sugar, granulated sugar, or jam.

P.S. You will need a Monk's Pan (Æbleskivepande) to make this sweet!

**BREADS**

### cinnamon puffs.

*Another winner from my sister, Harriet! Whenever I need a new recipe, she always has one to share! I prepared this delicious sweet for the 2007 January HSN Board meeting at my home. Easy to make – hard to resist – very addictive! You cannot eat just one!*

6 frozen biscuits (Harriet uses Pillsbury's Take and Bake Biscuit Dough.)
3 Tbsp butter, melted
1/2 C sugar
1 tsp cinnamon

Preheat oven to 375 degrees. Remove 6 frozen biscuits from the freezer and thaw only until each biscuit can be cut into 4 quarters (about 5 to 7 minutes). Melt butter and stir in sugar/cinnamon mixture. Spray *miniature* muffin tins. Roll each quarter in the mixture to coat and place in muffin tin. Bake 12 minutes or until bottoms of muffins are nicely browned. Yield: 24 puffs.

*For a savory instead of a sweet, Harriet substitutes ground Parmesan cheese for the cinnamon-sugar.*

**BREADS**

### french breakfast muffins.

*During the spring of 2010, Judy Armstrong, who was living in Florida, came to Nashville specifically to volunteer for the Chihuly installation. That exciting exhibition attracted people from all over the country! And, in 2020, another Chihuly Exhibition will be installed at Cheekwood!*

*Judy stayed with our friend, Suzanne Regen, who was also Judy's childhood friend from Princeton, Kentucky. That day, Gary and I joined Judy and Suzanne in installing The Sun on the lawn in front of the Cheek mansion.*

*Eight years later, Judy and her husband, Dwight, moved to Nashville. On New Year's Day 2018, Gary and I became reacquainted with Judy at a brunch at Suzanne's home. Judy had baked these delicious muffins for our get-together.*

| | |
|---|---|
| 1/3 C shortening | 1/4 tsp nutmeg |
| 1/2 C sugar | 1/2 C milk |
| 1 egg | 1/2 C sugar |
| 1 1/2 C flour or cake flour | 1 tsp cinnamon |
| 1 1/2 tsp baking powder | 1/2 C melted butter |
| 1/2 tsp salt | |

Heat oven to 350 degrees. Grease 15 muffin cups. Thoroughly mix the shortening, 1/2 cup sugar, and egg. Stir in flour, baking powder, salt, and nutmeg alternately with milk. Fill muffin cups 2/3 full. Bake 20-25 minutes.

Mix 1/2 cup sugar and cinnamon. Immediately after baking, roll muffins in melted butter, then in cinnamon-sugar mixture. Serve hot.

*****

*Gary and I enjoyed volunteering to install exhibitions at Cheekwood:* Chihuly Glass *in 2010,* Trains in G *in 2011, and* Bruce Munro Light *in 2013. In 2010, we helped British artist, Sophie Ryder, repair her* Crawling Lady Hare. *In 2015, we assisted Soo Sunny Park with her site-specific creation of* Silver Linings. *And, in 2016, we helped Crystal Wagner with her large-scale installation,* Radical.

## BREADS

### german breakfast cake.

*In 1897, the Cleveland Baking Powder Company published a practical cookbook of* Superior Receipts. *Mrs. Cheek's copy of this 76-page booklet is in the archives of the Cheekwood Estate and Gardens. Jane MacLeod, Cheekwood's President and CEO, shared a breakfast cake recipe from this booklet. Mrs. Cheek preferred this recipe and had marked it with an X. Following is the Receipt as originally printed.*

1 quart flour
2 tsp Cleveland Superior Baking Powder
2 Tbsp sugar
1 Tbsp butter
1 tsp ground cinnamon.
Salt

Mix all the dry ingredients together. Rub in butter and add enough milk to make a soft dough. Roll into two sheets. Put in pie tins, allowing to come up the sides. Sprinkle with sugar, cinnamon, and lots of butter. Bake and serve hot.

*Cheekwood was the home of Leslie Cheek and his wife, Mabel Wood. In 1928, the Cheeks purchased 100 acres in West Nashville and built a Country Place Era Estate. They hired Bryant Fleming, a residential and landscape architect. In 1929, while the land was being cleared, the Cheeks and Fleming sailed to England where they decided on the Georgian-style architecture for the house. The Cheeks purchased objects, architectural elements, furniture, and art to create the sense of legacy and longevity that characterized European mansions and estates. By creating a home in the Georgian style and filling it with objects from the 1700s, the Cheeks projected timeless wealth and social stature. When they moved into Cheekwood in the fall of 1932, the home looked as though generations of the Cheek family had lived there. Under the leadership of Jane MacLeod, the Cheek Mansion was refurbished to reflect the 1930s and debuted in 2017.*

## BREADS

### lavender and rosemary focaccia.

*Members of the Herb Society enjoy meetings at Susan Adams' home on Old Hickory Lake, especially in spring when Spanish bluebells bloom profusely by her front door. I've added these flowers to my garden!*

*Susan chairs the Herb Study Groups for the Nashville Herb Society. In July 2009, she prepared this bread for the study group's culinary event, Ladies in Lavender Luncheon.*

1 pound fast pizza dough or 1 pound frozen bread or pizza dough, thawed
2 Tbsp olive oil (extra-virgin)
1/4 C pitted and chopped imported black olives
2 tsp chopped lavender buds
1 Tbsp chopped fresh rosemary
2 cloves minced garlic
1 tsp coarse salt
Ground black pepper to taste

Lightly oil a large baking sheet. On a work surface, roll pizza dough out into an 8x14-inch rectangle. Transfer to prepared baking sheet and cover with a clean dish cloth. Let rise at room temperature for 20 minutes.

Preheat oven to 450 degrees. After a final rising on baking sheet, make dimples in dough with finger tips. Brush on 2 tablespoons olive oil. Then add mixture of lavender, rosemary, garlic, and olives. Press into place, and sprinkle with salt and black pepper to taste. Bake 12-15 minutes or until golden brown. Cool on wire rack. Cut into pieces to serve. Serves 6.

**BREADS**

### mitford orange-marmalade muffins.

*I became a Jan Karan-Mitford fan in 1994 with the publication of* At Home in Mitford. *In April 1999, Davis Kidd Bookstore manager, Bev Perry, hosted an 8am breakfast for the Nashville launch of* A New Song, *the fifth book in the series. I prefer to use my peach jam instead of the orange marmalade. (See Preserves Category.)*

1/2 C orange marmalade
2 C all-purpose flour
1/2 C sugar
1 Tbsp baking powder
1 large egg
1 C plain yogurt or buttermilk
1/4 C melted butter
1 tsp vanilla
3/4 C chopped pecans

Preheat oven to 375 degrees. Blend the flour, sugar, and baking powder. Combine egg, yogurt, butter, vanilla, and pecans. Whisk thoroughly until smooth. Pour egg mixture into the flour and fold 2-3 times until the dry ingredients are moistened. Do not over-mix. Spoon 1 tablespoon of batter into greased muffin tin. Using the back of the spoon, press a small dimple into the batter. Place 1 teaspoon of marmalade into the dimple and top with 2 tablespoons batter. Bake 25-30 minutes. Yield: 8 muffins.

*Mitford, the fictional version of Blowing Rock, North Carolina, is just a short distance from Boone where I often stayed with my sister, Harriet, in her log cabin. Frequently, we hiked sections of the Appalachian Trail. One summer, we enrolled in a dulcimer workshop at Appalachian State University. Instructors included folk song masters, Janita Baker and Betty Smith.*

**BREADS**

**mother's waffles.**

*In Bedford, my family were members of St. John's Evangelical and Reformed Church that was later merged into The United Church of Christ. In high school, I studied with the church organist, Dave Behers, and substituted for him on Sundays. During my junior year, I served as organist for the Methodist Church in Everett, a small-town east of Bedford. And I played the organ at the Lewis Geisel Funeral Home during my senior year.*

*For years, my father served as an Elder on the Church Consistory. Their annual fund-raiser was a Waffle Supper, prepared by the men of the church. These men manned dozens of waffle irons. Without fail, each year, they blew several fuses, delaying the waffle production!*

*At home, our Day-after-Christmas dinner always featured Mother's home-made waffles covered with left-over turkey gravy. While the rest of my family enjoyed waffles with gravy, I preferred mine with maple syrup or simply with butter. Leftover waffles - if any - freeze well!*

2 C flour
3 tsp baking powder
1 tsp salt
2 eggs, separated
1 1/4 C milk
6 Tbsp melted shortening

Preheat waffle iron. Beat egg yolks. Add milk, then sifted dry ingredients, and beat well. Add shortening, and fold in the well-beaten egg whites.

*In an emergency, I use Jiffy Blueberry Muffin Mix, and follow the recipe on the box for blueberry waffles. These are yummy! The recipe makes about three Belgian waffles.*

**BREADS**

### pizza margherita.

*For a light supper with friends during the holidays, Gary prepares this quick pizza. Perfect accompaniments are a green salad and fresh mixed fruit. A gooey dessert provides a perfect ending!*

1 can (10 oz) refrigerated pizza-crust dough
1 tsp extra-virgin olive oil, divided
1 clove garlic, cut in half
5 plum tomatoes, sliced thin
1 C shredded mozzarella cheese
1 tsp balsamic vinegar
1/2 C basil, thinly sliced

Preheat oven to 400 degrees. Unroll pizza crust on a baking sheet coated with cooking spray. Pat crust into a 13x11-inch rectangle. Bake for 8 minutes. Remove crust from oven.

Brush with 1/2 teaspoon olive oil, and rub crust with cut sides of garlic. Arrange tomato slices on crust, leaving a 1/2-inch border. Sprinkle evenly with cheese. Bake 12 minutes or until cheese melts and crust is golden.

Combine 1/2 teaspoon of oil and vinegar, and stir with a whisk. Sprinkle pizza with basil. Drizzle oil mixture on pizza. Cut into 8 pieces. Serves 4.

*****

*Ideas are like pizza dough, made to be tossed around.*
*-Anna Quindlen*

## BREADS

### real southern cornbread.

*In Naples, during the late 1980s, I met Paul Frank, who became a most interesting friend because of his stories of old Florida. His pioneer family hunted, fished, and lived on the land that now encompasses Wilderness Country Club in North Naples. They also owned the land where the Hole in the Wall Golf Course was built. Paul lived on that golf course and oversaw the maintenance of the grounds.*

*In the 1940s, Paul's father built the original swamp buggy to take him into the wilderness. In 1949, his father helped organize the Swamp Buggy Races, held annually in February, for over 70 years, at the Florida Sports Park near Naples. Paul raced his Tumble Bug in the 1950s.*

*In mid-November, Paul would retreat into the wild country to bag a wild turkey for his Thanksgiving dinner that we attended on several occasions. He also harvested hearts of palm and created a most delicious salad. The cornbread dressing was prepared following his mother's cornbread recipe.*

2 C white corn meal
1 tsp baking powder
1/2 tsp baking soda
1 tsp salt
2 eggs
2 C buttermilk
2 Tbsp bacon drippings or vegetable oil

Preheat oven to 425 degrees. Combine dry ingredients. Beat eggs into buttermilk. Add dry mixture and stir. Add oil. Mix well and pour into a well-greased, hot skillet or into muffin tins. Bake 25 to 30 minutes or until cornbread is brown and cake tester comes out clean.

**BREADS**

### sour cream coffee cake.

*Bessie Williams' sour cream coffee cake has become our traditional sweet for an early morning family birthday celebration or on Christmas morning, with a glass of champagne! Bessie was the librarian at Pyle Junior High School in Bethesda, Maryland, where I taught eighth-grade English in the 1960s.*

*During my three years there, I compiled a* ReciPyle Cookbook *of the staff's best recipes. Bessie's was definitely a winner! And I've been baking this cake for almost 50 years in an antique, green-glaze pottery Bundt pan. For a stunning presentation, fill the center of the cake with edible flowers, such as pansies or orchids.*

| | |
|---|---|
| 1 C sugar | 1/2 pint sour cream |
| 1/2 C butter | 1 tsp vanilla |
| 2 eggs | 1 tsp cinnamon |
| 2 C all-purpose flour | 1/4 C sugar |
| 1 tsp baking powder | 1/2 C chopped nuts |
| 1 tsp baking soda | |

Preheat oven to 350 degrees. Cream the sugar and butter. Add eggs and beat well. Sift the dry ingredients. Add the sifted mixture alternately with the sour cream and vanilla to the butter mixture. Spoon half of the batter into a well-greased Bundt pan and sprinkle with half of the cinnamon, sugar, and pecan mixture. Spoon rest of batter in, and add rest of cinnamon mixture. Bake 45 minutes to an hour.

To remove cake from pan, wet a kitchen towel with cold water and wring it out. Set cake pan on a cooling rack and carefully lift the sides of the towel up against the pan edges for 30 seconds. Let cake cool and remove by inverting the cake on a serving plate.

## BREADS

### zucchini bread.

*In 2011, I was invited by my friend, Liz Weller, to become a member of PEO Chapter E in Nashville. What a group of extraordinary women who share philanthropic and educational interests. Our chapter meets once a month. Fran Massey, a former Metro English teacher, facilitates our PEO Book Group that meets monthly to discuss member-selected books. We bring a sandwich and gather in a member's home, where the hostess provides a salad and dessert. Our annual fund-raising event is a Silent Auction that I chair each November. We all look forward to bidding on Fran's zucchini bread. Her* Hello, Dolly! Bars *(See Cookie Category.) also garner substantial bids!*

1 C grated zucchini
1 C sugar
2 eggs
1/2 C cooking oil (Fran uses 1/4 Canola oil and 1/4 grape oil.)
1 1/2 C all-purpose flour
1 tsp cinnamon
1 tsp baking powder
3/4 tsp soda
1/3 C raisins

Preheat oven to 350 degrees. In a mixing bowl, beat together zucchini, sugar, and egg. Add cooking oil and mix well. Stir together flour, cinnamon, baking soda, and baking powder. Stir into zucchini mixture. Fold in raisins. Pour into a greased 9x5x3-inch loaf pan and bake 50 minutes. Cool in pan.

*****

*The trouble is, you cannot grow just one zucchini. Minutes after you plant a single seed, hundreds of zucchinis will barge out of the ground and sprawl around the garden, menacing the other vegetables.*
*-Dave Barry*

During the summer in 1977, my friend, Renata Vaccari, and I toured Italy with our sons, Roberto and Billy. We visited with her brother's family in Pisa. In Venice, we traveled the Grand Canal by gondola, ate at the Caffe Florian, and lingered in the Piazza San Marco while Billy fed the pigeons.

joanne fletcher slaughter

In Italy, Renata and I, with Roberto and Billy, visited Rome. She and I threw three coins into the Fountain of Trevi. The second coin did ensure a new romance with Gary Slaughter, several years later in 1980. The third, ensured our marriage in 1981. But, I'm "on-wait" for the first coin, guaranteeing my return to Rome.

# soups

**Only the pure of heart can make good soup.**
*- Beethoven*

**A soup like this is not the work of one man.
It is the result of a constantly refined tradition.
There are nearly a thousand years of history in this soup.**
*- Willa Cather*

## SOUPS

### chilled cucumber dill soup.

*Molly Schneider and I became acquainted through HSN. Going to meetings at her home is a visual treat because she and her husband, Rick, were early collectors of Rookwood pottery. They have since donated a portion of their outstanding collection to Cheekwood.*
*In February 2010, the HSN Morning Study Group met at Sara Gillum's home for* A Dilly of a Luncheon. *Molly adapted this delicious cold soup from several recipes.*

2 Tbsp vegetable oil
10 cucumbers, peeled, seeded, and coarsely chopped
4 sweet onions (preferably Vidalia), coarsely chopped
5 cloves garlic
5 C rich chicken stock
1/2 C chopped fresh dill
Freshly ground white pepper to taste
2 C heavy cream
Additional dill for garnish

In a large saucepan, heat the vegetable oil over medium heat and sauté the cucumbers, onions, and garlic until the onions are transparent, about 5 minutes. Add chicken stock and simmer until the cucumber is soft, about 15 to 20 additional minutes.
Remove from heat and transfer soup to a food processor, in batches if necessary. Blend until smooth. Strain the mixture through a fine sieve. While the mixture is still warm, stir in the chopped dill and season with pepper. Chill the soup.
Stir in the cream just before serving. Garnish with dill sprigs. Serves 10.

## SOUPS

### cream of crab soup – maryland style.

*In 1975, Denny Diamond shared her deliciously simple soup recipe for the Georgetown Day School cookbook,* Kitchen Privileges. *Denny, a native Washingtonian, convinced me, a Pennsylvanian, that if you live in Maryland, this soup must be included in your recipe file!*


1 small onion, finely chopped
1 Tbsp butter
1 C strong chicken stock
1 quart rich milk
1 Tbsp parsley, finely chopped
1/2 tsp celery salt
Dash red pepper
Salt and pepper to taste
1 pound back-fin crabmeat, chopped
2 Tbsp flour
1/4 C sherry

Cook onion in butter until transparent. Add chicken stock and slowly pour in milk. Add herbs and spices. Stir in crabmeat and simmer for 15 minutes. Make a paste of flour and water, thinning it with a little hot stock. Stir into the soup to thicken slightly. Remove from heat and stir in sherry. Serves 4.

*****

*When Billy was in high-school, he was not too eager to prolong dinner. We would buy steamed crabs at Bethesda Crab House, spread them out on newspapers covering the kitchen table, and pick crabmeat from the shells. It's amazing how long it takes to eat crabs and how much Gary and I learned about Billy's life at Georgetown Day School through those prolonged dinner conversations. Serving boiled shrimp in shells is another idea, but the conversation won't last as long!*

## SOUPS

### cream of red pepper soup.

*Between 1985 and 1998, Gary and I lived in Naples, Florida. In 1992, I was selected as Executive Director of the Forum Club of Southwest Florida and served in that capacity until 1997. I enjoyed my associations with the board members and missed this interaction when we moved to Nashville.*

*Each season from November through April, the Board of the Forum Club invited prominent Fortune 500 CEOs, Supreme Court Justices, Congressmen, and Military Officers to speak to the membership at its luncheon meetings.*

*Among my main responsibilities, I coordinated the speakers' arrangements, arranged the luncheon logistics, planned Board meetings and Board events, maintained the Club membership records and luncheon attendee lists, and produced a monthly newsletter for the membership. Once a year, I arranged a dinner for the board members and their spouse, held at the Naples Yacht Club.*

*During my tenure, speakers included:*

- *Clarence Thomas, Associate Justice of the Supreme Court*
- *General Norman Schwarzkopf, Commander US Central Command*
- *James R. Jones, Chairman and CEO, American Stock Exchange*
- *Nicholas Katzenbach, Attorney General of the United States*
- *Ralph S. Larsen, Chairman of the Board and CEO, Johnson & Johnson*
- *Raymond W. Smith, Chairman and CEO, Bell Atlantic Corporation*
- *Tom Foley, former Speaker of the House of Representatives*
- *William W. Sessions, Director, Federal Bureau of Investigation*

*These Friday speaker luncheons were held at the Naples Beach Hotel on Gulf Shore Boulevard. I selected the menus and often included their Red Pepper Soup, served either hot or cold.*

## SOUPS

### cream of red pepper soup. (cont.)

3 large red bell peppers, chopped
1 medium onion, chopped
2 C chicken stock, canned
1/4 C heavy cream
1 Tbsp butter
1 tsp lemon juice
Dash cayenne pepper
Dash white pepper

Sauté onion in butter. Add bell peppers and chicken stock. Simmer 30 minutes. Place in blender to puree. Add remaining ingredients. Serve immediately, or store in refrigerator for a day.

*****

*The Naples Beach Hotel was originally constructed in the 1880s. Its guests came predominately from the Midwest, arrived for the winter season in December, and returned home in the spring.*

*In 1946, Henry B. Watkins, Sr. bought the original hotel along with the Beach Club and its golf course. Then. he proceeded to create a new beach resort between the golf course and the Gulf of Mexico. Many guests came to the hotel when they were younger and have made it a custom to bring their own children and grandchildren to the resort. This family tradition directly reflects on the Watkins family's love of the Naples area and the tropical paradise that they have preserved for their guests.*

## SOUPS

### hot tomato soup.

In January of 1985, Gary and I had decided to semi-retire and moved to Naples, Florida, where we bought a lovely home in Port Royal. It was located on the "cul-de-sac" of a canal that extended southward into Naples Bay. Frequently, we were entertained by manatees and porpoises in our watery backyard. Tarpon and catfish inhabited the waters under our long boat dock.

When we first arrived in Naples, we kept our IT Training business in Bethesda, Maryland, along with our burgeoning List business, managed by our CEO, Arnold Palley. By summer of 1986, we had become bored with playing tennis and walking the beaches, so we moved the Training to Naples. We acquired a condo office suite on Fifth Avenue in Downtown Naples and hired a secretary and two telephone-sales people. Once again, I managed the day-to-day operations while Gary taught IT Management and Communication Skills workshops until 1992.

In addition to managing GSC, I joined Friends of Art (FoA), led by Lucille Howe. Each season, we underwrote three traveling art exhibitions. In 1987, I became Vice-President of this organization.

Olga Hirshhorn served on our board, as well as Elke Schmid, George Wallace, and Betty Albrecht. On several occasions, Olga gave members of FoA a personal tour of her art collection. While her husband, Joe, collected for his museum in Washington D.C., Olga selected pieces for her collection. Most notable was Picasso's pottery. A magnificent Calder sculpture on her front lawn welcomed visitors to her Port Royal home.

Myra Janco Daniels, the founder of the Philharmonic Center for the Arts (now called ARTIS), had been the guiding force behind the Naples/Marco Island Philharmonic Orchestra. Myra undertook the fund-raising for the Philharmonic Center for the Arts and inspired the community by promising "to entertain you for the rest of your lives!" Gary and I signed on and endowed four seats in Hayes Hall, where we were entertained for ten years.

The PHIL had four art galleries, and I asked the members of the Friends of Art Board to endow one gallery. The Board then voted to use its assets to initiate a new Friends of Art organization at the PHIL. I served as its President from 1990 to 1994 and as ex-officio until 1998. During this

## SOUPS

**hot tomato soup.** (cont.)

*time, the FoA Board undertook several fundraising initiatives, including an Art History Lecture Series and Living with Art that featured a tour of three private art collections in Naples.*

*Between 1990 and 1993, I was committed to an annual, major fund-raiser for the Philharmonic Center. Kathleen Passidomo, currently Majority Leader of the Florida State Senate, and I co-chaired four annual Auctions-on-Stage. These events featured a silent auction and cocktails, a seated dinner on the Hayes Hall stage, and a live auction with Bruce Thalheimer as auctioneer. Each year, we netted over $100,000 for the PHIL. Not bad for the early 1990s.*

*Often, Myra relaxed by preparing dinner for friends in her Pelican Bay home. Prior to our move to Nashville, Myra served this delicious hot tomato soup at a dinner party for Gary and me and our friends.*

| | |
|---|---|
| 2 Tbsp olive oil | 1/2 C goat cheese |
| 6 fresh basil leaves | 1/4 C flour |
| 1 C diced sweet onion | 4 C fresh chicken stock |
| Fresh ground salt/pepper to taste | 1 tsp sugar (optional) |
| 5 C fresh tomatoes, seeded | Sour cream |
| 1/4 C finely chopped celery | Basil leaves |

Heat olive oil, onions, chopped basil leaves, salt and pepper. Cook stirring until onions are wilted. Add tomatoes and chopped celery, and stir to blend with flour and crumbled goat cheese. Simmer for 10 minutes. (Make sure it does not stick or scorch.) Add broth and heat thoroughly. Serve by topping each bowl with a dab of sour cream and a basil leaf.

## SOUPS

### mother's vegetable soup.

*In the 1950s during the winter when I arrived home from college, my requested supper was Mother's home-made vegetable soup with pimento-cheese, chicken salad, or ham-salad sandwiches. For me, this soup was comfort food for an exhausted student after the long trip on a Greyhound bus that stopped in every small town in route from Chambersburg to Bedford. Filled containers of soup usually made the return trip for a Sunday evening snack.*

| | |
|---|---|
| Soup bones | 2 large potatoes, diced |
| 1 can (8 oz) tomato juice | 1 pkg (10 oz) frozen corn |
| 2 ribs celery, chopped | 1 pkg (10 oz) frozen peas |
| 2 carrots, sliced | 1/2 head cabbage, shredded |

Cover soup bones with water. Add salt and pepper. Cook to boiling. Reduce heat and simmer on low for 3 to 4 hours. Refrigerate overnight. Skim fat from broth and discard it. Reserve meat from bones. Cook celery, carrots, onions, and potatoes in tomato juice over medium heat for 1/2 hour or until vegetables are tender. Add broth to the above. Add cabbage, peas, corn, and 1/2 teaspoon of sugar. Cook all ingredients for 1 hour on low. Add meat cut into small pieces and heat thoroughly.

*****

*In rural southwestern Pennsylvania on the farms, a hearty breakfast was served after cows were milked. The main meal, referred to as dinner, was served at noon. Generally, it was followed by a brief nap to refresh oneself for the long working afternoon and milking the cows again in the late afternoon. Supper, the evening meal, usually consisted of leftovers or a light meal of soup and sandwiches. People, living in the town, referred to the noon as lunch and the evening meal as dinner.*

**SOUPS**

### potato-corn chowder.

*When I lived in southern Pennsylvania or the Washington, D.C. area, this soup hit the spot after a day walking in the snowy woods, shoveling snow, or building a snowman. In Nashville, Gary and I enjoy the soup during a dreary, rainy December day.*

3 Tbsp chopped onion
1/2 C chopped celery
2 Tbsp butter
1 C pared, diced potato
2 C water
1/2 tsp salt
1/2 tsp paprika
1/2 tsp red pepper, optional
1 bay leaf
2 Tbsp flour
2 C milk
1 small can pimentos, drained and chopped
1 pkg (10 oz) frozen white corn in butter sauce
Chopped parsley to garnish

In a large saucepan, sauté onion and celery in butter until transparent. Add potatoes, water, and seasonings. Simmer until potatoes are tender, about 45 minutes.

In a separate pan, combine flour and 1/2 cup of the milk to make a paste. Bring the paste to a boil and add to the chowder. Reduce the heat. Stir the chowder until it thickens. Heat the remaining 1 1/2 cups milk. Add corn, pimentos, and milk to the chowder. Do not let it boil. Garnish with parsley. Yield: 6 cups.

## SOUPS

### shrimp bisque.

*After college, Harriet remained in Pittsburgh, working for the Pittsburgh Gas & Electric (PG&E) as a home economist. What a position! Her job was to test recipes and present public cooking demonstrations. Her testing provided our family with many delicious recipes, including this one for shrimp bisque. On Christmas Eve after church, I usually serve this soup in bread bowls, accompanied by a Waldorf or Cranberry Sour Cream Salad. (See Salads Category.)*

1 pkg (8 oz) cream cheese
2 C skim milk
1 can chicken broth
2 cans cream of celery soup
1 can zesty tomato soup
1/2 C dry sherry
1 tsp lemon juice
1 pound shrimp, cooked and diced
3 green onions, minced
2 Tbsp fresh dill
1 tomato, seeded and chopped

In a large saucepan, blend cream cheese and skim milk. Add chicken broth, celery soup, and tomato soup. Wisk ingredients, and add sherry and lemon juice. Add onions, dill, and tomato. Refrigerate until ready to serve. Add shrimp. Heat thoroughly. Do not let the bisque boil. Garnish with chopped parsley.

# SOUPS

### soupe au pistou.

*Gary and I enjoy this delicious soup on a cold evening, served with French bread, salad, and a decadent dessert! Originally from Provence, this soup is a vegetarian's delight!*

2 ½ quarts water
2 C carrots, sliced
1 C potatoes, diced
1 C onions, diced
1/2 C broken spaghetti
1 C pimento-stuffed green olives, sliced
1 can (17 oz) red kidney beans, drained
2-4 garlic cloves, crushed
1/2 C grated Parmesan cheese
1/4 C tomato paste
1 Tbsp dried basil leaves
2 Tbsp olive oil

Bring water to boil. Add carrots, potatoes, and onions. Cover and cook 10 minutes or until vegetables are tender. Stir in spaghetti and olives. Add kidney beans. Meanwhile, blend garlic, cheese, tomato paste, basil, and olive oil to make the pistou. Add 1 cup of soup gradually to the pistou, stirring rapidly. Pour in remaining soup. Or ladle hot soup into bowls and add a spoonful of pistou to the center, swirling gently.

*****

*Pistou is related to pesto but has no nuts.*

On July, 2, 1981, our family gathered at Mother's home in Meadowbrook Terrace in Bedford, Pennsylvania, to celebrate her 80th birthday.
- Front row: Kathryn Yake, Mother, Adam Yake
- Second row: Luke Ward, Sharon Yake, me, Gary
- Third row: John Ward, Harriet Ward, Billy Rainey, Tom Ward

# salads

It's so beautifully arranged on the plate –
you know someone's fingers have been all over it.
-Julia Child

**Cauliflower is nothing but cabbage with a college education.**
-Mark Twain

**It's certain that fine women eat
A crazy salad with their meat.**
-William Butler Yeats

## SALADS

### belle meade country club frozen tomato salad.

*In 2005, Nan Parish hosted a Luncheon and Baby Shower for my friend, Dianne May's daughter, Kim Sonday. Belle Meade Country Club prepared the lunch that included their fantastic iced salad!*

| | |
|---|---|
| 3 C tomato juice | 1/4 C cottage cheese |
| 3 C mayonnaise | 1 Tbsp Worcestershire sauce |
| 1 small onion, finely chopped | 2 drops Tabasco sauce |
| 3/4 C crushed pineapple | Red food coloring |
| 1/4 C cream cheese | Boston or Bibb lettuce leaves |

Combine 2 cups of the tomato juice, 1 cup of the mayonnaise, the onion, pineapple, cream cheese, cottage cheese, Worcestershire sauce, and Tabasco sauce in a blender. Blend until smooth and pour into a bowl. Combine the remaining tomato juice and mayonnaise in the blender and blend until smooth. Add enough food coloring so that it is the color of a very ripe tomato, otherwise the color will be pale pink. Add it to the mixture in the bowl and whisk until combined. Season with salt and pepper and more Tabasco if needed. (Use a sieve if you want a smoother texture.) Pour into a 2-inch deep baking dish and freeze. Arrange lettuce on 10 salad plates and place one or two scoops on top. Add a dollop of mayonnaise. Serves 10.

*****

*In 1807, John Harding purchased the Dunham's Station log cabin and 250 acres on the Natchez Trace, located near Richland Creek. He named the property Belle Meade, that is French for beautiful meadow. Over the next decades, he built a mansion and established a thoroughbred breeding farm and cotton plantation. In 1906, debt forced the family to sell. Belle Meade Land Company built the first road and developed the farm into a neighborhood that became the City of Belle Meade in 1938. Our home, built in 1920, is located in the former Deer Park of the Belle Meade Plantation.*

**SALADS**

### broccoli-raisin salad.

*My sister, Harriet, serves this salad for brunch or as a buffet table salad! And an easy recipe for the grandchildren to prepare. Beautifully healthful!*

3 bunches fresh broccoli, broken into flowerets
1 C cut cauliflower
1/2 C red onion, chopped
1 C celery, chopped
1/2 C hulled sunflower seeds
1/2 C raisins
1/4 C red bell peppers, chopped (optional)

salad dressing:
3/4 C mayonnaise
1/4 C sugar
2 Tbsp vinegar

Combine the salad ingredients in a mixing bowl. Thoroughly mix the dressing ingredients. Pour the dressing over salad ingredients. Stir to blend. Serve chilled. Serves 6.

*****

*I know when you think about the South, you think about fried foods,
but we eat a tremendous amount of vegetables.
I have my own garden, so vegetables have always been a big part
of my life. I love broccoli. I love fresh beets.
It's not all about the fried chicken and the biscuits.*
-Paula Deen

## SALADS

### chicken salad with creamy lemony herb dressing.

*The HSN Study Group enthusiastically endorsed this tasty chicken salad. You can serve the chicken salad in phyllo cups or in Scoops as an appetizer. Sara Plummer prepared this for our tasting luncheon in August 2007. In the summer, I often arrange a plate with a scoop of salad surrounded by slices of honeydew and cantaloupe, garnished with red raspberries and blueberries.*

1 pound chicken breast, cooked and cut into small, bite-sized pieces
3/4 C celery, thinly sliced
1/2 C sliced chives or green onions
3/4 C toasted pecan pieces or other nuts
1/2 C seedless grapes, sliced in halves
1/2 C golden raisins
Garnish with sprigs of lemon balm or Mexican mint marigold.

Mix and toss lightly with dressing. Makes 4 generous servings.

creamy lemony herb dressing:
Mix the following and chill overnight.

3/4 C sour cream
3/4 C mayonnaise
2-3 Tbsp lemon juice
1 tsp ground coriander seed
3 Tbsp honey
1 Tbsp grated lemon peel
2 Tbsp chopped fresh lemon balm
2 Tbsp chopped fresh Mexican mint marigold
2 tsp chopped fresh lemon thyme
2 Tbsp chopped fresh parsley
1/2 tsp salt and 1/4 tsp ground white pepper

**SALADS**

### chinese chicken salad.

*During the summer of 1980, I participated in a Montgomery County, Maryland teachers' workshop on ethnic diversity. The culminating activity was a potluck dinner. All participants prepared a dish that reflected their heritage. Fumie Yamamoto demonstrated the preparation of this dish. What a spectacular presentation! Kids are fascinated by the Mei-Fun noodle explosion!*

2 C cooked chicken, cubed
1 C celery, sliced
1 C green onions, slivered
1 head lettuce, shredded
Mei-Fun (rice sticks), fried according to directions
4 Tbsp sesame seeds, toasted

Combine chicken, celery, and onions. Moisten with salad dressing. Place rice sticks on a plate, add a layer of shredded lettuce, and top with chicken salad mixture. Sprinkle with sesame seeds before serving. Serves 4.

chinese dressing:

2 tsp salt
1/4 tsp pepper
5 Tbsp sugar
6 Tbsp vinegar

Heat above until sugar dissolves. Shake well before using. Make ahead of time and refrigerate.

**SALADS**

### chopped chicken salad.

*This has become one of my favorite dishes! I first tasted this chopped salad when Billy and I had lunch at Spago, shortly after he moved to Los Angeles in 1991. Later, I discovered that California Pizza Kitchen in Naples served a similar salad. This recreation comes close!*

3 C roast chicken (or turkey), diced into 1/4-inch pieces
1/3 pound thinly sliced salami, cut into thin 1/2-inch strips
1/2 pound thinly sliced Swiss cheese, cut into 1/2 -inch strips
1 C pitted black olives, sliced
1 can (15 oz) garbanzo beans, rinsed and drained
1 bunch scallions, trimmed and minced
6 plum tomatoes, seeded and diced
1/2 C shredded fresh basil
6 C shredded iceberg lettuce

Combine and toss all ingredients. Then, toss with enough balsamic vinaigrette to coat evenly. The salad may be served at once or refrigerated and served within 24 hours of preparing. Makes 10 servings.

balsamic vinaigrette:

2 cloves garlic, minced
2 Tbsp Dijon-style mustard
3 Tbsp white balsamic vinegar
2/3 C olive oil
Freshly ground pepper

Combine the garlic, mustard, and vinegar in a small bowl. Gradually whisk in olive oil, and season dressing with herbs and pepper.

**SALADS**

### covington potato salad.

*In May 2019, Gary and I joined John and Sherry Covington's families to celebrate their daughter Lauren's graduation from Trevecca University. The luncheon buffet was a spectacular display of Sherry and John's culinary expertise! Teenager and adult approved enthusiastically, Sherry's potato salad was deliciously flavored with bacon, fresh garlic, and Dijon mustard. Dessert was her fabulous Tiramisu. (See Desserts Category.)*

4 C water
1 tsp salt
4 C small new red potatoes, quartered
1/3 C sour cream
1/3 C mayonnaise
1/2 tsp dill weed
1/4 tsp salt
1/4 tsp pepper
2 Tbsp chopped fresh parsley
1 Tbsp Dijon mustard
1/2 tsp minced fresh garlic
4 slices cooked, crumbled bacon
2 Tbsp chopped green onion

Bring water and salt to full boil. Add potatoes and cook over high heat until tender, about 12 to 15 minutes. Rinse under cold water. Stir all remaining ingredients in a large bowl, except bacon and green onion. Add potatoes and toss to coat. Sprinkle with bacon and green onion just before serving. Serves 4.

## SALADS

### cranberry-sour cream salad.

*My mother usually served this salad for our Christmas dinner. Today, it's traditional in our home during the holidays, especially attractive when placed on Boston lettuce leaves. For an easy holiday buffet supper, serve the salad with Pat Nixon's Hot Chicken Salad. (See Chicken Category.)*

2 pkgs (3 oz each) raspberry Jell-O
1 3/4 C boiling water
1 can (16 oz) whole cranberry sauce
1 can (20 oz) crushed pineapple, un-drained
1 C sour cream

Dissolve Jell-O in boiling water. Stir in cranberries and pineapple. Pour half of the mixture into a rectangular dish. Chill. Spread mixture with sour cream. Cover with remaining Jell-O. Chill thoroughly.

*****

### crunchy cole slaw.

*Gary and I frequently ate at Princeton's in Green Hills after a movie. I really enjoyed their cole slaw and have recreated that crunchy quality.*

1/4 head green cabbage, thinly sliced
1/4 head purple cabbage, thinly sliced
1 turnip, peeled and cut in match sticks
1/2 red onion, cut in thin slices
1 carrot, peeled and cut in match sticks
3 Tbsp mayonnaise
2 tsp Dijon mustard
Juice of 2 lemons

Combine the mayonnaise, mustard, and lemon juice. Mix thoroughly. Pour over first five ingredients.

**SALADS**

### curry rice salad.

*This fabulous salad from Harriet can be served as an entrée or as an accompaniment to grilled chicken, beef, or salmon. I like this salad because of its unusual combination of flavors.*

1 pkg (6 oz) long-grain and wild rice mix
2 C chicken broth
1 C white raisins
1 C hot water
1/2 C sliced green onions
1 C chopped pecans, toasted
1 can (16 oz) garbanzo beans, drained
Lettuce leaves

Combine rice mix and broth in a saucepan. Bring to a boil. Cover, reduce heat, and simmer 20 to 25 minutes or until the rice is tender and liquid is absorbed. Combine raisins and water. Allow to stand for 10 minutes. Drain. Stir raisins, green onions, pecans, and beans into rice mixture. Serve on lettuce leaves. Serve dressing on the side, or mix the dressing into the salad. Salad may be served warm or cold. Serves 6.

curry dressing:

2/3 C mayonnaise (Or 1/3 C mayonnaise and 1/3 C sour cream.)
1 Tbsp curry powder
1 Tbsp honey
1 Tbsp vinegar
2 tsp prepared mustard
1 tsp Worcestershire sauce
1/8 tsp red pepper
Combine all ingredients. Chill. Yield: 3/4 cup.

## SALADS

### georgia peach chicken salad.

*This recipe is from Harriet who was transplanted to Marietta, Georgia, over 40 years ago from Valley Forge, Pennsylvania. I enjoy this recipe during the summer because it is so versatile. Omit the chicken for a delicious side salad, served with grilled chicken or fish.*

1/4 pound Chinese pea pods
1/2 C pecan halves
4 medium peaches
1 C red seedless grapes
4 chicken breast halves, cooked and cubed
1/2 C mayonnaise
2 Tbsp sugar
1 Tbsp poppy seeds
1 Tbsp lemon juice

Cook peas 2 to 3 minutes in 1-inch boiling water. Chill and cut each in half. Toast pecans. Peel peaches. Chop two and slice two into ¼ inch slices. Mix mayonnaise, sugar, poppy seeds, and lemon juice until blended. Place peaches and peas in a bowl. Add grapes and chicken cubes. Toss with dressing. Serve on a bed of lettuce and sprinkle with pecans. Serves 4.

*****

*When I was growing up, you could ask, "What kind of peach is this?" The answer could be, "Elberta." (Bright yellow, fuzzy freestone Georgia peach). But today the answer is "Georgia." A peach is a location? There are five different types of Georgia peaches (Flavorich, Fiesta Gem, Harvester, Flame Prince, and Elberta). Each peach serves a different purpose and deserves its own name.*

**SALADS**

### greek salad.

*In March 2002, our garden club toured Nashville's Parthenon and enjoyed a picnic lunch on the grounds of Centennial Park. Greek Salad, prepared by Dancey Sanders, was served with hummus, tabbouleh, pita pockets with lamb, spinach and cheese triangles, and baklava for dessert!*

2-3 small heads of romaine lettuce
8 cherry tomatoes
1/2 C feta cheese
Red onion, 6 thin slices
1/2 cucumber, peeled and sliced
8 Kalamata olives, pitted
3/4 C celery hearts, diagonally sliced
4 scallions, cut in 1-inch pieces
8 firm radishes, sliced
1 can (2 oz) anchovy fillets (optional)

greek salad dressing:

6 Tbsp olive oil
2 Tbsp lemon juice
1 tsp finely minced garlic
1 tsp dried oregano
Salt and pepper to taste

Whisk the salad-dressing ingredients together. Combine salad ingredients. Pour on dressing just before serving.

**SALADS**

### hartzell potato salad.

*This tasty salad was served at my sister, Sharon's daughter, Kathryn's wedding rehearsal dinner in Carlisle, Pennsylvania. Kathryn's future mother-in-law, Nancy Hartzell, prepared her son, Matt's, favorite potato-salad for the buffet. Just the right amount of horseradish!*
    *Kathryn and Matt's two sons, Ben and Jacob, enjoy creating "new" dishes for their parents. They have been chefs-in-training since they were old enough to wield a paring knife. I'm looking for them to appear on a cooking channel soon!*

5 medium-size red potatoes (about 2 pounds)
4 hard cooked eggs, diced
1 Tbsp chopped parsley
2 green onions
1/2 C mayonnaise
1/2 C sour cream
2 Tbsp horseradish
1/2 tsp salt
1/2 tsp pepper

Cook the potatoes in unsalted water for 25 minutes or until tender. Drain and cool. Cut potatoes in cubes. Combine potatoes, eggs, parsley, and green onions in a bowl. Combine the remaining ingredients. Pour over potatoes, tossing gently. Serves 4-6.

*****

*When we were young, my sisters and I enjoyed car rides and reading signs advertising Burma Shave, a brushless shaving cream. Between 1927 and 1963, Burma Shave erected a series of rectangular signs in fields along the road. The first four or five lines were a humorous verse:*
    He's the Guy – The Gals Forgot – His Style –
    Was Smooth – His Chin Was Not.
    *BURMA SHAVE!*

**SALADS**

### julie's poppy-seed chicken salad.

*Recently, my niece, Julie Ward's son, Jack, passed his driver's test. Now, he helps Julie chauffeur his sister, Katy, to her softball practices and his brother, Daniel, to his sports events. So, Julie has more time for her passion for cooking!*

*Her most often requested recipe is for Poppy-Seed Chicken Salad. In fact, every year, her mother-in-law, my sister Harriet, serves this salad at her bridge club luncheon at the request of the other 11 members.*

5 C cubes, cooked chicken
1 C chopped walnuts
1 C diced green pepper
1/4 C raisins
1/2 C chopped scallions
1 pound pasta, cooked

Mix together and add the dressing below.

poppy-seed salad dressing:

2 C mayonnaise
1/4 C poppy seeds
6 Tbsp sugar
1/4 C fresh lemon juice

*****

*A person who sows seeds of kindness enjoys a perpetual harvest.*
*-Anonymous*

## SALADS

### mom's coleslaw.

*Eileen Fels and I met through HSN. Eileen says, "While this recipe is rather mundane, it holds a dear place in my heart, because my mom continuously made coleslaw throughout the summer. It's very vinegary and light. It tastes like summer and reminds me of being home as a kid with the family. Of course, by the end of summer, we were tired of cole slaw!"*

Large head cabbage, shredded
1/2 C sugar
1/2 C apple cider vinegar
1/2 C cup water
4 carrots, shredded
Small red onion, chopped
2 small or 1 large green bell pepper, chopped
Mayonnaise (Eileen prefers Duke's.)

Boil the sugar, vinegar, and water together until the sugar melts, about 10 minutes. Cool off just a little. Pour over the cabbage. Cover by weighing it down with a heavy plate. Cool in refrigerator.

    Add the carrot, onion, and pepper to the cabbage when cool. Add as much mayonnaise as desired (1/3 to 1/2 cup or to taste). Cover. Place the slaw in the refrigerator.

    Eileen makes this a day ahead "to let the flavors get happy!"

## SALADS

### peach and tomato salsa.

*Gary and I serve this salsa as a side salad for chicken or beef. And we especially enjoy it as an appetizer - with Scoops or a thick salty Tostito.*

3 ripe peaches, chopped
1 pound cherry tomatoes, chopped
1/2 sweet onion, diced
1 ear corn, cooked and cut from the ear
1/2 C basil, chopped
1/2 C pecans, chopped
1/4 C peach or basil olive oil
1 Tbsp balsamic vinegar
1/2 C crumbled blue cheese

Combine all ingredients from the peaches to pecans. Save some basil for garnish. Combine oil and vinegar for dressing. Mix dressing with vegetable mixture. Top with cheese and basil. Serves 4 as a salad.

*****

*In 2012, Jessica and Stephen Rose launched The Peach Truck, a mobile-peach sales business. They began trucking peaches to Nashville from Fort Valley, Georgia, in Stephen's '64 Jeep Gladiator. This year, the Peach Truck will travel the country on its annual summer tour with stops in eight states, delivering peaches in season.*

*In May 2019, we attended the launch of their cookbook,* The Peach Truck Cookbook, *at City House Restaurant in Germantown. The party included a taste of City House Chef, Tandy Wilson's peach dishes and peach-based vodka and bourbon drinks. We enjoyed a conversation with the Roses, as they autographed an advance copy of their book for us. And, we even picked a bag of peaches from the back of their peach truck!*

## SALADS

### pickled beets and eggs.

*In my family home shortly before Easter, Harriet, Sharon, and I retrieved our Easter baskets from the attic. We always hoped there would be a few jelly beans from the previous year, hiding in the artificial grass.*

*The Easter Bunny's signature eggs were multi-colored, speckled eggs. I knew, for certain, there was NO RABBIT when I once tip-toed down the stairs the night before Easter morning and saw my father decorating those eggs.*

*After Easter, with an abundance of colored eggs, Mother prepared pickled beets and eggs, using some of the surplus. Other eggs became a delicious egg-salad sandwich spread.*

6 hard-boiled eggs
2 cans (15 oz each) cut beets, undrained
3/4 C sugar
3/4 C cider vinegar
1/8 C pickling spice

In a medium saucepan, combine sugar, vinegar, liquid from the beets, and pickling spice. Heat just above boiling. Pour over beets and eggs. Refrigerate for a few days before serving. You can keep adding beets for several weeks.

*****

*The day after Easter, Harriet and I arrived at the G.C. Murphy's 5 & 10 Store when it opened. Our mission was to buy left-over yellow marshmallow Peeps, now quite chewy and tough. But who could resist a bargain of two for a penny! We did not adhere to Daddy's words, "It's not a bargain if you don't need it."*

**SALADS**

### salad a la parisienne

*An excellent summer luncheon salad, especially with the addition of grilled chicken or steak!*

2 C cooked, sliced red potatoes
1 C scallions, chopped
2 C celery, sliced
12 sweet pickle slices
3 large tomatoes, quartered
1/4 C capers
6 hard-boiled eggs, quartered
1 large red or green bell pepper, sliced
Lettuce

Line a bowl with lettuce. Arrange all other ingredients on the lettuce. Toss with French dressing. Serves 8 as a first course. To serve as an entrée, add slices of grilled chicken or grilled steak. Serves 4..

classic French dressing:

2 cloves garlic
1/3 C vinegar
2 Tbsp mustard
1 C oil

Crush garlic in bottom of wooden salad bowl and discard the garlic. Add the remaining ingredients and whisk.

## SALADS

### seven-layer salad

*My younger sister, Sharon, was the family historian. She kept in touch with both the Dibert and the Fletcher branches of our family. Frequently, she brought this salad to family reunions.*

1/2 head shredded Iceberg lettuce
3 stalks celery, sliced
3 green onions, diced
1/2 green bell pepper, diced
1 pkg (10 oz) frozen peas
1 C mayonnaise
1/2 C grated Romano cheese

In a glass bowl, layer first six ingredients. Spread with mayonnaise. Sprinkle with cheese. Chill thoroughly before serving. Serves 8.

*Sharon's home in Camp Hill, Pennsylvania, was only a few hours east of Bedford. On week-ends, she and her son, Adam, drove to Bedford for the day. While Sharon visited with family and friends, Adam photographed Bedford's historic sites.*

*Sharon's interest in history was evident in her and Frank's two months-long, annual trips to visit historical, as well as off-the-beaten-path sites, throughout the United States and Canada. Each trip began by their playing Willy Nelson's on the Road Again as their rig pulled out of their driveway.*

*Her special interests were Indian mounds and lighthouses. Gary and I treasured our visits with Sharon and Frank here in Nashville and on Gasparilla Island, a barrier island on the southern Gulf coast of Florida. Gary and I have vacationed there for twenty years. In 1909, a railroad was built on Gasparilla Island to transport phosphate from the mainland to the Gulf f Mexico port on the southern tip of the island. Today the railroad bed is a walking-biking path.*

## SALADS

### tom's taco salad

*Harriet was an excellent tennis player and traveler. On a cruise in the 1960s, she met her future husband, Tom Ward, a CPA who retired from Peat Marwick in the late 1970s. Tom perfected this salad that became the Ward's Friday night supper.*

*Harriet and I really appreciated his preparing supper for us after our volunteer stints for the Atlanta Golf Classic, played at the Atlanta Country Club near their home or after our docent sessions at the Russian Art Exhibition in downtown Atlanta. And, Harriet welcomed this salad after her Friday volunteer day at the Atlanta Olympic Committee Headquarters between 1996 and 1998.*

1 can (16 oz) red kidney beans
1 Tbsp chili powder
1 head Iceberg lettuce, chopped or 1 head Romaine, torn
2 large tomatoes, chopped
1 medium onion, chopped
1 red or green bell pepper, sliced
Ripe olives and pimento-stuffed olives, sliced
2 C shredded Cheddar cheese
Ranch dressing
Tortilla chips

Place beans in a skillet and sprinkle with chili powder. Heat thoroughly and cool. Toss beans with lettuce, tomatoes, onions, olives, and cheese. Drizzle with Ranch dressing. Serve with tortilla chips.

## SALADS

### wild rice and cranberry salad.

*This delicious salad can be served at a dinner party and the leftovers for brunch. A delicious accompaniment for grilled chicken, baked ham, or roasted pork tenderloin!*

1 pkg (6 oz) long-grain and wild rice mix
2 C sweetened dried cranberries (Ocean Spray Craisins)
1 C fresh broccoli flowerets, chopped
4 green onions, chopped
3 celery ribs, thinly sliced
1 jar (2 oz) diced pimentos, drained
1/2 C sweet-and-sour dressing
1 C dry-roasted peanuts

Prepare rice according to directions simmering 20 to 25 minutes or until rice is tender and liquid is absorbed. Allow the rice to cool. Combine rice, cranberries, and the next four ingredients. Add dressing and stir gently. Cover and chill at least 2 hours. Stir in peanuts before serving. Serves 6.

## SALADS

### wilted lettuce.

*A Pennsylvania-Dutch classic! Spring lettuce from our kitchen garden in Bedford provided the basis for this salad. I was amazed to read an August 27, 2017 Wall Street Journal article by Louisa Shafiz, entitled* Live a Little, 'Kill' Your Greens. *It was about "kilt" lettuce or warm "wilted greens."*

*In the late 1940s, our babysitter, was an elderly lady, who we affectionately called Koontzie. She would pick a mess of dandelion greens from our backyard under the clotheslines and prepare "wilted greens" for our dinner. Harriet and I did not share her enthusiasm!*

*My mother made wilted lettuce. She served this salad with fried ham and hot boiled red potatoes. Sometimes, she added fried bacon to her mayonnaise or added fried bacon to the lettuce and onions.*

To prepare wilted lettuce, toss freshly picked spring garden lettuce or a head of shredded iceberg lettuce with a medium onion, sliced. Pour hot mayonnaise over the lettuce and onions.

### mother's cooked mayonnaise:

| | |
|---|---|
| 1 Tbsp sugar | 1 C milk |
| 1 Tbsp flour | 1 egg |
| 1 tsp dry mustard | 1 tsp vinegar |
| 1 tsp salt | 1 Tbsp oil |
| Dash pepper | |

Mix dry ingredients, and moisten with milk. Add the egg and beat well. Add milk and vinegar. Heat Wesson oil and add it to the mixture. Cook, stirring thoroughly until mixture thickens.

In November 1981, Gary and I passed through customs at Dulles Airport in Washington, D.C., returning from our European honeymoon that included business appointments in London, and Amsterdam and a stay at a beautiful inn tucked away in the deep forests of Holland near the Belgian border.

# sides

**Eat no garlic, for we are to utter sweet breath.**
-William Shakespeare


There's nothing wrong with sending a quick note
if you're busy or just want to flirt,
but it's hard to have any real interaction over text.
In the buffet of communication,
text messaging should be a side dish, not the entre.
-Greg Behrendt

## SIDES

### baked potato chips.

*These crispy chips can be used as sides or as appetizers!*

2 medium baking potatoes
1 1/2 tsp butter
3/4 tsp salt
1/2 tsp paprika

Heat oven to 425 degrees. Cut each potato into 20 1/4-inch disks. In a small saucepan, melt butter, then stir in salt and paprika. Brush one side of potato disks with mixture and place on buttered cookie sheet. Brush second side with butter. Bake 20-25 minutes or until crisp and brown.

*****

### baked zucchini slices.

*These are similar to the fried zucchini served with white pizza and Tuscan white beans at The Amalfi, our favorite Italian restaurant in Rockville, Maryland.*

1/2 C panko
1/4 C loosely packed fresh basil leaves
1/4 C finely grated Parmesan cheese
1/2 pound zucchini, cut into 1/4-inch rounds
1 Tbsp olive oil
Vegetable cooking spray

Preheat oven to 450 degrees. Process first 3 ingredients in a food processor until finely ground. Toss zucchini rounds in the oil. Dredge zucchini, one round at a time in the panko-cheese mixture, pressing it to adhere. Place rounds in a single layer in jelly-roll pan coated with spray. Bake 30 minutes or until browned and crisp.

**SIDES**

### billy's garlic-smashed potatoes.

*During the 1990s, my son, Billy, began the tradition of preparing a gourmet Thanksgiving dinner for his Los Angeles friends. For the first few years, guests brought their own silver, as well as chairs.*

*His stove was vintage green-and-white enamel, a late 1930s model. On the upper warming shelf, Billy stored his home-made apple and pecan pies. Billy experimented with many new recipes, including one that quickly replaced the traditional mashed potatoes. Preparing Christmas dinner for his wife Rene, their children, Fletcher and Sophia, and guests has become a tradition for his family.*

6 unpeeled garlic cloves
15 small (1 1/2-inch) new potatoes, halved
1 C heavy cream
1/2 C unsalted butter

Preheat oven to 300 degrees. Place the garlic in a baking dish and bake for 45 minutes. Set aside. Cook potatoes in water to cover until tender (15 minutes.) Place cream and butter in another pan. Cut ends off garlic. Squeeze pulp into this pan and heat until butter is melted. Keep warm. Puree potatoes. Stir in cream mixture. Serves 6.

*Billy was always interested in cooking. Before he could be legally employed, he volunteered to be the salad-maker and garlic-peeler at the Amalfi restaurant in Rockville, Maryland, owned by our friends, Moe and Renata. Renata's son, Roberto, and Billy were best buddies. You can imagine the amount of garlic Billy peeled in an evening. He and his clothes reeked. Fortunately, I drove a Fiat convertible and put the top down to transport him home, even in the winter.*

*In the summer of 1978, the four of us spent two weeks in Italy, visiting with Renata's family in Pisa and her favorite cities, including Venice where she had studied art while in college.*

**SIDES**

**garlic cheese grits.**

*This recipe comes from our neighbor, Celeste Lester's New Orleans family. Celeste says, "Of all the things I cook, it's my most requested recipe. It's easy and can be prepared ahead of time. And, it's Southern!"*

1 C quick grits
4 C water
1 stick margarine or butter
1 tsp salt
8 oz American cheese (Celeste uses cheese slices.)
2 eggs
Garlic powder
Milk (small amount)
Grated Cheddar cheese
Sour cream

Preheat oven to 325 degrees. In 4 cups of boiling, salted water, stir grits slowly. Return to boil, then reduce heat and cook 5 minutes. Add chunks of butter and American cheese, stirring to melt. Beat eggs and add enough milk to make 1 cup. Add mix to grits and stir in several dashes of garlic powder. Pour mixture into a greased casserole. Bake 30 minutes. Sprinkle with grated Cheddar cheese and dot with sour cream. Sprinkle with paprika and bake at 350 degrees for 30 minutes more.

When freezing, initially bake for 30 minutes at 325 degrees to set the eggs. Freeze. The night before serving, place the casserole in the refrigerator. Then bake at 325-degrees for about 25 minutes or until heated through. Add sour cream, paprika, and Cheddar cheese. Continue baking at 350 degrees for 25-30 minutes. Pull it out when the Cheddar is melted and before it burns!

**SIDES**

## hoppin' john.

*Cooking rice and beans together was brought to the South from Africa in the 19th century and became a staple in antebellum cooking. By the early 20th century, the dish was associated with the New Year and prosperity. Some say, because peas swell when cooked, they symbolize growing prosperity. Hoppin' John is eaten with collard greens, representing paper money and with cornbread, which represents gold. Keeping with that theme, some families place a penny under the dish of Hoppin' John when they serve it.*

*As a northern transplant to Naples and to Nashville, I adapted to the Southern cuisine. Rather than the traditional Pennsylvania-Dutch custom of eating sauerkraut on New Year's Day to ensure luck for the following year, I have adopted the Hoppin' John tradition and combined several recipes. I shop in early December, to make sure I have black-eyed peas for the new year!*

3 scallions, thinly sliced
2 Tbsp butter
2 oz smoked ham
1 celery stalk, diced
1/2 green pepper, diced
2 garlic cloves, minced
Pinch of cayenne
2 C black-eyed peas, rinsed
1 C chicken broth

Heat butter in a large skillet. Add scallions, ham, celery, green pepper, and some salt. Cook, stirring for 6 minutes. Add garlic and cayenne. Cook 1 minute. Add black-eyed peas and chicken broth. Simmer for 8 minutes. Stir in scallion greens.

## SIDES

### judy's curried rice.

*Chuck Nuechterlein, Gary's Michigan SAE fraternity brother, and his wife, Judy, really enjoy cooking together. A dinner at their Naples home always promises new and exciting dishes. This curried rice dish is exceptional!*

1 medium onion, diced
1/2 stick butter
2 tsp mild curry powder
1 1/2 C long-grain rice
1 tsp garlic powder
1 Tbsp chicken bouillon
3 C chicken broth
1 C golden raisins

Sauté the onion in butter until the onion is transparent. Add curry powder to the onion and stir. Mix in the rice and stir until coated. Add remaining ingredients. Bring to a boil. Reduce the heat, and cook uncovered until water is absorbed.

*Chuck and Judy were from Frankenmuth, Michigan. In the 1940s, the town was known for its two enormous, competing chicken restaurants, The Zehnders (Chuck's family) and The Fishers (Judy's family).*

*On Sundays, hundreds of people arrived there from all over Michigan for a family-style dinner. The diners alternated restaurants on successive week-ends, trying to decide which restaurant served the best chicken. This continued even after Fishers sold his establishment to the Zehnders, and the food for both restaurants was prepared in the same kitchen, a fact not shared with the public. Today, Frankenmuth is still known for its traditional, family-style chicken dinners!*

**SIDES**

### mother's baked beans.

*Mother usually prepared baked beans for our family picnics and always for the Fletcher or Dibert family reunions. In summer after church, our family drove into the country for a picnic at Fred's. This spot, down the lane from my father's boyhood home, was actually one of Fred Helsel's cow pastures. And, we always prayed that his cows hadn't grazed there recently.*

*First, we stopped at Fred's farmhouse to ask if we could use the field. Then, we drove into the field and parked the car near the stream so that we could wash the car later in the afternoon.*

*Our Sunday dinner was spread on a tablecloth under a towering maple tree. The menu rarely varied: fried chicken, potato salad or baked beans, carrot and celery sticks, and cake for dessert.*

*We spent the afternoon drifting on inner tubes in the stream, fishing, reading the Sunday papers, washing the car, or napping. Some Sundays before returning to Bedford, we stopped in Imlertown to visit Uncle Ralph or Aunt Mary, my mother's brother and sister.*

| | |
|---|---|
| 1 pkg Navy beans | 1 Tbsp dark Karo or maple syrup |
| 2 onions, cut into 1/8-inch slices | Black pepper |
| 1 Tbsp dry mustard | 1 C tomato juice |
| 1/4 C brown sugar | 4 strips bacon, cut in half |

Soak beans overnight covered with water. Preheat oven to 300 degrees. Cook beans until skins split when blown on. Spoon beans into casserole, so some water stays with them. Spread onions, mustard, sugar, Karo, and pepper over the beans, and stir in tomato juice. Top with bacon pieces. Bake 6 hours. Uncover for the last 30 minutes.

## SIDES

### sauerkraut cooked in beer.

*To assure each new year is filled with good luck, the Pennsylvania Dutch serve sauerkraut and pork on New Year's Day. Leftovers from this recipe are delicious when served cold with corned beef and hot mustard in a sandwich. Or, when the sauerkraut is served hot with grilled pickled franks. (See Entrées Category.)*

3 Tbsp butter
3 medium onions, sliced
1 garlic clove, minced
1 can (1 pound, 11 oz) un-drained sauerkraut
1 C beer
3 Tbsp brown sugar
1/2 tsp celery seed
1 bay leaf

Brown onions and garlic in butter. Add sauerkraut, beer, brown sugar, celery seed, and bay leaf. Stir together well. Cover and simmer about 1/2 hour, stirring once or twice. Uncover and cook to evaporate the liquid. Remove bay leaf. Serves 4.

**SIDES**

### squash casserole.

*I first tasted this recipe, from Martha Stamps' book,* The New Southern Basics, *at her restaurant, Martha's at Belle Meade Plantation in Nashville in the early 2000s. Martha says this is a great way to use large squash! The casserole keeps well and is as delicious the next day.*


2 pounds (6 overflowing cups) yellow summer squash
1 yellow onion, diced large
1 Tbsp salt
1 C breadcrumbs (plus more for topping)
3 eggs
1 C cream
2 Tbsp minced fresh basil
1 tsp black pepper
Dash cayenne pepper
1 C grated Cheddar cheese

Preheat oven to 350 degrees. Clean squash and cut in circular slices. Cover squash and onion with cold water. Add salt and bring to a boil. Reduce heat to medium and cook for 20 minutes or until very tender. Drain well and place in a large mixing bowl. Add breadcrumbs. Beat eggs with cream and mix into the squash. Stir in fresh basil and ½ cup of grated cheese. Add peppers.
    Pour into a baking dish. Cover the top with additional breadcrumbs and remaining 1/2 cup of cheese. Cover with aluminum foil. Bake for 30 minutes or until casserole is set. Remove foil and bake for 10 minutes more until brown on top. Serves 8.

**SIDES**

**sweet potato casserole.**

*My friends, Judi Smith and Liz Weller, coordinate showings of the cabi clothing collection twice a year. Usually, a preview for hostesses precedes the showings in their hostesses' homes, including my own. Several seasons ago, Judi prepared this dish for a cabi Preview Dinner.*

*Many years ago, Judi received this recipe from her mother, Ann Anderson Brown. Judi has served this traditional dish at each of the 37 Thanksgivings she has hosted in her home.*

3 C cooked mashed sweet potatoes (about 6 medium sweet potatoes)
1 C granulated sugar
2 eggs
1 tsp vanilla
1/2 C sweet milk
1/2 C butter (melted)
1 C dark-brown sugar
1/3 C all-purpose flour
1 C chopped pecans
1/3 C butter

Preheat oven to 325 degrees. Combine potatoes, granulated sugar, eggs, vanilla, milk, and melted butter. Placed in a greased casserole dish. For the topping, combine brown sugar, flour and then add butter and pecans. Mix together until crumbly and sprinkle over the top of the potatoes. Bake for 40 minutes.

**SIDES**

### syrian pilaf.

*After college, I taught at Mellon Junior High School in the Mt. Lebanon School System, a southern suburb of Pittsburgh, Pennsylvania. Frequently, we drove to the city's north side to a restaurant owned and operated by a Lebanese family. There we enjoyed green salad with a tart lemon dressing, chicken shish kabobs with pita bread, and their delicious pilaf, followed by a dessert of honeyed baklava.*

2 Tbsp butter
1/4 C vermicelli, uncooked
1 C long-grain rice
2 C chicken broth
1/4 C pignolia nuts, heated in 2 Tbsp butter

Melt butter. Lightly brown the vermicelli in butter. Soak rice in hot water. Rinse in cold water and drain. Add rice and water to vermicelli. Simmer 25 minutes or until water is absorbed. Add nuts before serving. Serves 3-4.

*****

*When Harriet, Sharon, and I were teenagers, we frequently went to Pittsburgh to shop downtown at Gimbels and Hornes department stores. In the late 1950s, Harriet was finishing her degree at Carnegie Mellon while I was teaching in Mt. Lebanon. Often, we met downtown for dinner at the Stouffer's restaurant that had been established in Pittsburgh in 1929. By 1990, the Stouffer's name was attached to 40 upscale resorts and hotels and 68 restaurants. Two years later, the company began selling its properties to focus on their frozen meals of baked ziti, chicken-and-broccoli pasta bake, and turkey tetrazzini.*

## SIDES

### tomato pudding.

*This family recipe is from the mother of Piper Brewer, Executive Director of the Shiawassee Arts Center in Owosso, Michigan. Piper told me that her mother served this tomato pudding as a side dish for Thanksgiving or Christmas dinner. Given the sweetness of this pudding, it could be a dessert! Tomatoes for dessert?*

4 C bread cubes, crusts removed (Dry bread works best.)
2 sticks butter
1 C light brown sugar
1/2 C water
2 C canned tomato puree
1/2 tsp salt

Preheat oven to 375 degrees. Place bread cubes in a greased baking dish. Pour melted butter over them, stirring carefully as you pour. Mix together brown sugar, water, tomato puree, and salt. Simmer for 5 minutes and then pour over buttered bread cubes. Set baking dish in pan of hot water and bake 45-50 minutes or until top is well-browned. Serves 6.

*****

*Botanically, a tomato is a fruit. True fruits are developed from the ovary in the base of the flower that contains the seeds of the plant. True fruits include blueberries, raspberries, oranges, and many kinds of nuts. The case of Nix v. Hedden, 149 U.S. 304 (1893), was a decision by the U.S. Supreme Court that, under U.S. customs regulations, the tomato should be classified as a vegetable rather than a fruit.* **Fruit or vegetable? You decide!**

**SIDES**

### wild rice casserole.

*For many years, Mary Strutz Fox kept my Naples pantry shelves stocked with gourmet wild rice when she returned from her childhood home in the Twin Cities, Minnesota. This delicious company casserole can be prepared in the morning and refrigerated. Allow it to come to room temperature (about 30 minutes) before placing it in the oven.*

1 onion, diced
1/3 C butter
2 C wild rice or 1 C wild rice and 1C white rice
4 1/2 C chicken broth, boiling
1 C sliced fresh mushrooms
2 fresh tomatoes, sliced
1/2 C slivered almonds
1/4 tsp thyme
1/4 tsp oregano

Preheat oven to 325 degrees. Sauté onion in butter. Add rice, coating with butter. Place rice in a 3-quart casserole. Add remaining ingredients. Cover with foil and bake for 1 hour. Uncover and bake for 15 minutes. Serves 10.

*****

*Women should not feel obliged towards any men for eternity.*
*They earned this privilege by gathering berries, digging roots,*
*picking wild rice, and chewing deer skin to make it soft for 999,000 years,*
*while the men were having fun in the open,*
*chasing deer and fighting among themselves.*
— Vinko Vrbanic

**SIDES**

**yellow squash casserole.**

*In Naples, Florida, from 1990-1994, I served as President of Friends of Art at the Philharmonic Galleries, and my good friend, Ginny Small was Vice-President. In 1994, Ginny succeeded me and initiated an Annual Public Lecture in Hayes Hall. Our first speaker was Thomas Hoving, the Director of the Metropolitan Museum of Art in New York City.*

*Ginny's husband, Bob, retired before they moved to Naples, and he assumed the role of chef in their home. Bob was especially renowned for his risotto. After he planned the evening menu, Bob drove to Wynn's Market for ingredients and the correct wine to accompany that meal. How lucky can you get?*

*This yellow squash casserole was a hit at Ginny and Bob's Naples dinner parties!*

3 pounds yellow squash
1 medium onion
1 stick of butter
1/2 C grated cheese
3 or 4 Ritz crackers, crumbled
Salt and pepper to taste

Preheat oven to 375 degrees. Cut squash in cubes and chop the onion. Cook together until tender. Mash thoroughly and add the butter. Mix in crackers, cheese, and salt and pepper. Place mixture in a casserole. Bake 40-45 minutes.

**SIDES**

### zucchini-potato casserole.

*This elegant French dish of layered vegetables is delicious warm or at room temperature. For a snack, heat any leftovers and place in warm pita bread.*

2 Tbsp butter
2 medium onions, chopped
Vegetable spraying oil
1 medium potato, sliced
1 medium zucchini, sliced
4 plum tomatoes, sliced
1/2 tsp black pepper
1/2 C fresh basil, chopped
2 Tbsp butter, melted
1/2 C Parmesan cheese, freshly grated

Preheat oven to 375 degrees. Melt butter and brown onions until they begin to caramelize, about 10 minutes. Spoon onions into a 10-inch quiche dish, sprayed with vegetable oil. Alternate potatoes, zucchini, and tomatoes around the outside of the dish over the onions. Overlap the vegetables slightly. Alternate the remaining vegetables in the center of the dish. Sprinkle with basil and pepper. Drizzle with butter. Cover with aluminum foil. Bake for 30 minutes. Remove foil and sprinkle with cheese. Bake 35 minutes or until golden brown. Wait 10 minutes before serving.

In June 1982, I resigned from teaching in the Montgomery County Schools and became Gary's business partner. While Gary traveled to teach and lecture, I managed both the List Business and the IT Professional Training Business. Frequently, we invited the staff to our home (pictured) for lunch or held a TGIF Party on the back lawn of our 4820 Montgomery Lane office in Bethesda, Maryland.

# brunch

**And yet, as course followed course, the king could not help feeling puzzled, for in spite of the variety of dishes, he perceived that they were all concocted of hens.**
-Giovanni Boccaccio

**The proof of the pudding is in the eating.**
-Joseph Addison

**A Sunday brunch well spent brings a week of content.**
-Anonymous

## BRUNCH

### apple pancake breakfast casserole.

*Dianne May and I met at the Cheekwood Docent Class in 1999. Our involvement at Cheekwood included the Friends of Cheekwood Annual Fashion Show at the Belle Meade Country Club. Dianne chaired the Fashion Show committee for two years and asked me to chair the Silent Auction that was held on the BMCC sunporch*

*In 2011, Dianne and Hinckley, her therapy dog, participated in a Lovey's Legacy program to teach pre-school children how to care for dogs. Dianne wrote a book,* Hinkley Goes to School, *to give to these children. Today, Dianne accompanies Hinckley on his visits to the Alzheimer residents at Abe's Garden.*

*Over the years, we have met for coffee or have invited one another for brunch. On one occasion, Dianne prepared this delicious dish for me.*

*Several years ago, Dianne joined with Gary, Suzanne Regen, and Julie Schoerke in extracting my promise that I would begin to write my memoir using recipes. Many thanks to all four for their encouragement.*

| | |
|---|---|
| 8 eggs | 1/2 tsp cinnamon |
| 1 1/2 C milk | 1/2 C margarine |
| 1 C flour | 2 Granny Smith apples |
| 3 Tbsp sugar | 4 Tbsp brown sugar |
| 1 tsp vanilla | Confectioners sugar |
| 1/2 tsp salt | |

Preheat oven to 450 degrees. Mix the first 7 ingredients together. Batter will be lumpy. Set aside. Melt margarine in a 4-quart baking dish.

Peel and slice apples. Place in pan and return to oven until butter sizzles. Remove and place brown sugar on top of apples. Pour batter over apples. Bake for 20-30 minutes. Dust with confectioners sugar. Serves 10.

**BRUNCH**

## basil tomato tart.

*Babs Freeman is a charter member of the Sew 'n Sow Garden Club. Through the years, Babs has planned many exciting club events. Most memorable was an Evening with Chihuly, held in Cheekwood's Potter Room. The party preceded an evening walk through the Chihuly Exhibition. Babs is an excellent cook, and many club members have enjoyed her tomato basil tart!*

1/2 C basil leaves
1/4 C parsley leaves
2 cloves garlic
1/3 C basil oil or a good olive oil
Salt and pepper to taste
14 oz Monterey Jack cheese, shredded
6-8 Roma tomatoes, sliced thin
1 sheet Puff Pastry, thawed
2-3 Tbsp Dijon mustard

Preheat oven to 400 degrees. Mince basil, parsley, and garlic. Mix with oil, salt, and pepper. Roll pastry on a floured board to a 13x17-inch rectangle. Place in an ungreased 11½ x15½-inch jelly roll pan, pressing into corners and up the sides. Brush mustard over the pastry and spread cheese on top. Arrange the tomato slices in rows over the cheese and brush with basil mixture. Bake for 25-30 minutes until pastry is well browned and cheese is bubbly. Best if served warm. Can be made ahead and refrigerated. Reheat in a 350-degree oven for 15 minutes.

*If you're in a hurry, Babs suggests using a ready-made pizza crust (Boboli) and any good pesto sauce.*

## BRUNCH

### becky's brunch casserole.

*Liz Weller and Judi Smith are partners and fashion consultants for cabi. Their 2013 Spring Preview Brunch began with mimosas. Liz served her sister-in-law's specialty, Becky's Brunch Casserole, and Judi prepared her Blueberry French Toast. This casserole is also delicious with Bloody Marys, fresh fruit, and sweet rolls.*

2 pounds bulk sausage (Liz prefers Bob Evans.)
Finely chopped green pepper and onion to taste
1 pound fresh mushrooms, thinly sliced
3 C milk
11 slices of bread, cubed
9 eggs, beaten
Salt and pepper
2 Tbsp dried mustard
1 pound shredded Cheddar cheese

Brown sausage. Remove the meat and drain. Cook peppers, onions, and mushrooms. Combine milk, bread, eggs, and spices. Beat with a fork. Mix with sausage mixture and place in 9x13x2-inch dish. Cover with foil and refrigerate overnight.

      Preheat oven to 350 degrees. Remove dish from the fridge and let it stand for 30 minutes. Top with cheese and bake for 45 minutes. Let stand for 15 minutes before serving. Serves 12.

## BRUNCH

### broiled grapefruit.

*Between 1970 and 1992, my mother enjoyed the best of all worlds, summers in Bedford, nestled in the mountains of southern Pennsylvania, and Florida winters in Sarasota or Naples. Usually, I drove her north and south with a stop at my sister, Harriet's home in Marietta, Georgia. Many times, an overnight stop was at Chalet Suzanne in Lake Wales, Florida, where we had dinner and visited their gift shop. Chalet Suzanne was the home of gourmet soups. Broiled grapefruit was their signature appetizer. While Chalet Suzanne closed in 2016, it remains a very pleasant memory of my many trips with Mother.*

| | |
|---|---|
| 1/2 grapefruit, room temperature | 1/4 tsp cinnamon |
| 1 Tbsp margarine | 2 Tbsp sugar |

Preheat oven to broil. Cut grapefruit in half. Then, cut the sections with a grapefruit knife. Fill the center with margarine. Sprinkle cinnamon-sugar mixture over grapefruit. Broil in baking pan 4 inches from heat for 8-10 minutes or until top browns and is bubbling hot.

*My first trips with Mother began in the fall of 1954, during my sophomore year at Wilson College. I had been selected Grand Worthy Advisor of the Pennsylvania State Assembly of the Order of the Rainbow for Girls. In that capacity, on most week-ends, I visited different Assemblies throughout the state. On Friday afternoons, my mother picked me up in Chambersburg and drove me to those meetings. In the summer of 1955, she and I drove to San Antonio, Texas, where I was an officer in the Supreme Assembly.*

*In the 1980s, Mother and I cruised on the Rhine from Amsterdam to Zurich. On another occasion, we sailed through the Greek Islands. On one more trip, we explored the capitals of Europe. All wonderful memories!*

## BRUNCH

### cheese enchiladas.

*In the late 1970s, I taught eighth-grade English at Belt Junior High School, located outside Washington, D.C., in suburban Maryland. Marie Sneed, the principal, prepared cheese enchiladas for faculty gatherings. This low-fat dish is a delight for a Mexican dinner. Delicious with a green salad and fresh fruit! Follow dinner with a decadent chocolate dessert!*

2 cans (10 oz) enchilada sauce
1 container (12 oz) reduced-fat cottage cheese
1 container (8 oz) reduced-fat sour cream
1 can (4 1/2 oz) chopped green chilies, un-drained
8 flour tortillas (8-inch)
1 C (4 oz) shredded reduced-fat Monterey Jack cheese
1 can (2 1/4 oz) sliced ripe olives, drained
1 C shredded, reduced-fat Cheddar cheese
Garnishes: Sour cream, sliced ripe olives, and chopped green onions.

Preheat oven to 350 degrees. Spread 3/4 cup enchilada sauce in lightly greased 13x9x2-inch baking dish. Combine cottage cheese, sour cream, and chopped chilies. Spoon about 1/3 cup down the center of each tortilla. Sprinkle evenly with Monterey Jack cheese. Roll up and place, seam side down, in the baking dish. Top with remaining enchilada sauce. Sprinkle with olives. Bake, covered, for 25 minutes. Uncover and sprinkle with Cheddar cheese. Serves 4

*For variety, add a tablespoon or two of diced chicken or shrimp to each enchilada.*

**BRUNCH**

### christmas cheese soufflé.

*In the early 1980s, Gary and I began a tradition of serving this souffle on Christmas morning! Wendy and Jennifer, Gary's daughters, referred to the dish as Cheese Pit because their Grandmother Parker's similar dish was so named. I recently discovered that Cheese Pit is actually the correct name. But, "souffle" sounds so much better to me. This is a terrific "Prepare the Night Before" recipe!*

*With the souffle, I often serve fresh fruit, Canadian bacon, and Sour Cream Coffee Cake. (See Breads Category.)*

| | |
|---|---|
| 10 white bread slices, cubed (6 cups) | 3 eggs |
| 1/2 pound sharp Cheddar cheese | 3 C milk |
| 1 tsp salt | Butter |
| 1 tsp dry mustard | |
| 1/4 tsp Worcestershire sauce | |

Cut the bread into cubes and grate the cheese. In a well-greased 13x9x2-inch baking dish, place bread cubes. Sprinkle evenly with cheese, salt, and dry mustard. Dot with butter. Beat the eggs with milk and pour over the layers. Let stand at least one hour or overnight. If chilled, let stand 30 minutes at room temperature. Preheat the oven to 350 degrees. Bake for 50 to 60 minutes or until brown and fluffy. Serves 6 - 8.

*****

*Cheese Pit is a classic family Easter dinner tradition.*
*Nothing better with your ham.*
*Don't even think about the fat and caloric content.*
*-Epicurious*

# BRUNCH

### crepes provençal.

*In 1972, the Women's Suburban Democratic Club (WSDC), planned a fundraiser for the McGovern Campaign. Our planning sessions were held at Timberlawn, Eunice Shriver's home, in Rockville, Maryland. Art for the auction included pieces by Alexander Calder, Sister Corita, and Sam Gilliam. Bea Prosterman, created this dish for the Art Auction and Dinner held at Hickory Hill, the home of Bobby and Ethel Kennedy in McLean, Virginia.*

| | |
|---|---|
| 1 pound smoked ham | 6 sprigs fresh parsley |
| 3 large ripe eggplants | 1 tsp dried oregano |
| 3 medium zucchinis | 1 1/2 tsp salt |
| 3 medium onions | 1/4 tsp freshly ground pepper |
| 3 green peppers | 1/4 C salad oil |
| 5-6 large tomatoes | 1 small can tomato paste |
| 2 large cloves garlic | Grated Parmesan cheese |
| 1 1/2 tsp dried dill | |

Preheat oven to 250 degrees. Dice ham into very small pieces. Sauté lightly in 2 tablespoons oil and set aside. Finely dice all vegetables and parsley. Place them in a pot. Peel garlic and mince finely. Add this to vegetables. Add tomato paste, dill, oregano, salt, pepper, and remaining oil. Mix contents until coated thoroughly with oil and seasonings. Cover and bake for 2 hours. Stir frequently until vegetables soften and juices flow. Add ham and mix with vegetables. Bake 1/2 hour without cover and stir occasionally.

    Preheat oven to 300 degrees. Fill 7-inch crepe with 3 tablespoons of mixture. Fold and place in buttered baking dish. Sprinkle with grated Parmesan cheese and bake until very lightly browned and cheese is melted.

**BRUNCH**

### egg and hash-brown casserole.

*Ginger Caldwell and I met at the Sew 'n Sow Garden Club where she is a charter member. For the 2000 Annual Business Meeting, she prepared this delicious casserole, served with fresh fruit and ham biscuits.*

1 pkg (32 oz) Ore-Ida potatoes
Cooking oil
1 pound mild sausage
12 eggs
5 green onions, chopped
¼ red pepper, diced
½ to 1 pound sharp white Cheddar cheese, shredded
Tomato-green onion salsa

Preheat oven to 350 degrees. Fry the potatoes in oil. Set aside. Cook, drain, and crumble the sausage. Scramble the eggs until they are halfway done. Add cooked sausage, green onions, and red pepper. Continue to cook until the eggs are done but still soft. Add salt and pepper to taste.

Spray a large casserole with Pam. Layer cooked potatoes on the bottom. Add eggs and sausage mixture. Top with shredded cheese. Bake for 30 minutes. If this casserole is baked ahead, reheat it in the oven longer and cover if necessary. Serve with a tomato-green onion salsa as a topping.

*In the 1970s, Ginger Caldwell and three other Nashville young women had the dream of sharing their love of sewing. This vision became Children's Corner Patterns. Back then, there were not many options readily available for sewing patterns for children, especially heirloom-inspired pieces. The women hired a Nashville pattern designer, Elizabeth Travis Johnson, who created for them patterns of classic children's styles and simplified techniques for home sewers.*

## BRUNCH

### low country tomato pie.

*My friend, Joan Pinkley is an enthusiastic real estate agent, as well as an energetic HSN member. At the 2009 Sherry Party, as well as at the culinary program for the HSN Morning Study Group, Joan prepared this pie, that resulted in rave reviews and recipe requests.*

1 pie crust, baked and cooled
1/2 onion sliced paper thin
1/2 - 1 C bread crumbs
1/2 - 1 C grated Parmesan cheese
Dried basil to taste
Dried oregano to taste
Salt and ground pepper to taste
3-4 large tomatoes, peeled and sliced 1/4-inch thick
3 C sharp Cheddar cheese (grated)
1/2 C mozzarella cheese (grated)
1/2 - 1 C mayonnaise

Preheat oven to 375 degrees. Peel, slice, and salt tomatoes. Drain for 30 minutes. Spread onion rings on the pie crust. Sprinkle onions lightly with bread crumbs and Parmesan cheese. Pat tomatoes dry and layer on top of onions making sure they overlap. Sprinkle tomatoes with basil, oregano, pepper, bread crumbs, and Parmesan cheese. Mix together cheeses and only enough mayo to make it spreadable but not too runny. Spread cheese mixture over tomatoes. Sprinkle with bread crumbs and Parmesan cheese.

Bake for 10 minutes and then turn oven down to 350 degrees. Bake for about 35-40 minutes longer or when just brown on top. Cool completely before cutting. Can be served warm or at room temperature.

**BRUNCH**

### penne with capers, olives, and tomatoes.

*Gary enjoys preparing this pasta dish, especially during the winter. Fresh basil, garlic, and capers mingle to create a mouth-watering experience! Left-over sauce is tasty in a baked potato, topped with sour cream and chopped green onions.*

1 Tbsp olive oil
1/4 tsp crushed red pepper
3 cloves garlic, finely chopped
3 C plum tomatoes, chopped
1/2 C kalamata olives, chopped
1 1/2 Tbsp capers
6 C hot, cooked penne (4 C uncooked)
1/2 C Parmesan cheese, grated
3 Tbsp fresh basil, chopped

Heat oil and sauté pepper and garlic for 30 seconds. Add tomatoes, olives, and capers. Reduce heat and simmer 8 minutes. Stir occasionally. Serve over penne, sprinkled with Parmesan cheese and basil.

This sauce is also delicious on grilled chicken or shrimp, placed on a bed of angel-hair pasta. Fresh fruit and a green salad would complete the meal!

*****

*Man's life's a vapor, and full of woes;*
*he cuts a caper, and down he goes.*
*-Latin Proverb*

## BRUNCH

### sequi inn baked French toast.

*Chuck and Judy Nuechterlein moved to Naples in the late 1980s. Judy and I became fast friends and enjoyed week-ends organized by the Florida Society for Historical Preservation. Historical sites we visited included Orlando, St. Petersburg, Key West, and St. Augustine.*

*The highlight of a 1994 May week-end was the private opening and dinner at the newly-restored St. Augustine Lighthouse and Maritime Museum. While there, Judy and I stayed at the Sequi Inn Bed and Breakfast. Each morning the innkeepers offered a gourmet experience, but our preferred dish was their Baked French Toast.*

1 loaf French bread, sliced 1 1/2 -inch thick
6 eggs, beaten
2 C half & half
1/3 C whipping cream
1 tsp vanilla
1/2 C sugar
1/2 tsp cinnamon

Preheat oven to 350 degrees. Spray a 9x13x2-inch pan. Place bread slices in pan. In medium bowl, whisk the eggs. Add half & half, whipping cream, and the vanilla. Whisk mixture until blended.

In a small bowl, combine sugar and cinnamon, and whisk into eggs. Pour mixture over the bread and soak for 10 minutes. Turn bread over and bake for 45 minutes or until custard is set. Cover with foil if it becomes too brown. Serve with grape jam or maple syrup. Serves 6-8.

**BRUNCH**

### spinach and spaghetti bake.

*This dish is another favorite of Harriet's family, that includes her husband (Tom), two sons (John and Mike), daughters-in-law (Hannah and Julie), and five grandchildren (Caroline, Jack, Luke, Katie, and Daniel). As toddlers, the grandchildren loved spaghetti, so Harriet created this dish for family brunches or dinners. Soon it became a staple for their family gatherings. Today, she prepares this dish for Tom's and her supper, with leftovers as a side dish the following evening.*

1 pkg (10 oz) frozen chopped spinach
4 oz spaghetti, uncooked
1 egg, beaten
1/2 C sour cream
1/4 C milk
2 Tbsp grated Parmesan cheese
2 tsp minced dried onion
1/2 tsp salt
Dash pepper
2 C (8 oz) shredded Monterey Jack cheese
2 Tbsp grated Parmesan cheese

In separate pots, cook spinach and spaghetti, according to package directions. Drain both well. In a large bowl, combine egg, sour cream, milk, 2 tablespoons Parmesan cheese, onion, salt, and pepper. Add Monterey Jack cheese and mix well. Add drained spinach and drained spaghetti. Mix well. Turn mixture into an ungreased 10x6x2-inch baking dish. Sprinkle with 2 tablespoons Parmesan cheese. Bake covered for 15 minutes. Uncover and bake 15-20 minutes more or until heated through. Serves 4.

## BRUNCH

### swiss cheese bake.

*The mother of Joan Cole, my next-door neighbor in Potomac, Maryland, was an antique dealer in Hammondsport, New York. One summer, she interested Joan in buying antique wicker at upstate New York auctions to sell in the Washington, D.C. area. Joan did just that and became a very successful D.C. wicker dealer.*

*Before our move to Naples in 1985, I acquired some Newport pieces circa 1900 and Lloyd Loom pieces circa 1920 from Joan. In Naples, I placed these exquisite pieces on our enclosed sun porch. Today, they form conversational areas in our bedroom and in the foyer of our home, built circa 1920.*

*The cover of a 1992 coffee-table book,* Living with Wicker, *featured Joan's front porch at The Elms, her Keuka Lake summer home, as well as many photographs of her wicker collection both at The Elms and at her former home in Potomac, Maryland.*

*At the lake, Joan often served this delicious luncheon dish with a green salad and an icy dessert.*

| | |
|---|---|
| 1 loaf unsliced white bread | 1 Tbsp poppy seed |
| 1 pkg (6 oz) Swiss cheese slices | 3 Tbsp prepared mustard |
| 1/2 C butter | 2 tsp lemon juice |
| 1/3 C instant minced onion | 2 bacon slices |

Preheat oven to 350 degrees. Cut the bread into 1/4-inch wide slices, almost through. Cream together the butter, onion, mustard, poppy seeds, and lemon juice. Spread it on the bread slices. Insert 1 slice cheese into each cut. Press the loaf back into its shape. Place loaf into a greased 9x13x2-inch baking dish. Cut bacon slices in half and arrange over the top of the loaf. Bake for 20 minutes or until bacon has cooked and cheese is bubbly. Serves 4 to 6.

**BRUNCH**

### tomato-cheese-spinach strata.

*Gary and I enjoy this dish as a luncheon or supper dish, accompanied by a green salad and a really sinful dessert. If there are strata leftovers, heat and cut into small cubes to serve as appetizers. Gary has perfected this recipe!*

Tomato slices
Garlic salt
Italian or Rosemary-Olive bread, cut into 1-inch thick cubes
2 C chopped spinach
Fresh basil to taste
4 eggs
1 3/4 C milk
White pepper
Grated 6 Italian cheeses

Broil tomato slices, sprinkled with garlic salt. Set aside. Place bread into a buttered 8x8-inch baking dish. Chop spinach and basil and place over bread. Beat eggs and milk with white pepper and garlic salt to taste. Pour over spinach. Sprinkle with cheese to cover. Place tomato slices on the cheese. Refrigerate the strata.

    Preheat oven to 350 degrees. Bring the refrigerated strata to room temperature before baking. Bake for 50-60 minutes or until set. Serves 6.

*****

*I'm strong to the finish, 'cause I eats me Spinach.*
*I'm Popeye the sailor man! Toot, Toot!*
*-Popeye Theme Song*

In 1998, celebrating Christmas with Billy. In early December, I visited Billy in Boston where he was working, following his graduation from Boston University. Billy's job was sound engineer for Videocraft, a film-production company. That weekend, I observed their filming of a PBS documentary, recording the annual Candlelight Stroll at Strawberry Banks in Portsmouth, New Hampshire. A light snowfall completed the scene.

# entrees

## pheasant and chicken

**A sparrow in hand is worth a pheasant that flieth by.**
-French Proverb

**I want there to be no peasant in my realm so poor that he will not have a chicken in his pot every Sunday.**
-King Henry IV of France

**The difference between involvement and commitment is like ham and eggs.**
**The chicken is involved; the pig is committed.**
-Martina Navratilova

## PHEASANT

### smoked pheasant crepes with a huckleberry gastrique.

Jane Marcum and I met in the Herb Society of Nashville. Jane is consulting chef and partner at Jack's Place Bistro in Florence, Alabama, as well as a personal chef. Her culinary life is so amazing that I'm hoping she'll record it – soon! Meantime, here is one of her stories,

"While working at a hunting lodge in South Dakota, I created this for the hunters' first dinner. When I arrived, unlike many other places I had worked, there was no kitchen, as one would expect. There was a cast-iron wood stove and a large open fireplace, with crane for using a Dutch oven, and a spit. And very rudimentary utensils. Needless to say, I had to come up with some ideas and pretty quick. After this, I learned to ask what cooking amenities were available on site – assuming none!

"Primarily, the hunters were there for pheasant but there were also some areas for grouse hunting. The camp had some pheasants hung in the cooler, and there was plenty of sagebrush to be harvested. I proceeded to smoke 14 pheasants and used these as the main ingredient in a number of different dishes in the coming days. The hunters, all men on this particular trip, were a bit disappointed at my announcement of crepes for dinner. Yet, I have to say, they all converted and actually begged me to repeat the crepes on their final night a week later! And I provided the recipe for them to take home.

"I had provisions brought in with me - various spices, cheeses, a few herbs, oils and vinegars, etc. I have adjusted this recipe for 4 persons. You can smoke the pheasant yourself, or you can buy them online from MacFarland Farms in Wisconsin. I had brought blue cheese but any cheese along those lines will work. Two men, who said they hated blue cheese, loved it in the crepes."

*****

*As an aspiring, unemployed actor in New York City, Jack White worked for a catering company and discovered a career in food styling. During his 27-year career in Los Angeles, he styled food for over 100 TV sets and films. In June 2018, he opened Jack's Place Bistro in Florence, Alabama, where he had graduated from the University of North Alabama with a degree in broadcasting.*

**PHEASANT**

## smoked pheasant crepes with a huckleberry gastrique. (cont.)

Crepe Filling
1 smoked pheasant, shredded
1 large onion
1 large fennel bulb
1 C ripe cheese

Huckleberry Gastrique
1/2 C cider vinegar or dry wine
1 C huckleberries

Crepe Batter
3/4 C flour
1 tsp baking powder
Pinch salt
2 eggs
2/3 C milk
1/3 C water

Caramelize one large onion and one large fennel bulb, shaved or fine sliced. Sauté with butter/oil slowly until a deep color is achieved.

Crepe Batter: Sift flour twice with baking powder and salt. Fold into the mixture of eggs, milk, and water. Grate a little orange rind in if you have it. Whisk all together quickly, about 10-12 strokes, Batter will be lumpy. Let it sit at least three hours or better yet overnight.

Huckleberry Gastrique: Reduce about 1/2 C cider vinegar or a dry wine. When it becomes viscous, add 1 C huckleberries. Cook down. Taste if sugar or honey is needed, so taste is slightly sweet but retains its tartness. Either strain through cheesecloth or leave it natural.

Crepes: Whisk the rested batter. In a hot sauté pan, crepe pan or iron flat, pour batter while moving to coat (swirl) so you have a very thin crepe once turned over. Place some shredded smoked pheasant, caramelized onion/fennel and blue cheese mixture into the crepe. Amount will depend on size of crepe. For a 6-inch crepe, use about 3 heaping tablespoons. Drizzle some gastrique over crepe. The crepes can be prepared and held in a warmer or oven. Plate and serve 2 crepes per person.

## CHICKEN

### chicken sniff.

*Lee Fairbend is a dear friend whom I met through WNBA. Periodically, we meet to catch up at a restaurant that serves crab cakes, our addiction!*

*Recently, she shared with me a recipe most dear to her heart. Lee says, "I am not a fancy cook, or even a happy cook. If a recipe has more than 8 ingredients, I usually choose something else."*

*Lee told me, "My mother learned to cook inexpensive meals when my career Navy Dad was stationed in California. Since my mother gave up her job in Massachusetts so we could travel with him, she had to be very efficient with the food budget. This is one of her 100 recipes that used a pound of hamburg, the most inexpensive meat at that time. I still make it. But to make it even easier, I cheat on the ingredients. It's not healthy, but I have a good time reminiscing!"*

1 pound hamburg
1/4 small onion, chopped
1 package Minute Rice
1 can cream of chicken soup
1 can carrots

Brown hamburg and chopped onion while cooking the Minute Rice. Combine hamburg and rice and add chicken soup and carrots. Heat and serve with a healthy salad!

## CHICKEN

### chicken thighs with banana peppers.

*During the 1970s, Rita Psomadakis was my neighbor in Olney, Maryland. Her two daughters were friends with my son Billy. Rita's husband, Terry, was an American Airlines pilot. On his flights from Amsterdam to Dulles, he would surprise us with tulips in the winter. What a treat!*

*Rita was a fantastic cook and shared many of her family's Italian recipes. This dish has become one of Gary's favorites, usually a once-a-week treat. Generally, I serve it with wild rice and a green salad.*

4 chicken thighs, boneless or with bone
1/2 C chicken broth
Splash of low-sodium soy sauce
1 Tbsp butter
Yellow banana peppers or banana pepper rings

Preheat oven to 375 degrees. Place chicken thighs in an 8x8-inch baking dish. Baste with chicken broth mixed with soy sauce, and dot with butter. Bake 45 minutes, basting often. Top each thigh with banana peppers, and continue to bake 15 more minutes. Serves 2.

*A few days ago, I wanted to prepare this dish, but I discovered that there were no banana peppers in the pantry. What to do? I had some honey-ham slices and peach chutney in the fridge. I placed a strip of ham on each boneless thigh, rolled it up, and placed it, seam-side down in the baking dish. I followed the above instructions and, after 45 minutes, spooned some peach chutney over each thigh and continued baking for 15 minutes. Delicious over a bed of rice with more chutney, if desired. (See Preserves Category for Peach Chutney recipe.)*

# CHICKEN

### panko chicken with hummus.

*In Naples, Gary and I were loyal Publix customers and missed the store's friendly ambiance when we moved to Nashville. In 2010, Publix began to open stores here. This recipe is adapted from an Apron's Simple Meals recipe that I tasted at our Belle Meade Publix.*

Juice of 2 limes (3 Tbsp)
4 chicken cutlets, about 1 pound
1/2 tsp kosher salt
1/4 tsp pepper
1 container (8 oz) jalapeno hummus
3/4 C panko bread crumbs
3 Tbsp canola oil
1 Tbsp water

Season chicken with salt and pepper. Coat both sides of the chicken with hummus, about 1 tablespoon for each cutlet. Place panko in a shallow dish. Dip chicken to coat both sides. Wash hands.

Preheat large sauté pan on medium heat 2-3 minutes. Place oil in the pan, and add chicken. Cook each side 3-4 minutes. Combine remaining 1/2 cup hummus with lime juice and water. Drizzle sauce over the chicken and place chicken cutlet over a bed of rice. Serves 4.

## CHICKEN

### pat nixon's hot chicken salad.

*When I lived in the Washington, D.C. suburbs during the 1960s and 1970s, I attended functions at the Congressional Club with Joan Cole, whose father-in-law was U.S. Representative Sterling Cole from upper New York State. A Club highlight was the tasting party held in conjunction with the publication of each new* Congressional Club Cookbook.

*During the 1970s, we "tested" Patricia Nixon's dish that had been prepared by the White House for the tasting. This dish has become a company-requested dish. It is especially delicious made with turkey and served with Cranberry-Sour Cream Salad (See Salads Category.) for supper during the holidays. Liz Weller and I prepared this for the 2012 PEO Christmas Luncheon.*

4 C cooked chicken chunks
2 Tbsp lemon juice
3/4 C mayonnaise
1 tsp salt
2 C chopped celery
4 hard-cooked eggs, sliced
3/4 C cream of chicken soup
1 tsp onion, finely minced
2 pimentos, cut fine
1 C Cheddar cheese, grated
1 1/2 C crushed potato chips
2/3 C toasted almonds, chopped

Combine all ingredients except cheese, potato chips, and almonds. Place in large rectangular dish. Top with cheese, potato chips, and almonds. Let stand in refrigerator overnight. Preheat oven to 350 degrees. Bring casserole to room temperature. Bake 30 to 35 minutes or until cheese has melted and bubbles form. Serves 8.

## CHICKEN

### peach and basil chicken breasts.

*In August, when I was growing-up, my family would take a Sunday drive to Chambersburg, Pennsylvania, when the peaches were at their peak. We bought bushels! We three daughters were pressed into service to peel and slice the peaches for Mother. She canned peach halves for winter desserts, cooked peach jam for toast, and froze peach slices for pies. Our family savored this fruit all winter long and into the spring.*

*Today, I eagerly await the arrival of The Peach Truck in Nashville, transporting peaches from southern Georgia. In late summer, I haunt the Produce Place for peaches from Michigan so I can make more peach jam or chutney and continue enjoying this recipe into fall. This dish makes a beautiful presentation for your dinner guests!*

6 skinned, boneless chicken breasts
3/4 tsp ground pepper
3 Tbsp oil
1 onion, thinly sliced
3 cloves garlic, finely minced
16 basil leaves, chopped
1 1/2 C low-sodium chicken broth
6 large peaches, peeled and cut in slices

Preheat oven to 350 degrees. Heat oil and brown the chicken on each side, about 2 minutes on each side. Remove chicken from pan. In pan drippings, add onion and garlic. Sauté about 45 seconds. Add basil, chicken broth, and peaches to the mixture. Place chicken in a baking dish and cover with the peach sauce. Bake 15 minutes or until the chicken is done. Sprinkle with more chopped basil before serving.

**CHICKEN**

### savory chicken and ham bake.

*In May 2015, the HSN Morning Study Group completed its study of savory with a luncheon. Liz Weller and I adapted this recipe to incorporate savory. Both of us have prepared this for dinner parties, with rave reviews!*

| | |
|---|---|
| 6 chicken breast halves | 1 head Belgian endive |
| 6 slices ham (very thin) | 2 small onions, chopped |
| 1/2 C all-purpose flour | 1 C chicken broth |
| 1/2 tsp salt | 1 tsp fresh savory, chopped |
| 1/4 tsp black pepper | 1/2 tsp minced garlic |
| 4 Tbsp vegetable oil | 1 tsp fresh parsley, chopped |
| 12 small fresh mushrooms | 1/2 C orange juice |

Preheat oven to 350 degrees. Place flour, salt, and pepper in a paper bag. Drop chicken breasts, one at a time, into the bag and shake to coat. Heat 3 tablespoons oil in a large frying pan over medium-high heat. Add chicken breasts and brown on both sides. Drain on paper towels. Then, place chicken in a large rectangular dish.

Roll up ham slices and arrange around the chicken breasts. Tuck in mushrooms and Belgian endive around the chicken and ham.

In 1 tablespoon oil, sauté onions until beginning to brown. Then add chicken broth, savory, garlic, and parsley. Simmer 1 minute and pour mixture over chicken, ham and mushrooms, and greens. Cover with foil and bake for 1 hour 15 minutes.

## CHICKEN

### sesame chicken.

*This outstanding recipe is from one of Harriet's food demonstrations when she was a home-economist with Pittsburgh Gas and Electric Company. Prepare this delicious dish for a very special occasion.*

*Begin the evening with Mushrooms Escargot. (See Savories Category.) Serve the Sesame Chicken with asparagus or green beans. Heath Torte (See Desserts Category.) would be a perfect ending for the dinner.*

4 whole chicken breasts, skinned and boned
Baked ham, cut into 1-inch strips
Swiss cheese, cut into 1-inch strips
1 egg
1 Tbsp water
3/4 C breadcrumbs
1/4 C butter
1 Tbsp soy sauce
1/2 C chicken broth
Sesame seeds

Preheat oven to 350 degrees. Fill chicken breasts with ham and cheese. Press edges firmly together and secure with toothpicks. Beat the egg with water. Dip chicken in the egg and then in breadcrumbs. Sauté chicken in butter until golden brown. Place in a baking dish. Combine melted butter, soy sauce, and chicken broth. Brush chicken with sauce, and sprinkle with sesame seeds. Bake for 35 to 45 minutes or until tender, occasionally basting with remaining sauce. Serves 4.

*****

For a luncheon, I enjoy serving chicken dishes on my Blue Willow plates. My fascination with this china began with Gary's Grandma Mitchell's gift of a Blue Willow antique serving platter in the early 1980s. Since then we have collected the luncheon plates, as well as occasional Blue Willow and cloisonné pieces.

## CHICKEN

### tommy's chicken barbecue sauce.

*In the early 1960s, Tommy and June Jackson arrived in the Washington, D.C. area from Baton Rouge, Louisiana. At the same time, we had moved there from Pittsburgh, Pennsylvania. June and I met as new English teachers at Springbrook High School in Silver Spring, Maryland.*

*We four became close friends and planned "themed" birthday parties for one another. Most memorable was a Roman theme – complete with guests arriving in togas and dinner served while guests reclined on low couches, sipping wine and munching grapes.*

*Tommy brought his family barbecue-sauce recipe and his grilling expertise with him. We spent many summer Saturday evenings enjoying Tommy's grilled chicken on the shaded terrace of their Fox Hall Road home.*

1 stick butter
1/2 C Wesson oil
1 Tbsp Worcestershire sauce
2 Tbsp vinegar
Dash tabasco
1 lemon, juice and peel
Salt
Pepper

Combine all ingredients and simmer for 15 minutes. A few hours before grilling, marinate chicken in lemon juice and peel. Baste chicken often with the sauce.

In early August 1990, Mother and I toured the Greek peninsula, cruised the Greek Islands, stopped in Istanbul, and visited the ruins at Ephesus, pictured here. In 1980, on a Rhine Cruise, we visited Lucerne, attended the Passion Play in Oberammergau, and toured Garmisch-Partenkirchen, Munich, Salzburg, and Vienna. What memorable trips with Mother!

# entrees

## meat

**A tale without love is like beef without mustard: an insipid dish.**
-Anatole France

**The way you cut your meat reflects the way you live.**
-Confucius

**If I had to narrow my choice of meats down to one for the rest of my life, I am quite certain that meat would be pork.**
-James Beard

**MEAT**

**BLT bacon.**

*In June 2019, Green Door Gourmet, an on-farm market on River Road in Nashville, hosted a BLT Party. Yes, Bacon, Lettuce and Tomato! The owner, Sylvia Ganier, invited five premier Nashville chefs from Grilled Cheeserie, Oak Steakhouse, Earnest Bar and Hideaway, Black Rabbit, and the Green Door Gourmet to prepare BLT originals! Nathan Gifford provided Gifford Bacon for the chefs. What a gastronomic evening!*

    *Richard Jones, Green Door Gourmet chef, shared with me how he prepared the bacon for his BLT Salad.*

preparing the bacon:

Marinate bacon strips overnight in Korean BBQ Sauce. Preheat oven to 365 degrees. Cover a jelly-roll pan with parchment paper and place the bacon strips, almost touching, in the pan. Brush bacon with the BBQ sauce. Bake 8-10 minutes. Turn over the strips and brush with the sauce. Bake another 8 minutes. Remove the strips from the pan, and place them in a second pan, lined with parchment paper. Return to the oven and bake until done.

His BLT Salad is a blend of unique flavors:

Korean BBQ sauce for the bacon
Chopped tomatoes with Bourbon Barrell Foods Smoked Togarashi
Bread cubes with roasted garlic
Fermented green tomato relish
Drizzle of Yum Yum Sauce

This BLT salad in an endive leaf is a perfect savory. Or serve it on a bed of Boston lettuce as a gourmet salad! Or make a BLP sandwich by substituting fresh peach slices for the tomato.

# MEAT

### BLT bacon. (cont.)

While you can purchase Korean BBQ Sauce and Yum Yum Sauce, I've decided to make my own.

<u>korean BBQ sauce:</u>

1/2 C low-sodium soy sauce
3/4 C brown sugar
2 Tbsp minced garlic
2 Tbsp rice wine vinegar
1 Tbsp chili paste

1 tsp minced ginger
1 tsp oil
2 Tbsp water
1 Tbsp cornstarch

Heat the first 7 ingredients over medium heat and stir. Whisk cornstarch and water together and then whisk it into the soy mixture. Continue whisking and bring to a boil. Cook until mixture thickens, about 5 minutes. Remove from the heat. Refrigerate.

<u>yum yum sauce:</u>

16 oz mayonnaise
2 Tbsp ketchup
2 Tbsp butter, melted
1 Tbsp garlic powder
2 tsp onion powder
1 Tbsp smoked paprika
1/4 C water
2 Tbsp sugar
Hot sauce to taste

Mix all ingredients and refrigerate overnight before using.

## MEAT

### besse's ham loaf.

*Besse Lysinger, our East Watson Street neighbor in Bedford, Pennsylvania, was revered for her perennial flower gardens surrounding her gracious home. On most summer afternoons, Besse could be found, pulling weeds from her beds of roses, poppies, day lilies, daisies, and peonies.*

*What a treat to be invited to Besse's home for dinner, served in her elegant dining room! Her son, Bill (four years older than me), was the perfect host. Everyone was especially fond of her ham loaf that has become one of our family favorites. My sister, Sharon, perfected this recipe.*

*The next day, cold ham loaf, if some remains, is delicious in a sandwich with mayonnaise and crisp lettuce leaves.*

1 1/2 pound ham
1 pound lean pork
1 C bread crumbs
2 eggs, beaten well
1 C milk

Ask the butcher to grind the ham and pork together. Preheat oven to 350 degrees. Mix the meat with the remaining ingredients. Form into a loaf and place into a large loaf pan. Bake for 2 hours. Baste every 15 minutes with the following mixture:

1 C brown sugar
1 1/2 tsp dry mustard
1/4 C water
1/4 C vinegar

Serve with Bea van Gundy's Whipped Mustard Sauce that follows.

**MEAT**

### bea's whipped mustard sauce.

*Bea van Gundy's sauce is delicious to serve at a buffet with thinly sliced baked ham for sandwiches. And the sauce is a perfect accompaniment to Besse's Ham Loaf.*

3 Tbsp horseradish
1/2 tsp salt
1 Tbsp prepared mustard
1/2 C whipping cream

Whip cream until it forms standing peaks.  Fold in horseradish, salt, and mustard. Chill before serving.

*After college, I taught junior-high school English in Mt. Lebanon, a southern suburb of Pittsburgh, Pennsylvania. Apartments were non-existent there, so I lived with Bea van Gundy in her spacious Victorian house on Castle Shannon Boulevard. That fall, she returned to teaching, so we had a lot in common. Often, we prepared dinner together, shared on many occasions with her son James, a student at the University of Pittsburgh.*

*My eighth-grade students had a double period with me (one hour of English/Spelling, followed by an hour of American literature). So, I only met with three groups of students, about 75 in all.*

*The English department emphasized correct grammar and punctuation. If a student forgot a word in a composition, I suggested placing a caret on the line and writing the word above it. Billy Scarlata complied by drawing carrots with leafy tops on the line and inserting the missing word above the carrot. How I wish I had kept that paper!*

## MEAT

### covington mexican lasagna.

*Gary and I met John Covington in February 1999 at the Nashville Home Show where John's company, Bid Express, had a booth. Bid Express was only one of John's many part-time endeavors, as we would learn over the years. He was quite capable of balancing these with his primary job as the top information technology (IT) manager at the U.S. Postal Service area office and later as the top IT manager at the Veterans Administration (VA) Hospitals in Nashville and in Murphreesboro, Tennessee.*

*During our twenty-year relationship with the Covingtons, we have shared many experiences. The most remarkable was watching the development of John and Sherry's daughter, Lauren, from a one-year old baby into a beautiful and multi-talented, twenty-two-year old young woman. On May 4$^{th}$, we saw Lauren graduate from Trevecca University with a degree in graphic design.*

*I have fond memories of the many summers when Sherry dropped off Lauren around 7:00am on her way to Freeman Webb in Green Hills where Sherry is the Benefits Manager. Lauren, Gary, and I played cards or dominos until 8:45am when we drove her to Cheekwood to attend summer camps. In the afternoons, we went to lunch, took trips to the zoo or other attractions, and went to the movies or shopping. Sometimes, she and I baked cookies or worked on various crafts.*

*Later, Lauren spent summers as a camp counselor at Cheekwood, using our house as a base until camp started. Our summers with Lauren came to an abrupt halt when she obtained her driver's license. But so it goes with a capable and bright young woman with many talents and interests.*

*Through the years, we have enjoyed many brunches and dinners at the Covingtons. Both are exceptional cooks. This lasagna recipe is one of John's tasty creations!*

*****

*Garfield, the lazy, Monday-loving, lasagna-loving cat was created by Jim Davis over 40 years ago. Garfield's quotes include "With due respect to Will Rogers, I never met a lasagna I didn't like." And "When the lasagna content in my blood gets low, I get mean."*

**MEAT**

### covington mexican lasagna. (cont.)

| | |
|---|---|
| 1 small onion | 1 1/2 pounds ground beef |
| 1 tomato | 1 pkg taco seasoning |
| 1 bell pepper | 1 pkg corn tortillas |
| 2 jalapenos (optional) | 1 large can refried beans |
| 1 small bunch cilantro | 1 bottle taco sauce |
| 2 cloves garlic | 1 container (8 oz) sour cream |

1 block of quesadilla melting cheese
1 can Ro-Tel chopped tomatoes and green chilies

Preheat the oven to 350 degrees. Chop onion, tomato, bell pepper, jalapenos, and cilantro. Mince garlic cloves. Shred cheese, be generous. Drain the Ro-Tel. Set all aside. In a frying pan, brown and drain ground beef. Return beef to pan. Add the Ro-Tel, minced garlic, and 1/2 of the chopped vegetables. Stir in the taco seasoning and simmer.

    Lightly oil the 9x13x2-inch baking pan. Cover the bottom with 6 tortillas. Spread 1/2 refried beans over tortillas. Spread 1/2 beef-vegetable mixture over beans. Cover beef mixture with shredded cheese. Spoon taco sauce around the perimeter. Repeat the entire layering process. Sparingly, sprinkle some fresh cilantro over the top. Bake for about 30 minutes. Mix remaining vegetables and cilantro.

    To serve, cut into 6 slices. Top each serving with taco sauce, fresh vegetables with cilantro, and a dollop of sour cream. Serve tortilla chips and salsa on the side.

*****

*After my first year of teaching, I spent the summer of 1958 on the island of Oahu. I lived with two secretaries who prepared casseroles, similar to John's, on the week-end. These were dinners for the coming week.*

    *My purpose in being in Hawaii was to take an Audio-Visual Aids class so I could be certified to teach in Pennsylvania. I did attend classes but missed some workshops, on threading a projector, etc. The final exam was mostly related to the mechanics of the equipment. Needless to say, too much beach time and not adequate study netted me a D. The first and only one of my academic life. At least, I passed.*

## MEAT

### flank steak teriyaki.

*Gary's recipe for this melt-in-your-mouth treat is to marinate a flank steak for several hours or overnight in a mixture prepared by combining the following ingredients:*

| | |
|---|---|
| 1/4 C oil | 2 minced garlic cloves |
| 1/4 C soy sauce | Juice of 1 lemon |
| 1 minced green onion | 1 Tbsp cider vinegar |

Remove steak from marinade; grill or broil for 5 minutes on each side. Thinly slice on the diagonal, and serve with rice, green salad, and warm pita bread.

*****

*At Wilson College, students were known as Odds or Evens, depending on the year that the class would graduate. As members of the Class of 1957, we were Odds and our big sisters, the juniors, were Odds. There were endless competitions between the Odds and the Evens. In October of 1953, the Class of 1958 was our nemesis. We freshman were to become the* **Heinz 57 Varieties**. *I wrote Hazing Daze (below) for my freshman composition class.*

### Hazing Daze

In the literature that Wilson College sends to its perspective students, I had read nothing about hazing. Until the Sophomore Hazing Committee came to our Class of '57 meeting last week, I regarded hazing as a campus activity at universities. Wilson was a mere "college." When I learned that I, too, would be subjected to this ordeal, my attitude was not one of anticipation.

The committee informed us that we would be required to dress like dogs, complete with tail, nose, ears, collar and leash, whiskers, mittens, and even a flea. Then, we were taught a song, *How Much Is That Heinz Dog*

### **hazing daze.** (cont.)

*down at Wilson?* These lyrics were written by the sophomores to be sung, on demand, by their hounds, the freshman.

The days elapsed and, finally, the dreaded morning arrived. Attired in the required paraphernalia, I went to breakfast. Inside the dining room, I was one of a hundred, attired in odd varieties of doggy costumes. When I attempted to sit at the table, my trouble began. I had constructed my tail from a metal coat hanger. At first, I found it impossible to sit on it. Then I discovered a way to stick my tail through the back of the chair. The greatest challenge occurred when I tried to drink my fruit juice. The mouth of the glass was so small that my cardboard whiskers spilled the juice onto my shirt.

More difficulties arose in chapel. We had been asked to wear mittens for paws. But since I had no mittens, I used a pair of socks. With this as a paw, finding the correct page in the hymnal became quite a task.

During the day, I did all that was required of a freshman. When a male professor passed, I panted. When a sophomore threw a newspaper, I fetched. When commanded to roll over or beg for a bone, I obeyed. When whistled to by a sophomore, I barked.

I thought to myself, I've lived through one day of this ordeal, and I will probably survive the remaining days. But I can hardly wait until next year when I will seek my revenge on the Class of '58.

## MEAT

### pickled franks.

*This recipe of Gary's is terrific for a cookout or for New Year's Day with Sauerkraut Cooked in Beer. (See Sides Category.)*

| | |
|---|---|
| 1/4 C thinly sliced onions | 1 C white vinegar |
| 1/2 tsp peppercorns | 1 Tbsp sugar |
| 6 cloves | 1 clove garlic |
| 1 1/2 Tbsp salt | |

Slice franks into three pieces. Cover with boiling water to which has been added onions, peppercorns, cloves, and salt. Cook slowly until tender. Drain and pack in sterilized jars, and cover with vinegar, sugar, and garlic. Keep refrigerated until ready to serve. Or, prepare as directed above without slicing. Charcoal. Serve with mustard butter.

*****

### sunday night supper:

*When Harriet and I were in junior-and-senior high school, our Youth Fellowship met at the church on Sunday evenings. Harriet's age group met at 5pm and my group at 6pm. A sit-down supper for the family was impossible. Generally, we ate supper at the bar in the kitchen. Our usual foods were hotdogs or hamburgers, potato salad or baked beans, and potato chips. These chips were always served in a red-black-and-gold painted, wooden Russian bowl that had been in Mother's family. We referred to it as "The Potato Chip Bowl." I have the original one that is over 100 years old. In 1992, when I was in Russia, I purchased two "new" bowls for Harriet and Sharon. I was amazed that the same "golden wood" bowl is still being produced in the village of Khokhlom.*

**MEAT**

### pizza casserole.

*In 2011, Carolyn Campbell and I became friends through PEO, and I enjoyed serving on her Board during her 2014-2016 presidency. She related that her husband, Joe, had been on the faculty of Darlington, a boarding school in Rome, Georgia. Carolyn never knew how many students he would invite home to share dinner with them. Out of necessity, she created a casserole that teenagers would like. She credits this quick recipe with saving the day, on numerous occasions. Undoubtedly, Carolyn kept a supply on hand of her Forgotten Cookies, stored in an air-tight container, to serve as dessert! (See Sweets Category.)*

1 pound ground hamburg
1 jar (14 oz) pizza sauce
2 C shredded mozzarella cheese
3/4 C Bisquick mix
2 eggs
1/2 C milk

Preheat oven to 400 degrees. Cook ground hamburg and drain. Place meat in an 8x8-inch baking dish. Pour pizza sauce over the beef and sprinkle the beef with cheese. Combine the Bisquick, eggs, and milk. Pour over the top. Bake for 30-35 minutes.

*Joe was a 12-year member of the Brentwood Academy Faculty and a lifetime educator, who dedicated his life's service to teaching young people. Each year Carolyn presents The Joe Campbell Service Award to a Brentwood Academy student who, like Joe Campbell, serves others where and when needed.*

## MEAT

### spaghetti alla carbonara.

*Paula Snyder and I met through our garden club. She is very active in the General James Robertson Chapter of the DAR and sponsored me for membership in her chapter. Diligently, she shepherded my application through the National process. In June 2019, I was thrilled to be accepted for membership.*

*Paula shared this recipe and said, "This (recipe) became a family favorite after trips to Italy in the 70s. This is my personal recipe, but I'm afraid my son John's recipe/technique may outshine mine."*

1/4 C extra-virgin olive oil
1/2 pound bacon (6 to 8 slices), slices halved length-wise, then cut crosswise into ¼ inch pieces
1/2 C dry, white wine
3 large eggs
1 C Parmesan cheese, finely grated
1 Tbsp dry parsley
3 small cloves garlic, pressed in garlic press or minced to paste
1 pound spaghetti
1 Tbsp table salt
1 tsp sea-salt flakes or 3/4 Tbsp table salt
Black pepper
Pecorino Romano cheese, finely grated

Bring 4 quarts of water to a rolling boil in a large Dutch oven or stockpot. While the water is heating, heat oil in a large skillet over medium heat until shimmering, but not smoking. Add bacon and cook, stirring occasionally, until lightly browned and crisp, about 8 minutes. Remove bacon and add wine and simmer until alcohol aroma has cooked off and the wine is slightly reduced, 6 to 8 minutes. Remove from heat and cover to keep warm.

Beat eggs, cheese, parsley, and garlic together with a fork in a small bowl. Set aside.

When water comes to boil, add pasta and 1 Tbsp table salt. Stir to separate pasta. Cook until al dente. Reserve 1/3 cup pasta cooking water and drain pasta for about 5 seconds, leaving pasta slightly wet. Transfer the

**MEAT**

**spaghetti alla carbonara.** (cont.)

drained pasta to pan containing wine. If pasta is dry, add some reserved Pasta Water (See below.) and toss to moisten.

Immediately pour egg mixture over hot pasta, sprinkle with 1 teaspoon sea-salt flakes or 3/4 teaspoon table salt. Toss well to combine. Pour reserved bacon pieces over pasta, season generously with black pepper, and toss well to combine. Serve immediately. Serves 4-6.

Save the Pasta Water. If the sauce is to spread evenly, the pasta must be moist. Add up to 1/3 cup reserved Pasta Water if the pasta is dry or sticky.

*****

*James Robertson, frontiersman and a founder of Tennessee, was born in 1742. Raised in North Carolina, he lived there until he led a group of settlers to Tennessee in 1769. In 1779, Robertson explored the Cumberland River country, present-day Middle Tennessee, and helped found Fort Nashborough. Under the Cumberland Compact, he was the chief civil and military officer of the community. His shrewd leadership was largely responsible for its survival.*

*In 1790, Congress created the Territory South of the Ohio River. In 1791, President George Washington appointed Robertson Brigadier General of the U.S. Army of the same region.*

*When the State of Tennessee was organized in 1796, Robertson helped draft its first Constitution. Later, he served in the state senate in 1798 and as agent to the Chickasaw Nation. James Robertson died at "the Chickasaw Agency" in 1814 and was reinterred in Nashville's City Cemetery in 1825.*

*Our DAR chapter maintains the family burial ground of General Robertson, locates and preserves historic sites, observes historic events, and supports the U. S. military by frequently writing notes and sending packages to troops deployed abroad.*

In the early 1990s, deep-sea fishing or fishing in the mangroves south of Naples was exciting and rewarding. Especially, when a black-spot snapper became our dinner!

# entrees

## seafood

**I'm on a seafood diet. I see it, I eat it.**
-Dolly Parton

**A loaf of bread, the Walrus, said,
Is what we chiefly need:
Pepper and vinegar besides
Are very good indeed –
Now if you're ready, Oysters, dear,
We can begin to feed!**
-Lewis Carroll

**The only kind of seafood I trust is the fish stick,
a totally featureless fish that doesn't have eyeballs or fins.**
-Dave Barry

## SEAFOOD

### casserole rockefeller.

*From kindergarten until high-school graduation in 1984, my son Billy was a student at Georgetown Day School (GDS), located on MacArthur Boulevard in Washington D.C. My friend, Denny Diamond's twin sons, were in his class. She and I served on the GDS Cookbook Committee that published* Kitchen Privileges *in 1975. The hand-written recipes and the detailed illustrations were created by an artist living in San Francisco, whose son had recently graduated from GDS. I didn't recall hearing her last name.*

*In 1983, Gary and I hired Arnold Palley, for whom Gary worked in the 1970s, as CEO of our List-Rental Business. When Arnold and Brenda moved back to Bethesda, I learned in conversation with Brenda that she, in fact, was that talented artist. Small world!*

*Denny and I worked tirelessly as room-mothers, preparing food for special holiday lunches (King's Cake for Mardi Gras, egg rolls for Chinese New Year, dozens of cookies for Christmas, etc.) and chairing the end-of-the year swimming party at our home in Olney, a northern Maryland suburb of Washington D.C.*

*We also were members of the Country Market Day Committee, an annual fall festival of gourmet foods, autographed books by GDS students' parents (Art Buchwald. George Will, Judith Martin, Frank Mankowitz, and Judith Viorst), and a silent auction.*

*Denny was a superb cook and her Casserole Rockefeller became a tasty side dish for our holiday dinners. This recipe can also be used as a supper dish served with a green salad and crusty warm bread. Or serve as an appetizer with toasted French bread slices.*

\*\*\*\*\*

*The world is your oyster. It's up to you to find the pearls.*
*-Chris Gardner*

SEAFOOD

### **casserole rockefeller.** (cont.)

2 pkg frozen chopped spinach
2 Tbsp butter
2 Tbsp lemon juice
1 Tbsp Worcestershire sauce
Tabasco, to taste
1/2 medium onion, grated
1 clove garlic, crushed
1 C coarse cracker crumbs
4 Tbsp butter
1 quart drained oysters
1/4 C freshly grated Parmesan cheese

Preheat oven to 350 degrees. Cook spinach and drain thoroughly. Stir it into the hot butter over moderate heat to evaporate the moisture. Mix lemon juice, Worcestershire sauce, and Tabasco. Blend into spinach. Brown onion, garlic, and crumbs in the 4 tablespoons of butter. Combine with oysters and spinach. Spoon mixture into a shallow casserole, top with cheese, and bake for 20 minutes. Serves 8.

*****

*"As I ate the oysters with their strong taste of the sea and their faint metallic taste that the cold white wine washed away, leaving only the sea taste and the succulent texture, and as I drank their cold liquid from each shell and washed it down with the crisp taste of the wine, I lost the empty feeling and began to be happy and to make plans."*
-Ernest Hemingway

## SEAFOOD

### grandma york's oyster dressing.

*My friend, SueAnn Norris, is a terrific gardener, as well as an excellent cook. This recipe for oyster dressing originated with her Great Grandmother Gwen Cartwright York. According to the original recipe, Grandma York probably added creole seasoning. SueAnn's Grandpa Charlie was a preacher. The congregation didn't have money to pay him for preaching, so he was paid with animals - pigs, chickens, and cows.*

*SueAnn is of the opinion "every great recipe deserves to be tweaked. Add more or less of any ingredient to make it your own. If you like heat, use hot sausage instead of mild."*

*Over the years, her grandmother, her mother, and SueAnn, herself, have tweaked the original recipe. Today at holiday gatherings, SueAnn's family savors her version of Great Grandma York's oyster dressing. SueAnn's last word is "By itself, this one is delicious!" Serve with a green salad as an entrée or as a side at Thanksgiving or Christmas.*

1 pound mild, sweet sausage
6 slices thick cut bacon, cooked and crumbled
1 stick butter
1 sweet onion, chopped medium
1 1/2 C celery, chopped
2 cloves garlic, chopped fine
2 cans (8 oz each) oysters drained, save liquid (Cut, if oysters are too big.)
8 C white bread cubes (1 large loaf)
3 C chicken broth
1/2 cup evaporated milk
2 large eggs, beaten till frothy

**SEAFOOD**

**grandma york's oyster dressing.** (cont.)

oyster dressing seasonings:

1 Tbsp dried parsley
1 tsp dried sage
1/2 tsp dried thyme
1 tsp poultry seasoning
1/2 tsp celery salt
1/4 tsp onion powder
1 tsp fresh ground black pepper
1/4 tsp creole seasoning (optional)

Preheat oven to 350 degrees. In a large frying pan, sauté sausage. Remove with a slotted spoon, and drain the sausage thoroughly. Crumble into 1-inch pieces.

    Wipe out frying pan, and cook the bacon. Drain, crumble, and set bacon aside. Wipe the pan and melt butter. Add onions and celery, and cook until translucent. Add garlic and cook until soft. Add the seasonings. Add sausage, bacon, and oysters. Keep the mixture warm.

    In a large bowl, place bread cubes, chicken broth, milk, meats, and seasonings. Taste and adjust seasonings, if needed. Add oyster liquid if you want a stronger oyster flavor. Taste again. Add eggs beaten until frothy. Do not over stir.

    Butter a 9x13x2-inch glass casserole dish, and spoon stuffing into the dish. Cover with foil and bake for 1 hour. If you want the top crispy, remove the cover and cook 10 minutes more.

**SEAFOOD**

**grilled shrimp.**

*In the mid-1960s, I taught eighth-grade English at Pyle Junior High School in Bethesda, Maryland. Each year I compiled and edited* ReciPyle, *a faculty cookbook, reproduced on the ditto machine. Today the copies are a faint purple, but thankfully still readable enough to preserve this shrimp recipe which I often serve during the summer. A gorgeous gorge!*

1 1/2 pounds raw jumbo shrimp
1/3 C Wesson or Canola oil
1/3 sherry
1/3 C soy sauce
1 clove garlic, crushed

Wash shrimp, and keep them in the shell. Mix the oil, sherry, soy sauce, and garlic. Marinate the shrimp in the mixture for 3 or 4 hours, turning now and then. Drain and arrange on skewers. Cook over a bright bed of glowing coals for 4 or 5 minutes on each side, basting with marinade. Serve shrimp in the shells with melted butter. Guests shuck their own. Serves 4.

*****

*During the summer of 1964, I was on summer vacation from teaching in a Washington, D.C. suburb. So, I had an opportunity to participate in the pilot program for Head Start. May 18, 2015 marked the 50th anniversary of President Lyndon B. Johnson creating this program. Head Start was designed to help meet the emotional, social, health, nutritional, and psychological needs of preschool-aged children from low-income families. I was privileged to assist in structuring the initial program.*

**SEAFOOD**

### lavender grilled salmon.

*In pursuing the culinary uses of lavender, the HSN Study Group members discovered many delicious uses of the herb. Joan Pinkley prepared this recipe for the* Ladies in Lavender Luncheon.

3 pounds salmon fillet
4 Tbsp honey
6 Tbsp virgin olive oil
1 Tbsp lavender, crushed or run through a coffee grinder
1/4 C white wine
1 Tbsp Worcestershire sauce
1 Tbsp lime or lemon juice

Preheat grill. Place all ingredients, except salmon, in a saucepan over moderate heat, stirring with wire whisk at all times until ingredients are reduced by one-third. Brush slightly cooled sauce on salmon. Grill or bake salmon until flaky, about 10 minutes, basting with the sauce. Pour the remaining sauce over the salmon before serving.

*An HSN discussion of its historical aspects revealed that lavender has been documented for over 2500 years. Ancient Egyptians used it for mummification and perfume. Romans used it in soaps and carried it throughout the Roman empire. In Medieval and Renaissance France, women who took in washing were known as "lavenders." Clothes were washed in lavender and laid to dry on lavender bushes. A few years ago, I draped some clothing on my lavender bushes to dry. I was disappointed that the scent was not stronger. Each June, I harvest the lavender blossoms. After they dry, I place them in small dishes where I store woolens. This method successfully deters moths!*

## SEAFOOD

### mother's seafood – tidewater/mobile style.

*Patsy Weigel's mother was a Mobile, Alabama native and a Virginia Tidewater transplant. "A wonderful cook for a family that loved to eat!" Patsy says. "Mother is the only person I know who made fruitcake before candied fruit was available. She worked weeks on her fruitcakes. During the Korean War, she sent them to my brother in the Air Force. Mother baked with love!"*

1 Tbsp butter
2 Tbsp all-purpose flour
1/2 tsp salt
1/4 tsp pepper
2/3 C undiluted evaporated milk
1 Tbsp chopped onion
1/2 C chopped celery (optional)
1/4 C chopped pimento
2 C cooked seafood (any combination of crab, shrimp, tuna, lobster)

Melt butter in saucepan. Blend in flour and other seasonings. Stir until well-blended and add milk. Cook over medium heat until mixture thickens, stirring constantly. Add celery, pimento, onions, and seafood. Mix well. Heat to serving temperature. Serve over rice, chow mein noodles, or buttered toast.

## SEAFOOD

### pike place salmon.

*In 1998, Billy was directing* Real World *in Seattle, Washington. Gary and I spent a long week-end there. A highlight was visiting the Pike Place Market, a seven-acre National Historic District. At Pike Place Fish, the clerks, out front working the crowd, would pull a salmon or halibut from the icy display pile and toss it skyward. Without exception, their cohorts behind the counter managed to catch the slippery fish, to the cheers of the crowd! At Christmas that year, Billy sent us a Dungeness Crab feast that we enjoyed with Liz and Frank Berklacich, our neighbors in Belle Meade. The following is the Pike Place recipe for salmon fillet.*

4 pound salmon fillet
6 cloves garlic
1 C mayonnaise
Salt and pepper to taste

Mix garlic and mayonnaise. Spread the mixture on the fish. Add salt and pepper. Grill skin side down for 22-25 minutes. Test by inserting fork into the thickest part of the fillet. If fillet flakes when turning the fork, it's done.

I usually serve the salmon with a Cucumber-Dill Sauce, using a mix I order from the Biltmore House in Asheville.

*To freeze fish, place fish into a sealable freezer bag. Fill the bag with just enough water to cover the fish. Freeze. The water surrounding the fish will prevent freezer burn. Allow the water to drain while thawing.*

**SEAFOOD**

### rosemary shrimp scampi skewers.

*Shrimp threaded on rosemary branches imparts a subtle herb flavor to the grilled shrimp. This herb of remembrance and fidelity is believed to be a love charm. Stand by for raves from your guests when you serve this aromatic dish as an appetizer or as a main dish!*

1 Tbsp dry white wine
1 tsp fresh lemon juice
1 tsp olive oil
1 garlic clove, minced
18 large shrimp, peeled and deveined
6 (six-inch) rosemary branches

Combine all ingredients, except the rosemary, in a zipped plastic bag. Seal and shake. Place in the refrigerator 30 minutes to marinate.

Hold a rosemary branch by the leafy end in one hand. Strip leaves from the branch, keeping 1/2-inch of leaves attached to the end. Thread 3 shrimp on each skewer.

Heat the grill pan over medium heat. Coat both sides of shrimp with cooking spray. Cook 2 minutes on each side or until the shrimp are done. Serve with fresh green beans or asparagus.

## SEAFOOD

### seafood casserole.

*This delicious casserole is from Harriet! How many times have I called her for a new dish for a dinner party? For a stunning presentation, serve this with Mother's Cranberry-Sour Cream Salad (See Salads Category.) and steamed haricots vert.*

1 medium onion, chopped
1/2 pound mushrooms, sliced
1/2 stick butter
1 pound fresh shrimp, shelled
8 oz imitation crabmeat
1/4 C sour cream
1/4 C mayonnaise
1 C Cheddar cheese
1 C stuffing mix or cracker crumbs

Preheat oven to 350 degrees. Sauté onion and mushrooms in butter. Add shrimp and sauté. Add crab. Mix the sour cream and mayonnaise and add to the mixture. Place in a greased 9x13x2-inch casserole. Top with cheese and stuffing mix. Bake 30 minutes. Serves 4.

**SEAFOOD**

### shrimp and asparagus pasta toss.

*Each October, Marilyn Whitmore, our mother's back-door neighbor, hosted my sisters and me for the annual Bedford Fall Foliage Festival. 2019 will mark its 55$^{th}$ celebration. For the first two week-ends in October, over 400 craftsmen and artists line the historic streets of downtown Bedford, including live music performances and food venders. But, the highlight of our weekend was conversation and a recipe swap. Marilyn not only swapped this recipe, she prepared it for dinner!*

6 oz uncooked angel-hair pasta
2 Tbsp butter
2 Tbsp flour
1 tsp chicken flavor instant bouillon
1 1/2 C milk
1/2 C shredded Swiss cheese
1/4 C grated Parmesan cheese
1/2 pound fresh cooked shrimp
18 spears cooked asparagus, cut in 1-inch pieces
1 C sliced fresh mushrooms

Cook the pasta. Drain and rinse with hot water. Keep warm. Melt butter. Blend in flour and bouillon, cooking until smooth and bubbly. Gradually add milk cooking until the mixture boils and thickens, stirring constantly. Add cheese, stirring until smooth. Stir in shrimp, asparagus, and mushrooms. Cook until thoroughly heated. Serve over cooked pasta. Serves 4.

**SEAFOOD**

### shrimp and feta cheese casserole.

*In 1998, Gary and I listed our Naples home with realtor, Paula van Zuidan. When she learned we were moving to Nashville, Paula suggested that we call Suzanne and Rick Regen because they "know everyone in Nashville." And they did! We and the Regens became best friends. Tail-gating before Titans games became a ritual. And for 20 years, we have enjoyed Christmas Eve dinner in one another's home.*

*Suzanne prepared this fabulous dish for our 2015 Christmas get-together. So delicious over a bed of wild rice and served with a green salad dressed with lemon olive oil and champagne mimosa balsamic vinegar!*

| | |
|---|---|
| 1 large onion, chopped | 1/2 tsp cumin seeds |
| 2 cloves garlic, minced | 1/4 tsp salt |
| 2 Tbsp butter, melted | 1/8 tsp pepper |
| 6 large tomatoes, chopped | 1 pound unpeeled medium shrimp |
| 1 Tbsp chopped fresh basil | 1/4 C butter, melted |
| 1/2 tsp sugar | 2/3 C crumbled feta cheese |
| Chopped fresh parsley | |

Preheat oven to 375 degrees. Sauté onion and garlic in butter in a large skillet until tender. Add tomatoes and next 5 ingredients, stirring well. Cook, uncovered, over low heat for 20-30 minutes, stirring occasionally. Remove from heat. Set aside.

Peel, devein, and butterfly shrimp, leaving tails intact. Sauté shrimp in ¼ cup butter in a medium skillet for 3 minutes. Remove from heat. Combine shrimp and tomato mixture. Place in a 13x9x2-inch baking dish. Sprinkle with feta cheese. Bake for 20 minutes or until bubbly. Garnish with chopped fresh parsley. Serves 4.

**SEAFOOD**

**shrimp and grits.**

*On May 5, 2019, Suzanne and Rick Regen hosted a celebration dinner for Gary and me on the launch of our book,* The Journey of an Inquiring Mind, *which had taken place that afternoon at Parnassus Books.*

*Before dinner, our friends toasted us with glasses of Blanc de Noirs, and we enjoyed Suzanne's savories. While Suzanne prepared her signature dish, shrimp and grits, Julie Schoerke tossed a tasty green salad. The evening passed all too quickly in animated conversation and culminated with Judy Armstrong's dessert, Derby Pie. (See Desserts Category.)*

cheesy grits:

1 tsp salt
1 C grits
1/2 C butter
4 oz mild Cheddar cheese, grated
6 oz sharp white Cheddar cheese, grated
1/2 tsp garlic powder
3 eggs
3/4 C half & half

Preheat oven to 325 degrees. Grease a 2-quart casserole dish and set aside. In a large pan, add salt to 4 cups of water and bring to a boil over high heat. Slowly stir grits into the boiling water. Lower heat to maintain a simmer and cook, stirring constantly until the grits thicken, about 8 minutes. Remove from heat and stir in butter, cheese, and garlic powder.

In a medium bowl, lightly beat eggs with half & half. Stir into the grits. Pour into the casserole and bake 45 minutes.

**SEAFOOD**

**shrimp and grits.** (cont.)

shrimp and gravy:

1/2 C butter, divided in half
1 medium onion, chopped
1 pound large shrimp, peeled and deveined. (Suzanne usually uses more.)
1 tsp Herbes de Provence seasoning
1 tsp Cajun seasoning (optional)
4 strips of bacon cooked until crisp
1/4 C parsley, minced fine
Lemon wedges

In large skillet melt 4 tablespoons butter over medium high heat. Add onions and cook until the edges brown. Add shrimp, seasonings, and remaining butter. Increase heat to high. Cook stirring constantly to a gravy-like sauce and until the shrimp are pink and cooked through. (5-10 minutes) Pour over grits and garnish with bacon, parsley and lemon. Serves 4.

*****

At our wedding in 1981, Gary and I served Domaine Chandon's Blanc de Noirs, a sparkling white wine from Napa Valley in California. Traditionally, we mark special occasions with this wine. Since 1981, we have visited the Domaine Chandon vineyard several times.

On our first trip to Napa in 1982, we stayed at the Burgundy House in Yountville. This charming, antique-filled Inn, built in 1904, was on the National Register of Historic Places. Our upstairs room and bath had fieldstone walls, a claw-foot bathtub overlooking the vineyards, and decanted wine by the bed. We were dismayed to learn that the inn was sold in 2007 and restored as an art gallery and wine-tasting center.

That evening in 1981, we enjoyed a gourmet experience at Chef Thomas Keller's *French Laundry*, established in 1978. This was before he earned a three-star Michelin rating and was discovered! Lunch or dinner today costs about $800 a couple. Yes. Gary frequently buys lottery tickets!

During the 1990s, to escape the Naples summer heat, I enjoyed spending a few weeks, with my sister, Harriet, at her cabin in Boone, North Carolina. There we hiked on the Appalachian Trail, lunched in Blowing Rock, and made forays into the countryside's peach and apple orchards.

# preserves

**Kissing don't last; cookery do!**
-George Meredith

**They dined on mince, and slices of quince,
Which they ate with a runcible spoon;
And hand in hand, on the edge of the sand,
They danced by the light of the moon.**
-Edward Lear

**On a hot day in Virginia, I know nothing more comforting
than a fine spiced pickle, brought up trout-like
from the sparkling depths of the aromatic jar
below the stairs of Aunt Sally's cellar.**
-Thomas Jefferson

## PRESERVES

### apple butter.

*Each fall, my mother searched the Bedford County orchards for the freshest apple cider and apples, either Jonathan or MacIntosh. Her sister, Mary, boiled apple butter outdoors in a huge copper kettle over a wood fire. But mother cooked her apple butter in a large iron kettle on the kitchen stove. During the following winter, we would enjoy spreading apple butter, Pennsylvania-Dutch style, over cottage cheese on a slice of bread, to make an open-face sandwich.*

*Like so many other recipes, this one was never written down. I have been experimenting to recreate her recipe and believe that this one produces the consistency and the taste of Mother's.*

6 pounds apples, peeled and quartered
5 C fresh cider or apple juice
1 C cider vinegar
4 C sugar
2 tsp cinnamon
1/2 tsp cloves
1/2 tsp Allspice

Combine apples, vinegar, and cider in a large pot. Cover and simmer for 30 minutes. Remove from the heat, and process in a food processor or sieve. Return to the pot. Stir in the sugar and spices. Bring to a boil, and reduce the heat. Cook uncovered over low heat for 2 hours. Stir often. Apple butter is cooked long enough when it sheets from a spoon or when placed on a plate and there is no rim or liquid around the edge of the apple-butter sample. Fill hot jars, and cover with hot lids. Seal according to the manufacturer's directions. Yield: 7 (6 oz) jars.

# PRESERVES

## brandied cherries.

*Pat Jones shared this recipe at* Preserving Summer, *the 2009 HSN culinary workshop. These brandied cherries are delicious over vanilla ice cream and/or pound cake. (See Desserts Category.)*

3 pounds black cherries, pitted
3 pounds sugar or less, depending on the sweetness of the cherries
Brandy

Combine the cherries and sugar. Allow to stand until the juices form. Cook slowly over medium heat until cherries are soft, about 20 minutes. Remove cherries and spoon them into sterile jars. Reduce the remaining syrup until slightly thickened. Measure syrup and add 1/4 C brandy for every cup of syrup. Pour into jars and seal, according to manufacturer's directions. Yield: 4 (6 oz) jars.

*****

## bulla tomato relish

*While Josh Bulla is cutting my hair, we frequently talk about recipes and food. Josh's grandmother's recipe is a delicious accompaniment to chicken entrees.*

1 quart fresh tomatoes (peeled and chopped lightly)
1 C sugar
1 C vinegar
1 tsp salt
1 hot pepper (thinly chopped)
1 C chopped onion

Combine all ingredients in large saucepan. Cook on high, stirring constantly with a wooden spoon. Reduce heat until it thickens like preserves. Pour into hot, sterilized jars, and keep refrigerated or seal according to manufacturer's directions for use during the winter.

**PRESERVES**

### concord grape butter.

*This recipe is from my Uncle Ralph Dibert, who grew grapes on his farm in Imlertown. I discovered that grape butter thickens as it cools, as do other jams and jellies. The first time I made this grape butter, I cooked it until it was thick. When it cooled, the butter had a tar-like consistency that was impossible to remove from the jar! So, boil only until the liquid starts to thicken.*
     *My friend, Joan Cole, submitted this recipe for publication in the 1993 edition of the* Congressional Club Cookbook *(page 285).*


2 quarts Concord grapes
2 quarts sugar
4 Tbsp water

Combine the ingredients. Stir and allow ingredients to blend. Bring to a slow, rolling boil. Cook 25 minutes, only. Put through a sieve to remove the skins and seeds. Return to boiling and remove from the heat. Pour it into hot jars. Cover with hot lids. Seal according to manufacturer's directions.
Yield: 6 (6 oz) jars.

**PRESERVES**

### dilly beans.

*Garlicky, crisp, snappy, somewhat spicy! Joan Cole's Dilly Beans were always a hit during the cocktail hour preceding her dinner parties in Potomac, Maryland. Each summer, Joan cans them at her Keuka Lake home, using her "secret" recipe. One summer, Doris Hansen and I decided to replicate her recipe. Joan had to admit our recipe is close!*

2 pounds small tender green beans
1 tsp red pepper
4 garlic cloves
4 large heads dill
2 C water
1/4 C salt
1 pint distilled white vinegar
4 pint jars

Stem the beans. Place a hot, pint jar on its side, and pack beans into the jar. To each pint, add ¼ teaspoon red pepper, 1 clove garlic and 1 head dill. Heat together water, salt, and vinegar. Bring to a boil, and pour over the beans, leaving 1/2-inch headspace. Cap each jar when filled. Seal according to manufacturer's directions. Yield: 4 pints.

**PRESERVES**

### lavender bundles.

*Molly Schneider crafted a spectacular display from lavender for* Gifts from the Herb Garden, *the HSN 2013 summer workshop.*

Arrange lavender in bunches, keeping the flower heads at the same level. Add pieces to the bundle to form a funnel shape. Tie each bundle with wire about 4 1/2 inches below the flower heads. Twist to tighten. Trim the edges until perfectly even so the bundle can stand on its own. Finish by tying a bow of wire-edged ribbon under the flower heads.

*****

### lavender wand

*A Lavender Wand keeps a drawer fragrant and will repel moths in a closet. As fragrance fades, squeeze the wand to release oils. Start with slightly wilted lavender so stems are pliable! Mary Cartwright demonstrated wand-making at the HSN July 2013 meeting.*

Gather an even number of stems, 18, 22, or 26. Take the end of 2 yards of 5/8-inch wide-ribbon and tie a knot below the flowers at the end of the ribbon.

Turn the bundle upside down and carefully bend each stem down. Grasp stems below the flowers and form a loose cage around the blooms.

Pull the ribbon from the center and weave it over and under the stems. Start at the top and weave over two and under two. Keep the ribbon snug against the rows above and wrap it tightly. At the bottom of the flowers, wind the ribbon around the stems a few times and tie a bow.

After a week or two, start at the top and tighten the ribbon all through the weaving and retie it at the bottom.

**PRESERVES**

## peach chutney.

*Becky Talbot, a member of HSN, created this savory chutney recipe, and passed it to her daughter, Jana. I've tweaked the recipe a little.*
  *This chutney is perfect over grilled chicken or on a ham or chicken sandwich. A versatile preserve, it is also delicious over a wedge of cream cheese as an appetizer or over vanilla ice cream for a dessert!*

4 pounds peaches, about 4 cups, coarsely chopped
1/2 C cider vinegar
1/4 C lemon juice
1 C black or white raisins
1/3 C chopped onion
1 tsp Allspice
1/2 tsp cinnamon
1/2 tsp cloves
1 tsp ground ginger
1/2 tsp cayenne pepper
4 1/2 C sugar
3/4 C brown sugar

Chop the pitted and skinned peaches into small pieces and add to other ingredients. Bring to a rolling boil and cook, uncovered, for 15 minutes or until the mixture thickens slightly. The chutney will look liquidly but will thicken as it cools. Fill the hot jars and cover with hot lids. Seal according to manufacturer's directions. Yield: 6-7 cups.

*An apple is an excellent thing ...*
*Until you've tried a peach.*
*-George du Maurier*

**PRESERVES**

### peach jam.

*Mother usually added finely chopped Maraschino cherries to her jam, but I prefer it without. This jam is also terrific over cream cheese as an appetizer or over vanilla ice cream for dessert.*

18 ripe peaches, pitted, skinned, and quartered
1 navel orange, sectioned with rind
Sugar

Chop peaches and orange in a food processor. Measure cups of fruit. Add 1 1/2 times as much sugar as fruit. Bring to a rolling boil and cook until syrup sheets from a silver spoon or until a spoon makes a clear line through a Tbsp of cooled jelly placed on a plate. Fill hot jars and cover with hot lids. Seal according to manufacturer's directions. Yield: 6 (6 oz) jars.

*****

### red pepper jelly.

*This jelly is especially delicious as an appetizer, spread over a block of cream cheese and served with crisp crackers.*

3 C red bell peppers, chopped
3 1/2 C sugar
1 1/2 C vinegar
1 Tbsp crushed red pepper

Combine all ingredients. Boil 15 minutes, stirring constantly. Cool slightly. Place in a food processor, and blend. Bring to a boil, and boil 10 minutes. Fill hot jars, and cover with hot lids. Seal according to manufacturer's directions.

**PRESERVES**

### red raspberry jam.

*When I was in grade school, I accompanied my mother to Imlertown where she had "engaged" (ordered) red raspberries from Essie Imler. Essie always waited until we arrived to pick the berries. Patiently, I waited to be invited into her fenced raspberry patch, but I never was so lucky!*

| | |
|---|---|
| 1 quart red raspberries | Sugar |
| 1/4 C water | Juice of 1/2 lemon |

Combine berries and water. Bring to a boil, stirring constantly. Remove from heat and measure. Add 3/4 cup of sugar to each cup of berries. Add lemon juice, and boil for 15 minutes. Remove from heat. Fill hot jars and cover with hot lids. Seal according to manufacturer's directions. Yield: 3 (6-oz) jars.

*****

### strawberry jam.

*In the late spring, our family spent many Sunday afternoons at Uncle Ralph and Aunt Gladys' farm. Uncle Ralph would pick ripe strawberries for my mother. One summer in France, I bought strawberries at a farmer's market and made jam while we barged on the Canal du Nivernas.*

| | |
|---|---|
| Strawberries | Juice of 1 lemon |
| Sugar | 1/2 tsp butter |

Chop berries in a food processor. Measure. Add 1 cup of sugar for each cup of fruit and juice. Add the lemon juice. Bring to boil, and add butter. Boil for 15 to 18 minutes or until mixture sheets from a silver spoon. Remove from the heat. Fill hot jars and cover with hot lids. Seal according to manufacturer's directions.

## PRESERVES

### quick, low-cal jam.

*The preceding jam recipes are my mother's. But you might prefer a jam with less sugar. Judith Bracken shared her method for a low-cal version. Frequently, Judith's bread-making assistant is her grandson Quinn, who prefers toasted bread with her jams. Judith prepares low-sugar jams from any extra fruit she has in her kitchen. This is a loose, light, sweet, fruity, delightful jam or topping. In the winter, Judith makes small batches "for a quick lift!"*

3 C fruit (strawberries, figs, peaches, grapes or any combination)
Juice (pineapple, cranberry, blueberry, pomegranate)
Meyer lemon juice (Or use lemon or lime, not as sweet as Meyer.)
1/3 C raw sugar
Kuzu (kudzu) root thickener (optional)

Clean and cut fruit. Halve strawberries and grapes or cut smaller if needed. Place fruit in a sauce pan with a small amount of juice, about 1/2 inch on the bottom of the pan.

    Squeeze in Meyer lemon juice or even throw in chunks of Meyer lemon flesh. (Judith loves to eat those lemons straight!). Sometimes she uses Satsuma mandarin orange segments. The acid in the lemon, lime, or tangerine causes the jam to jell. Add about 1/3 cup of raw sugar and just let it boil down to a fairly thick consistency. If she really wants it thick, Judith adds a little kuzu root thickener, "like cornstarch but better," she says.

    Spoon jam into jars, and refrigerate or freeze because of the low sugar content. Jam keeps a month or more in the fridge.

## PRESERVES

**sweet mango preserves.**

*Nancy Coleman shared this recipe at* Preserving Summer, *an HSN culinary workshop. This 2009 event focused on creating gifts for holiday giving from our summer gardens. As HSN culinary chair, I organized these workshops in 2008 and 2009 for members and friends and then reproduced the recipes for the HSN membership.*

*Nancy and her sister, Pat Coleman, lived in Panama when their father was a senior grade engineer for the Panama Canal Company, a branch of the Civil Service similar to TVA. This recipe has been a family favorite since Pat and Nancy, energetic HSN members, lived there.*

4 ripe mangoes, peeled and finely chopped
1-2 red chilies, seeded and chopped
2-inch ginger root, peeled and grated
2 lemons, juice and zest of, grated
2 1/2 C water
1 pound light brown sugar
1 C sultana or golden raisins
1-3 Tbsp balsamic vinegar

Place the mangoes, chilies, and ginger in a large pan. Add the lemon zest and juice, and stir in the water. Bring to a boil, and simmer for 20 minutes. Add the sugar, and heat gently until the sugar has completely dissolved. Bring to a boil for 10 minutes or until a thick consistency is reached. Stir in the raisins and balsamic vinegar. Cook an additional 5 minutes. Let cool slightly and pour into hot sterilized jars. Seal according to manufacturer's directions. Yield: 6 to 8 (6 oz) jars.

**PRESERVES**

### sweet pickle slices.

*My ancestors originally came from Germany and settled in southern Pennsylvania. Pennsylvania-Dutch cooking includes preserving vegetables in the summer so that "sweet and/or sour" dishes accompany meals during the winter.*

*The idea of seven sweets and seven sours stems from an ancient European custom based on the belief that everything should be properly balanced. Traditional "sweets" are based on locally-grown fruits such as apples, berries, or even candied watermelon rind. The "sours" are pickled vegetables (onions, cauliflower, and beets), tomato-relish, sliced cucumbers, and other recipes that grew from the German Old-World Influence.*

*Many recipes were family secrets, not to be shared with others. It took years for my mother to perfect a sweet-pickle recipe, which had been closely guarded by a friend.*

*Mother's process involved soaking the whole cucumbers for seven days in a cool cellar. Since I have no cellar, I place the soaking cucumbers in the refrigerator. I add a few (2 or 3) drops of green food coloring to the pickling syrup to enhance the color of the pickle slices.*

20 cucumbers (6-7 inches long, 1 1/2-inch diameter), sliced crosswise
1/4 C Mrs. Wages Pickling Lime
1/2 gallon distilled water
4 C distilled white vinegar, 5% acidity
4 C sugar
2 tsp mixed pickling spices

Soak clean, sliced cucumbers in water-and-lime mixture in a crock for 12 hours or overnight. Remove sliced cucumbers from limewater, and rinse three times in fresh cold water. Soak slices for 3 hours in fresh, distilled ice water.

## PRESERVES

### sweet pickle slices. (cont.)

Combine vinegar, sugar, and pickling spices in a large pot. Bring to a low boil, stirring until sugar dissolves. Remove syrup from the heat and add sliced cucumbers. Soak 5 to 6 hours or overnight.

Boil slices in the syrup for 35 minutes. Fill hot, sterilized jars with hot slices. Place 3 or 4 white raisins on the top slices. Pour hot syrup over slices, leaving 1/2-inch headspace. Cap each jar when filled. Seal according to manufacturer's directions.

*****

### sweet refrigerator pickles.

*When you don't have time to make sweet pickles, try this fast recipe. My sisters, Harriet and Sharon, and I all love these pickles. So easy to prepare and so delicious as a salad or a side!*

| | |
|---|---|
| 1 C distilled white vinegar | 6 C sliced cucumbers |
| 1 Tbsp salt | 1 C sliced onions |
| 2 C white sugar | 1 C sliced green peppers |

In a saucepan, bring vinegar, salt, and sugar to a boil. Boil until the sugar is dissolved. Place cucumbers, onions, and peppers in a large bowl. Pour the vinegar mixture over the vegetables. Transfer to sterile containers and store in the refrigerator.

Between 1990 and 1995, Kathleen Passidomo and I co-chaired the annual Auction-on-Stage, a fundraiser for the Endowment Fund at the Naples Philharmonic Center for the Arts, now known as ARTIS. In 1991, our theme was *Phantom of the Opera*. *The lights went out and a spotlight fell over the Casavante pipe organ. The* Naples Daily News *reported "Wearing a black cloak and white half-mask, James Cochran, the Phil's organist, began playing Bach's* Toccata and Fugue in D Minor. *This Third Annual Auction was another tour-de-force for 'producers' Kathleen Passidomo and Joanne Slaughter. They are still being applauded for the previous year's Elizabethan gala featuring trumpet fanfares and musicians in medieval dress."*

## christmas morsels

Christmas is the only time of year you can sit
in front of a dead tree eating candy out of socks.
-Anonymous

The best of all gifts around any Christmas tree:
the presence of a happy family all wrapped up in each
other.
-Burton Hillis

It's not what's under the Christmas tree that matters.
It's who is around it.
-Tom Baker

## CHRISTMAS MORSELS

The month of December was filled with family, school, and church-related activities. These random thoughts are from the 1940s when my family (Harry and Irene Fletcher and daughters, Joanne, Harriet, and Sharon) lived at 214 East Watson Street in Bedford, Pennsylvania. I played a vitally important role in the myriad of activities.

### checking the cookie supply.

In early December, Mother began baking numerous types of cookies that she stored in the walk-in pantry just off the kitchen. There were pink-and-white striped candy canes, date pinwheels, and pressed-out wreaths and trees. But our preferred cookie, by far, was the sand tart. This cookie came in different shapes: camels dusted with cinnamon sugar, Santa Clauses covered with multi-colored sprinkles, trees sprinkled with green sugar, and stars with cinnamon sugar and a pecan or almond placed in the center. Following his annual ritual, Daddy would hold a Santa Claus sand tart upside down and insist that it was a rooster. It was our duty to hold it right side up and convince him that it was, indeed, a Santa Claus. I wonder how Mother had time and patience to bake so many cookies during this busy month.

*In 1918, Mother graduated from the Bedford Normal School. (A normal school offered a one-year training and certification program for teachers.) Then, Mother taught in a one-room schoolhouse, located near the lake on the Bedford Springs Hotel property. She roomed and boarded in a log-house near the school. On week-ends, she took the train in Bedford to return to her family farm near Imlertown. Winter mornings, she arrived at school early to build a fire in the pot-belied stove to heat the classroom. Her teaching career abruptly terminated when both of her parents became ill, requiring her to return to her home to care for them.*

*Following their deaths, Mother moved to Altoona where she worked as a secretary to a stock broker and lived with her brother, Ralph Dibert, and his family. One Christmas, Daddy "came to call." Mother's two young nephews, Fred and Gerald, stood at the top of the stairs and peered through the railing. Gerald bellowed boorishly, "Care for another sand fart, Fred?"*

## CHRISTMAS MORSELS

### decorating our elementary-school classrooms.

In early December, we students spent hours after school turning red and green construction paper links into chains that we strung high on the walls enclosing our classroom. Then, we decorated the Christmas tree and created murals with colored chalk on the blackboards. Later, we drew the name of a classmate, from a hat, and bought a gift to give that person at a party, held on the last afternoon before the Christmas vacation. The price of the gift was limited to twenty-five cents!

*I attended first grade at the elementary school on Juliana Street. A fire destroyed the high school during my second grade, and the high school moved into our elementary school. The first six grades were then housed in the Bedford churches. Rebuilding the high school was a long process, because this was during World War II when building materials and labor were in short supply. Finally, during sixth grade, we moved back into the elementary school.*

*In the war years, savings stamps and bonds were sold at school. Schools also served as the collection points for newspapers and cans of used cooking fat. Harriet and I transported our recyclables to school in our red Radio Flyer wagon.*

### shopping for our teacher's gift.

During my elementary-school years, I presented each teacher with a snow globe as a Christmas present. Gables Department Store in Altoona had the best selection. And each year, I spent considerable time shaking prospective globes to determine which one had the largest and most snowflakes.

### attending the annual shrine christmas party.

On a Friday afternoon in mid-December, we sisters were excused early from school. We went home to change into our party dresses and black patent-leather shoes. Our family arrived in Altoona at the Jaffa Shrine

## CHRISTMAS MORSELS

Temple. A turkey dinner was served by Shriners in the downstairs of the building. Then, we were entertained upstairs in the auditorium by various Shrine groups, including their band, drum-and-bugle corps, chanters, and clowns. The culminating event was the arrival of Santa, who brought boxes of chocolates for everyone. On our return to Bedford, if there was fresh snow or ice, Daddy had to stop to put chains on the tires. As we grew older, we were allowed to stand beside him outside to watch while he worked.

*Daddy was a 32$^{nd}$ Degree Mason and a Grand Master of the Bedford Lodge. Then, he became a member of the Jaffa Shrine in Altoona. His brother Charles lived there and was a member of the Shrine Band.*

*When Daddy attended a Shriners' meeting, we all went along to Altoona and shopped for the day. Afterward, we had dinner, usually at the restaurant in Gables Department Store. Then, we attended a movie and waited for Daddy in our car, parked in a lot behind the theater.*

### decorating the outside of our house.

We hung spruce and pine garlands intertwined with lights surrounding our front door. We also covered the bushes near the porch with bright lights. My preference was to use only blue lights that gleamed through the December ice and snow covering the bushes.

### searching for the christmas tree.

On the second Sunday in December, we traveled the backroads near Imlertown and tramped through the woods in search of a Christmas tree. Even the best candidate required Daddy to add a branch or two where the tree was sparse. These must have been the original Charlie Brown trees. Personally, I would have preferred to purchase a perfectly shaped tree. But, this method of selection was a family tradition.

### trimming our christmas tree.

The Christmas tree was placed in the sunroom, adjacent to the living room. This room also served as Daddy's home office. The tree was decorated with ornaments, saved from one year to the next and stored in the attic. Some ornaments were from Mother's home, and similar ones hung on the trees of her brother, Ralph, and her sister, Mary.

The tree trunk, set in its stand beneath the tree, was surrounded by a platform about two feet above the floor. On the platform, a model train chugged slowly in a circle, as it traveled through a tunnel, around a small village of tiny houses lit from behind, and past a pond (a mirror) with ice-skaters. Sometimes this layout was covered with moss. Other years, the cotton-covered platform was dusted with artificial snow. On several occasions, angel hair (spun glass), resembling a covering of light snow, was added to the tree after the ornaments and lights had been hung on the tree.

### making a gum-drop tree.

On our trip to the woods, we also looked for a tiny thorn bush to be used as a table decoration. Mother first dipped the bush in starch, shook artificial snow onto its branches, and placed it in a flowerpot filled with sand. Our job was to stick small colored gumdrops on each thorn. The gumdrops, that survived our pilfering, hardened and were savored as snacks when the tree was disassembled in January. This treat was almost as good as finding a stray jellybean or two in the Easter-basket grass from the year before.

### shopping for mother's and daddy's gifts.

In the early 1940s, we shopped for our parents' presents at the G. C. Murphy Company, the local dime store on Juliana Street. Purchases were usually Coty's face powder and a powder puff for Mother and a handkerchief for Daddy. Later, these items became stocking stuffers. Then, we shopped at Murdock's for a decorative glass piece for Mother and at Straub's Men's Store for a tie for Daddy.

### receiving dried fruit from california.

For several years, Daddy received wooden boxes of dried fruit from the Sinclair Oil Company. For 35 years, Daddy was the Bedford County Distributor for Sinclair Oil products. This was the first time that I had seen

## CHRISTMAS MORSELS

dried fruit artistically displayed, which probably explains my craving for Hadley's Medjool Dates today.

*One wooden fruit box became Mother's button box, kept in the sewing room. This small room, at the top of the second-floor landing facing south to catch the light, also served as the ironing room. An outside door led to an upstairs porch where we sunbathed as teenagers.*

### buying citrus fruit at bedford monument works.

Each Christmas, Mother made her signature Boston Cream Candy. Some was packaged specifically for the Snyder Family that owned the Bedford Monument Works. During the week before Christmas, the Snyders trucked citrus fruit from the Orlando, Florida area, where they owned groves of orange, tangerine, and grapefruit trees.

Early in December, Daddy "engaged" (ordered) our fruit, because the supply was limited. This was the only source of citrus fruit in Bedford during the early 1940s. I was stunned that the citrus baskets were placed among the headstones.

### christmas shopping in johnstown.

Before leaving Bedford for Johnstown, Daddy would call his brother-in-law, Howard McGraw. The call informed him when we would arrive, so he could reserve a space for us in his downtown parking lot near Penn Traffic Department Store. Uncle Howard's lot filled early on Saturday, especially during the Christmas season. After shopping, we usually had dinner with Daddy's sister, Emma, and Uncle Howard.

*The men who drove Daddy's gasoline trucks enjoyed small-game hunting. While my family never cared for wild game, Aunt Emma really enjoyed rabbit and squirrel. On one occasion, she prepared "fried chicken" for our dinner. On the trip home, we asked mother why she hadn't eaten any chicken for dinner. Daddy revealed that the "fried chicken" was really rabbit that he had brought to Aunt Emma as a gift from his Bedford hunters.*

## CHRISTMAS MORSELS

### rolling calendars.

Each December, Daddy gave his customers calendars for the coming year. Those living in Bedford received a small desk calendar, and those living in the country were given a large wall calendar adorned with a pinup girl. These were usually hung in the barns, away from the eyes of farm women and children. The task for Harriet and me was to roll the wall calendars and secure them with rubber bands. Then, the route men delivered them to their customers.

### planning my annual christmas party.

When I was in fourth grade, I began the tradition of hosting an annual Christmas party for nine of my girlfriends. In early December, we drew names, keeping the name a secret. Part of the fun was guessing who had given you the gift. This tradition continued through college.

### delivering a christmas box to koontzie.

Harriet and I filled a Christmas tin with cookies and candy. And we wrapped cans of soup, boxes of Jell-O and tea, etc. Then, we packed the items in a decorated box or basket and delivered it to Koontzie who lived in a tiny, two-room apartment behind Ray Stayers' Old Bedford Inn on Pitt Street. Our visit with Koontzie always included playing cards or Chinese checkers with her before we walked home.

*We considered Koontzie (Mary E. Koontz) as a member of our family. She was our babysitter when Mother and Daddy went to Altoona, Johnstown, or Pittsburgh to shop. On their return, she always informed them that Harriet and I had been asleep for hours. In reality, we were still awake and had only become quiet when we heard the garage door open. Koontzie lived a very meager existence. Ironically, after she died, it was discovered that she was quite wealthy, owning bank stock that she had apparently forgotten about or thought to be worthless.*

## CHRISTMAS MORSELS

### bringing in the yule log.

In the late 1940s following World War II, Bland Hoke became the manager of the Bedford Springs Hotel. At Christmas time, Mr. Hoke brought mistletoe and holly from Virginia to decorate the public rooms of the hotel. During the week before Christmas, the wreathed, front doors were opened for the Bedford residents to attend the annual Colonial Christmas celebration.

This event featured the tradition of bringing in the yule log, festooned with holly. Four men, attired in Colonial dress, held the huge log aloft, carried it through the lobby, and placed it in the main fireplace where it was lit with great ceremony. Wassail and cookies were served in the upstairs dining-room. The hotel had magically been restored to its former splendor.

In the early years of the war, the hotel had been used as a Communications Training Center for the U. S. Navy. Bedford residents provided housing for the Navy's civilian instructors. My second-grade classmate was Margo Boocock whose father was the Commanding Officer of the school. His family lived in the Buchanan House on the hill above the hotel. What a treat to be invited there for lunch. Later, my sister Sharon was a classmate of the hotel manager's son. She, too, was often invited there for lunch.

One of our first "roomers" was Dick Shoap, an instructor for the school who had been an AT&T employee from Shippensburg, Pennsylvania. After the war, Dick returned to Bedford with AT&T, rented an apartment from Daddy, and then built a home in Meadowbrook Terrace. At another time, two instructors lived with us. Dave Ruth from Pittsburgh had a ham radio in his room. Leslie Davis was from Oswego, New York, where his family owned a canning factory.

Our Watson Street house had four bedrooms and a finished attic room. Harriet and I gave up our bedrooms and moved into the attic. Seven people sharing a single bathroom was a stretch. Our home had only one bathroom on the second floor and a powder room on the first floor.

Harriet and I operated a profitable business selling Daddy's green promotional Sinclair pencils to the sailors who walked into Bedford on Saturday evening, passing our corner of Watson and Richard Streets.

## CHRISTMAS MORSELS

However, our entrepreneurial endeavor was short-lived when Daddy learned of our "business." We could not find the sailors to return their money. But Daddy did accompany us across Watson Street to Mrs. Riley's home to return money she had given us. Her husband was the local attorney. We assumed that we had broken the law.

*Toward the end of the war, the Bedford Springs became a residence for the Japanese Diplomats from their embassy in Germany. (Many resort facilities, including the Greenbriar Hotel in West Virginia served this function.) The Springs' extensive grounds were enclosed in barbed-wire fencing and guard towers were built. A chef was hired from Washington D.C., and local residents provided daily services. Needless to say, many Bedford residents opposed the idea of hosting the Japanese in such fine style because their sons and daughters were serving with the U. S. Armed Forces fighting against Japan in the Pacific. On V-J Day, everyone from Bedford piled into their cars, drove around the Springs Hotel, and honked their horns in celebration. Soon, after the departure of the Japanese diplomats and the war's end, our home life returned to normal. Harriet and I moved back into our rooms on the second floor.*

*During the 1950s, the hotel operated as a convention center and as a summer resort. I worked as a waitress in the main dining room during my college years when the hotel was open only during the summer months. The dining room and kitchen staffs generally alternated between a hotel in Florida during the winter season and Bedford in the spring through fall.*

*The Bedford Springs Hotel, a National Historic Landmark, was founded in 1806, and is set on 2200 acres of rolling hills. The sprawling red brick façade supported by white columns, has been restored by combining the past with today's luxurious amenities. Dating back to the mid-19$^{th}$ century, in original glass windows of the Crystal Ballroom are the inscriptions of the names of brides who married at the resort. And, the original mineral springs that drew Native Americans, early settlers, and wellness-seekers, inspired the nearby Springs Eternal Spa.*

*Today, the Omni Bedford Springs Resort and Spa is one of the last and finest examples of American 19$^{th}$ century opulent resorts. Once again, the hotel provides guests a luxurious and restful experience.*

# CHRISTMAS MORSELS

### participating in st. john's church activities.

Over the years, Harriet and I spent many hours after school and on weekends practicing for the church's annual Youth Fellowship Christmas plays. We also decorated Christmas trees in the Sunday School room and in the church sanctuary. Then, we placed pine boughs and a candle on each windowsill under its stained-glass window. We also sang in the choir and caroled with the Youth Fellowship.

*In the 1940s, upon returning to the church from caroling, we learned that Hyndman, a small-town north of Bedford, was being destroyed by fire. Below freezing temperatures made firefighting almost impossible. We canceled our YF party, gathered the sandwiches and cookies, made a pot of coffee, and took food to Hyndman for the firemen.*

Daddy was a member of the Consistory, the governing body of St. John's Church. He ushered at the midnight Christmas service, while Harriet and I sang in the youth choir. At midnight, the electric lights were dimmed, and the ushers lit the candle of the person seated on the center aisle. Each member of the congregation lit his candle from the next person until all candles were lit. The service concluded with the singing of *Silent Night*.

The drive home was especially beautiful. We viewed many homes whose exterior lights illuminated doorways, walkways, and trees. On returning home, our family enjoyed a late supper of oyster stew and potato salad. Daddy ate the oysters while we floated oyster crackers in the broth until they became soggy and melted in our mouths.

### following the christmas morning ritual.

On Christmas morning, we first opened the stocking gifts, the last of which was the tangerine nestled in the stocking toe. Then, Mother stuffed the turkey and put it in the oven. Daddy then prepared breakfast. He began by fixing grapefruit halves. He cut out the core and along the edges of each of the sections leaving them in the rind. He always placed a soft green or pink mint in the center. Bacon and eggs followed. After we ate breakfast, we opened our presents.

## CHRISTMAS MORSELS

### sharing christmas dinner.

Most Christmas dinners were spent in our home with guests, usually Fletcher family members. I recall going to Uncle Bob and Aunt Bobbie's home for a Christmas dinner. The six children (we three, Nancy and Robert Hammer, and Peggy Lou Grissinger) ate at a separate table. Dessert was molded ice-cream figures of Christmas angels and Santa Clauses. What a treat!

According to tradition, we listened to Uncle Bob's personalized rendition of *Hark! The Herald Angels Sing*.

> *Hark! The Herald Angels sing,*
> *Timmons' pills are just the thing.*
> *Peace on earth and mercy mild,*
> *Two for a man and one for a child.*

*For the record, Dr. Timmons was one of three doctors in Bedford. All doctors made house calls and had office hours in the evenings. Patients were seen in the order of their arrival. The waiting room scene in the movie,* Doc Hollywood, *is very familiar.*

### going to aunt mary's house.

During the Christmas season, we drove to Imlertown to visit my mother's sister, Mary, and Uncle Howard. Their daughter, Goldie Holderbaum, and her daughter, Patty, lived with them. Another daughter, Flora Stickler, and her son, Joel, who lived in Imlertown, were there as well. Their son, Paul, and his family lived in the springhouse next to Aunt Mary's house.

This house was built over a spring. Its walk-in basement served as the farm refrigerator. Here the filled milk cans were stored in a trough, filled by flowing spring water, awaiting pickup by the truck from the Bedford milk plant.

Aunt Mary would offer us her bountiful array of Christmas baking, including slices of popcorn cake, molded in an angel-food cake pan, with popped corn, nuts, and bits of red candied cherries, bound together by a boiled sugar syrup.

## CHRISTMAS MORSELS

### seeing the tree.

Being invited to "see the tree" was a popular social event. This was probably a carry-over from the old Pennsylvania-Dutch custom called Belsnickeling. In those times during the Christmas season, a family would travel from farm to farm, dressed in old clothes or costumes and wearing false faces. The neighbors would guess their identity and invite them in for a visit and special Christmas food. This is similar to Halloween, but celebrated during the winter when the farmers had more time to socialize.

At Uncle Ralph's house, we checked his tree to see where the antique Dibert family glass ornaments were hanging that year.

While most trees were traditional, Mother's friend, Emma Sellers, decorated her tree differently each year. One year, Emma cut down a six-foot, leafless deciduous tree, strung lights along the branches, wrapped those branches with cotton batting, dusted the cotton with sparkling artificial snow, and hung multi-colored balls from the white branches.

Emma's husband, Charlie, grew up near Fletcher's family farm where we cut spruce and hunted for teaberries. In the 1970s, Charlie and Emma bought the Fletcher farm and planted its hills with Christmas trees.

*Daddy told of skiing over those hills to a one-room schoolhouse in Imlertown. He also worked with his father, a carpenter, to build the Reformed Church across the road from Uncle Ralph's home. When Daddy was thirteen, his father died. Daddy quit school, moved to Altoona where he lived with his brother, Charlie, worked in the railroad shops, and sent money home to his mother. The older brothers and sisters provided financial support and helped educate their younger siblings.*

In the 1980s, we three sisters and our families would return to Bedford to celebrate Mother's July 2nd birthday and to attend a Dibert or Fletcher family reunion. Many of these celebrations were held at Charlie's farm. A highlight was the bouncing jeep ride with Charlie over the hills, those same hills that Daddy, in the 1900s, had walked or skied over to reach elementary school!

I savor these memories of the 1940s Christmases in Bedford, Pennsylvania.

1988. Frequently, we met at sunset for drinks at the Pelican Bay Beach Club or for dinner in one another's homes. Left to right: Judy Nuechterlein, Barbara Fletcher, Elke Schmid, Penny Given Love, Karen Kelly, and me.

joanne fletcher slaughter

In August 1992, I arrived at the Moscow Airport to join an AmeriRuss Tour of Russia. American and Russian entrepreneurs cruised the Golden Ring (the cradle of Russian Culture), explored Moscow, and took an over-night train to St. Petersburg. The purpose of the tour, sponsored by the Mormon Church, was to stimulate conversation between American and Russian business people, following the collapse of the Soviet Union. Translators facilitated our sessions on topics, including women's issues, health, education, how to start a business, etc. Most of the Russians I met had never been outside Moscow's city limits.

# sweets

## cookies

A balanced diet is a cookie in each hand.
-Barbara Johnson

In the cookie of life, friends are the chocolate chips.
-Salman Rushdie

The Vice-Presidency is sort of like the last cookie on the plate.
Everybody insists he won't take it, but somebody always does.
-Bill Vaughan

## COOKIES

### caramel brownies.

*In November 2002, Ray Bowers from the Williamson County Agricultural Extension Service spoke to our garden club. His topic was how to make our backyards more hospitable and inviting to wildlife. After a lunch of Jack Daniel's Stew, Liz Weller served her decadent caramel brownies for dessert.*

*Each Christmas, Gary and I look forward to Liz's visit when she arrives with an awesome assortment of her holiday baking. We are indeed lucky to have such a talented baker as a friend.*

1 box German chocolate cake mix
3/4 C margarine, melted
2/3 C evaporated milk, divided 1/3, 1/3
1 C chopped pecans
1 pkg (6 oz) semi-sweet chocolate chips
1 pkg (14 oz) Kraft Caramels

Preheat oven to 350 degrees. Combine cake mix, margarine, and 1/3 cup of evaporated milk. Mix well. Press half of the mixture into the bottom of a 9x13x2-inch pan. Bake in preheated oven for 5 minutes.

Sprinkle pecans and chocolate chips over the crust. Melt caramels with 1/3 cup milk. Stir until smooth. Spread caramel mixture over the chocolate chip-pecan mixture. Top with remaining cake-mix mixture. Bake 20 - 25 minutes. Do not over-bake. Cool in the pan before cutting in squares.

German chocolate cake is not named after the country, but after Samuel German, the inventor of a type of dark chocolate.

# COOKIES

### cheese-cake bars.

*Carol Wattleworth brought this recipe from her Bend, Oregon PEO Chapter. In September 2015, she hosted our PEO Chapter E Bookies luncheon and served these luscious cheese-cake bars. We sisters always anticipate bidding on her delicious items at our November Silent Auction.*

1/3 C butter
1/3 C brown sugar
1 C sifted flour
1/2 C walnuts, finely chopped
1/4 C sugar
1 pkg (8 oz) cream cheese, room temperature
1 egg
2 Tbsp milk
1 Tbsp lemon juice
1/2 tsp vanilla

Preheat oven to 350 degrees. Cream the butter, brown sugar, flour, and walnuts. Reserve 1 cup for topping, and press remainder into a greased 8x8-inch pan. Bake for 12 minutes.

Blend sugar and cream cheese. Add egg, milk, lemon juice, and vanilla. Beat well. Spread over baked crust, sprinkle with the reserved crumb mixture. Return to the oven and bake 25 minutes. Cool and cut.

## COOKIES

### chocolate-chip cookies – sil.

*In early December, Gary and I know that Christmas is coming when Sil Hartzog, our Howell Place neighbor, delivers her delicious chocolate chip cookies! What a treat!!! Sil says that she follows the basic Toll House recipe, but doctored it a little!*

2 sticks unsalted butter
3/4 C brown sugar
3/4 C white sugar
2 eggs
1/2 tsp salt
1 tsp vanilla
2 C old-fashioned oats
1 1/4 C unbleached, all-purpose flour
1/2 to 3/4 C semisweet chocolate chips
1 C dried cranberries or dried cherries

Preheat oven to 350 degrees. Put the butter in a heat-resistant bowl and place it in the oven to melt the butter.

Add brown sugar and white sugar to melted butter and stir. Add eggs and mix. Stir in salt and vanilla. Mix in oatmeal, then flour. Stir in the chocolate chips and fruit, and mix.

Drop teaspoon of batter onto the cookie sheet. (You can place parchment paper on the cookie sheet to keep from sticking.) Pat down each cookie with tines of a fork, dipped in water or flour, to allow cookie to bake evenly. Bake for 10 to 12 minutes until edges are golden. Remove from the cookie sheet immediately and place on waxed paper to cool. Yield: 42-44 cookies.

# COOKIES

## chocolate-chip cookies – susan.

*In January 2006, I began docent training for the September 9, 2006 opening of the Schermerhorn Symphony Center in downtown Nashville. A gala concert, conducted by Leonard Slatkin, was broadcast by PBS affiliates throughout the state.*

*Our docent class included Drake Carlton, Karen Drier, Judith Hodges, and Nancy Zuccaro. Susan Williams, the Symphony Volunteer Coordinator, always had a smile and a cheery word for each of us!*

*In January 2007, we docents held a wedding shower for Nancy Zuccaro in the SSC Board Room. Susan shared her chocolate-chip recipe and baked the cookies for the event.*

1 C shortening (Crisco)
3/4 C white sugar
3/4 C dark-brown sugar, packed
2 eggs
2 1/4 C all-purpose flour
1 tsp salt
1 tsp baking soda
1 pkg (12 oz) semi-sweet chocolate chips
1 C chopped nuts, optional
1 tsp vanilla
1 tsp hot water

Preheat oven to 375 degrees. Cream shortening and sugars. Add flour, salt, and baking soda and mix. Stir in the remaining ingredients. Drop onto an ungreased cookie sheet with a teaspoon. Bake 8-10 minutes. Yield 3 1/2 dozen. Enjoy!

## COOKIES

### chocolate-chip oatmeal cookies

*In 2006, Julie Schoerke and I met at a Nashville WNBA meeting. Since PR was her business, I asked Julie to help me with publicity for Gary's second novel,* Cottonwood Fall. *She arranged for signings at Davis-Kidd and at Barnes & Noble. The book was selected by* The Scene *as the Critic's Book Pick for June 1, 2006. Julie's interest in books evolved into establishing a public relations firm for authors, JKS Communications.*

*I was impressed with Marissa DeCuir, editor of* The Tennessean's Food Section *and suggested that Julie hire her. And, because Julie had no business experience, she asked Gary and me to advise her about finances, contracts, and practices needed to achieve business success.*

*In 2007, JKS managed the publicity for* Cottonwood Winter *with book signings at book stores and reviews in* NFocus *magazine,* The Tennessean, *and* The City Paper.

*In 2012, I worked closely with JKS to promote* Cottonwood Summer '45. *Instead of the traditional city-to-city book tour, marketing was a Virtual Tour. Marissa DeCuir, heading the JKS team, scheduled Internet blog sites, book giveaways, radio interviews, Internet and print reviews, as well as the traditional newspaper and magazine coverage. Between April and June, our virtual book tour featured "appearances" in 23 different sites.*

*In working with JKS in 2016, I discovered that publicity had changed considerably since the Virtual Tour. My JKS contact was Angelle Barbazon. Because* Sea Stories *covered Gary's Naval career, she launched a publicity campaign geared to military websites for reviews and endorsements, as well as blogs to their website followers. Some blogs had followings in the 100,000's.*

*On Labor Day Sunday in 2016, Ginger Nalley coordinated the Parnassus launch for* Sea Stories. *That afternoon gathering of our Nashville friends was standing-room-only! Julie paid us a huge compliment, "It's safe to say that our book publicity firm wouldn't exist today if it weren't for these two amazing people."*

*Gary and I enjoy knowing Julie's children, Chan and Amanda, and sharing meals with them on many occasions. And, we've had the pleasure of meeting many Nashville book people through Julie's literary gatherings.*

# COOKIES

### chocolate-chip oatmeal cookies (cont.)

*Julie Schoerke's grandmother, Ethel Kuntz, baked these chocolate-chip oatmeal cookies beginning in 1915, long before Nestle and Hershey thought of adding oatmeal to their cookie recipes. Both of Julie's children have called her for this recipe for special college occasions. Julie says, "The kids continued to be voted 'Best Ole Miss Chocolate-Chip Cookie Bakers' by all their friends. Gary and I have enjoyed these cookies at Julie's home, as well as in her frequent Cookie Care Packages!*

1 C margarine (not butter)
1 C Crisco
1 1/2 C sugar
1 1/2 C brown sugar
3 eggs, whisked together
1 1/2 Tbsp *real* vanilla (best quality possible)
3 C all-purpose or pre-sifted white flour
1 1/2 tsp baking soda
1 1/2 tsp salt
3 C old fashioned oatmeal
20-24 oz chocolate chips, depends how chocolatey you prefer

Preheat oven to 375 degrees. In a large bowl, place margarine, Crisco, sugars, eggs, and vanilla. Beat until smooth. Sift the flour, baking soda, and salt. Add the sifted dry ingredients to batter. Add oatmeal and chocolate chips. Mix until well-blended.

    Grease a cookie sheet lightly with Crisco. Drop heaping spoons of dough onto the sheet. Bake 6-8 minutes, if you want chewy cookies. They will look slightly underdone. Allow them to sit for a minute. Remove cookies onto a cool counter, with a spatula that has been cooled by running water, after each cookie or two. Yield: 6 dozen.

## COOKIES

### christmas wreaths.

*Mother and I enjoyed making these cookies together. While she pressed out a wreath, I decorated them with green gumdrops and red cinnamon drops. Today, I press and Gary decorates. Very time consuming but well worth the effort!*

| | |
|---|---|
| 1 C shortening | 1/2 tsp baking powder |
| 3/4 C sugar | 1 tsp lemon extract |
| 1 egg | Green gumdrops cut in strips |
| 2 1/4 C sifted flour | Tiny red cinnamon drops |
| 1/4 tsp salt | |

Preheat oven to 350 degrees. Cream the shortening. Add the sugar and cream well. Beat in the egg and extract. Gradually add flour sifted with salt and baking powder. Fill a cookie press using the star shape. Press out and form a wreath. Place 4 gumdrop strips as two leaves and center 5 tiny cinnamon drops (holly berries) between the two leaves. Bake for 8 minutes or until lightly brown. Cool on rack. Yield: 6 dozen.

*****

*Listening to David Foster's* A Christmas Album *certainly puts Gary and me in a cookie-baking mood. In the summer of 1993, Billy's job was to film a documentary during the recording of Foster's album. Among the artists Billy filmed were Wynonna (*Blue Christmas*), BeBe and CeCe Winans (*The First Noel*), Michael Crawford (*O Holy Night*), Tom Jones (*Mary's Boy Child*), and Tammy Wynette (*White Christmas*). Who knew that a few years later, Gary and I would be living in Music City U.S.A. (Nashville)!*

## COOKIES

### crisp oatmeal cookies.

*Judith Hodges and I met in January 1999 at the Cheekwood Docent training. We also trained as docents for the Schermerhorn Symphony Center in 2006. Gary and I attended the Schermerhorn "Plank Signing" with Judith and her husband, Mark, in 2004. Our signatures, along with those of major Symphony donors, are preserved on planks supporting the Center's roof.*

*Because her mother did not like to cook, Judith did not have homemade cookies often. As a teenager, she decided she would learn to bake and used an oatmeal-cookie recipe of her mother's best friend. Over the years, the recipe evolved, using half white flour and half whole wheat. Later, she added finely chopped walnuts.*

*Judith said, "While I was going through chemo after my lumpectomy, I wasn't eating much myself but craved crisp oatmeal cookies. Friends brought some, but they were just too soft. As I adjusted to the chemo, my energy level increased. After the third chemo, I decided it was time to bake oatmeal cookies. That I could do it was such a victory for me!"*

| | |
|---|---|
| 1/2 C butter | 1 tsp baking soda |
| 1/2 C shortening | 1/2 tsp salt |
| 1 C brown sugar | 1 tsp vanilla |
| 2 C rolled oats | 1/4 C boiling water |
| 1 C all-purpose flour | 1 C walnuts, finely chopped |
| 1 C whole wheat flour | |

Preheat oven to 400 degrees. Cream butter, shortening, and sugar in large mixing bowl. Blend in dry ingredients. Add vanilla and boiling water and mix. Stir in finely chopped walnuts. Form into 60 balls and place on greased baking sheets. Press down with fork, floured or watered. Should be quite thin. Bake 10-12 minutes or until golden brown. Yield: 5 dozen cookies.

## COOKIES

### date pinwheels.

*During the Christmas season, the date pinwheel was a Fletcher family favorite! In the past, I eagerly awaited the annual cookie box from my sister, Sharon, who included these in her holiday baking. Today her daughter, Kathryn, and her sons, Ben and Jacob, are the cookie-bakers, making dozens and dozens to share with friends and co-workers.*

2 1/4 C chopped dates
1 C granulated sugar
1 C water
1 C chopped nuts
1 C shortening
2 C brown sugar
3 eggs, well beaten
4 C sifted flour
1/2 tsp salt
1/2 tsp baking soda

Combine dates, white sugar, and water. Cook over low heat until thick, about 10 minutes. Add nuts and cool. Cream the shortening by adding brown sugar gradually. Add well-beaten eggs, and beat mixture well. Add the remaining ingredients sifted together, and mix well. Chill thoroughly.

    Divide mixture into 2 parts, and roll each separately into a rectangle ¼-inch thick. Spread each with some of the date filling and roll up into 2 long rolls. Chill overnight. Preheat oven to 400 degrees. Cut into ¼-inch thick slices. Bake for 10 to 12 minutes.

*****

*Sharon graduated from the University of Pittsburgh with a degree in Journalism. Meticulously, she edited and proofed our five* Cottonwood *books. Her expertise certainly contributed to the awards for this series. I miss the collaboration that we enjoyed for those 15 years and would have loved to share this book with her.*

## COOKIES

### forgotten cookies.

*With their crisp, glossy exterior and fluffy center, these meringue cookies are perfect for the busy baker, because you just turn off the oven and forget them until morning. The cookies continue to bake as the oven cools down.*

*Carolyn Campbell often bakes these cookies for our annual PEO Silent Auction in November. Because meringue does not hold up in humid weather, these cookies are best made in winter. Perfect for Christmas gifting!*

2 egg whites
Pinch salt
2/3 C sugar
6 oz chocolate chips
1 C chopped nuts

Preheat oven to 350 degrees. Beat the egg whites and salt until soft peaks form. Slowly add the sugar. Continue beating until very stiff. Fold in chocolate chips and nuts. Drop by teaspoon of batter on a foil-lined baking sheet. Place the baking sheet in preheated oven. Turn oven off and leave the cookies in the oven overnight. Store in an airtight container.

*To vary the recipe, add 3 tablespoons of unsweeted cocoa into the egg whites with the sugar. For a toffee twist, replace the chocolate chips with milk chocolate toffee bits.*

## COOKIES

### fresh lemon squares.

*These yummy lemon squares were perfected by Helen Terrill, my sister Harriet's neighbor, when she lived in Valley Forge, Pennsylvania. This has always been Gary's daughter, Wendy's preferred dessert.*

| | |
|---|---|
| ¼ pound butter | 2 eggs beaten |
| 1 C flour | ¼ tsp baking powder |
| ¼ C powdered sugar | 2 Tbsp lemon juice |
| 1 C granulated sugar | Grated rind of 1 lemon |

Preheat oven to 325 degrees. Mix butter, flour, and powdered sugar. Place in an 8x8-inch baking pan. Bake for 15 to 20 minutes. Mix remaining ingredients and pour over cooked crust. Bake for about 30 minutes. Sprinkle powdered sugar over baked mixture when warm. Cut into small squares.

*****

### *1976 american bicentennial:*

*In July 1976, Harriet, Sharon, and I took our children to Mother's home in Bedford, Pennsylvania, for the arrival a Bicentennial Wagon Train. This train of Conestoga wagons had begun traveling east from Blaine, Washington, on June 8, 1975. By fall, wagons from nine northwestern states were on the Oregon, Bozeman, Mormon, and Lewis and Clark trails, headed for winter layovers in Wyoming and South Dakota. During the winter, wagons from the southern states began rolling and by spring, wagons from all 50 states were moving in five caravans toward a Fourth of July rendezvous at Valley Forge, Pennsylvania, where President Ford led the ceremonies.*

## COOKIES

### helen's brownies.

*During the early 1970s, Helen Hess and I were neighbors living on Post Oak Road in Potomac, Maryland. We exchanged many recipes during those late afternoons while our preschool children played in the sandbox and on the swings in our backyards. Among those Helen shared with me is this recipe for her luscious brownies.*

2 squares unsweetened chocolate
1 stick margarine
1 C sugar
2 eggs, well beaten
1/2 C flour, sifted and then measured
1/2 C chopped walnuts or 1 cup Rice Krispies
1/2 tsp vanilla

Preheat oven to 375 degrees. In a saucepan over very low heat, melt chocolate and margarine. Remove from heat, and add the remaining ingredients. Pour into a greased and lightly floured 8x8-inch baking pan. Bake for 25 minutes or until a straw stick comes out dry when inserted in the center. Cool the pan on a wire rack before cutting into squares.

*In the late 1970s, Helen's husband, Wally, joined the corporate offices of Balfour in New York City. The night before the Hesses moved to Darien, Connecticut, Helen and I slept on mattresses on the floor of their empty home, reminiscing and talking the night away.*

## COOKIES

### hello, dolly! bars.

*Dense, gooey, and sweet! Fran Massey baked these bars for the dessert following a PEO luncheon. A sweet-tooth indulgence for Christmas Gifting.*

*Hello, Dolly! Bars date back to the 1960s when the musical,* Hello Dolly, *starring Carol Channing was on Broadway. These decadent bars are also known as Magic Squares or Seven-Layer Bars. The bars are assembled in seven layers, and they go together magically because drizzled condensed milk holds the layers together.*

1 C chocolate chips
1 C butterscotch chips
1 C coconut
1 C pecans or walnuts, chopped
1 C graham-cracker crumbs
1 stick butter
1 can Eagle Brand Sweetened Condensed Milk

Preheat oven to 350 degrees. Melt the butter in a 13x9x2-inch pan. Sprinkle graham-cracker crumbs evenly in bottom of the pan. Add layer of coconut, layer of pecans, layer of chocolate chips and pour Eagle Brand milk over top. Bake for 20-25 minutes. Cool before cutting into squares.

*To vary the recipe, replace the butterscotch chips with more chocolate chips, peanut-butter chips, toffee chips, or white-chocolate chips.*

## COOKIES

### marilyn's sugar cookies.

*Marilyn Whitmore was my mother's neighbor in the Meadowbrook Terrace area of Bedford, Pennsylvania, and her husband John was Mother's doctor. Marilyn, a visiting nurse, stopped to chat with Mother almost every afternoon on her way home from work. Most times, Mother had cookies or a pie waiting for her. Mother always cut out a slice. She just had to make sure that the pie was "fit to eat!"*

*Marilyn was very active in the Bedford Garden Club. Harriet and I joined her at the annual Philadelphia Flower Show when Marilyn was President of the Pennsylvania Federation of Garden Clubs. She also served as a member of the Garden Clubs of America's Board of Directors.*

*She shared this light, sugar-cookie recipe, from her family in North Dakota. This cookie was popular with the Cheekwood docents and staff. No one can eat just one!*

| | |
|---|---|
| 1 C butter | 4 C all-purpose flour |
| 1 C oil | 1 tsp baking soda |
| 1 C powdered sugar | 1 tsp cream of tartar |
| 1 C sugar | 1 tsp salt |
| 2 eggs | 1 tsp vanilla |

Preheat oven to 350 degrees. Cream together the sugars and shortening. Add eggs. Add sifted dry ingredients and vanilla. Chill dough. Form into small balls and flatten with the bottom of a glass coated with butter and dipped in sugar. Bake cookies for 10 to 15 minutes or until brown around the edges.

*****

*In 1999, I joined the Cheekwood docent program and continued to conduct tours until January 2019, accumulating over 3500 hours. Gary became a docent in 2008, with 1,500 hours. In 2008, I was the recipient of the Catherine van Eys Award. Gary accepted this award in 2012. We were the only couple to receive this annual award for volunteers!*

## COOKIES

### mellon's snickerdoodles.

*In the late 1950s, home economics students, at Mellon Junior High School where I taught English, planned, prepared, and served a luncheon for their teachers. Traditionally, these soft, chewy, and buttery cookies were served for dessert.*

1/2 C shortening
3/4 C sugar
1 egg
1 1/3 C sifted flour
1 tsp cream of tartar
1 tsp baking soda
1/2 tsp salt

Preheat oven to 400 degrees. Mix thoroughly shortening, sugar, and egg. Sift together flour, cream tartar, soda, and salt. Chill the dough. Roll into balls. Roll balls in a mixture of sugar and cinnamon. Place 2 inches apart on an ungreased cookie sheet. Bake for 8 to 10 minutes.

*Adding cream of tartar to a sugar cookie creates a snickerdoodle. These drop cookies were cited in print by 1889 and were popular in New England and Pennsylvania. Some believe that the name is a corruption of the German Schneckennudeln, meaning cinnamon-dusted rolls. Others believe that the name came from a series of tall tales about Snickerdoodle, a folk hero who was the champion of the little guy and was known for his sense of humor.*

# COOKIES

**mexican wedding cookies.**

*In January 2009, Karla Ruiz, a Nashville chef, presented* Using Herbs in Traditional Mexican Cooking *for an HSN culinary workshop at Martha's at Belle Meade Plantation. Following the Mexican luncheon, Karla served these traditional cookies, also called Sandies or Pecan Balls, for dessert.*


1 C butter
1/3 C sugar
2 tsp vanilla
2 tsp water
2 C all-purpose flour, sifted
1 C chopped pecans
Confectioners sugar, sifted

Preheat oven to 325 degrees. Cream the butter and sugar. Add vanilla and water. Add flour and mix well. Stir in pecans. Shape dough into small balls. Bake for about 20 minutes. Cool slightly. Roll in confectioners sugar.

*****

*While teaching English in the Mt. Lebanon junior high school during the day, I also taught a beginning Spanish class for adults in the evenings. My minor in Wilson College had been Spanish, and I wanted to further my studies.*

*During the summer of 1959, I enrolled in classes in Mexican History and Mexican Cultural Arts at Mexico City College in Mexico City. During the week, I lived with a Mexican family in the city, not far from Lake Xochimilco. Colorful excursion boats, decorated with flowers, and some boats with mariachi bands plied the lake's picturesque canals. On weekends, I traveled to various Mexican states to experience the full flavor of Mexico. The most memorable weekend was spent in a hotel, formerly a convent, in Oaxaca, where the swimming pool was filled with fresh gardenias each morning!*

## COOKIES

### oatmeal lace cookies

*In April 2006, the Sew 'n Sow Garden Club members met at the John Deere Landscape Garden Center on Hillsboro Road. Robanne Legan assisted in a "hands on" container gardening demonstration. Afterward, our lunch, prepared by the committee, was served at the picnic tables under the vine-covered arbors. Judi Echols' Oatmeal Lace Cookies completed the leisurely, al fresco luncheon.*

*Judy acquainted Gary and me with the volunteer opportunities for the Salvation Army's Angel Tree. For the last ten years, we have volunteered for six or seven 2pm-6pm shifts at the Green Hills Mall Angel Tree. We look forward to this rewarding activity each year and, especially, to seeing our friends who bring their children and grand-children to select "angels" for whom they shop for clothing and toys.*

2 sticks butter
1 C sugar
1 C brown sugar
2 eggs
1 tsp baking powder
1 tsp vanilla
2 C quick oats, ground in blender
1 C sliced almonds, finely ground

Preheat oven to 350 degrees. Mix butter and both sugars thoroughly. Add beaten eggs. Then add baking powder, vanilla, oats, and nuts. Mix well. Drop by 1/3 teaspoon far apart, because they spread, on foil-covered cookie sheet and bake for 6-10 minutes. Remove from oven and cool slightly. Handle carefully and remove from pan. Makes 6 dozen.

*****

*If you're feeling really creative, fold over the two sides of the HOT cookie to form a cylinder. When cool, tie a red ribbon around the center for a spectacular addition to your Christmas cookie platter!*

## COOKIES

### orange-spice cookies.

*I met Mary Myers through our garden club and succeeded her as president. A former English teacher, Mary now has the time to indulge in her favorite pastimes, hiking and traveling. Frequently, she participates in the Road Scholar programs and shares her recent adventures with us at garden club meetings. Mary shared her recipe for these delicious cookies and baked them for the lunch that followed our October 2005 meeting.*

1 box spice-cake mix
1/2 C vegetable oil
1/2 – 3/4 C orange marmalade
1 large egg
1 tsp ground ginger

Preheat oven to 350 degrees. Mix ingredients and blend on low 1 minute, scrape sides and mix 1 minute more.

     Grease a cookie sheet or use parchment paper (better). The dough is thick. Drop by rounded teaspoon, 2 inches apart, on cookie sheets.

     Bake on middle rack 12-15 minutes, until they start to brown, NO MORE. Let rest 1 minute before removing to cool. Cookies can be stored up to 1 week or frozen for 3 months. Yield: 48 two-inch cookies.

## COOKIES

### pumpkin bars.

*On a very drizzly morning in October 2004, our Sew 'n Sow Garden Club toured Nashville's Mt. Olivet Cemetery. Dale Powell's gooey pumpkin bars proved a perfect dessert for our luncheon.*

1 box yellow cake mix
1 egg
8 Tbsp butter, melted
1 pkg (8 oz) cream cheese, softened
1 can (15 oz) pumpkin
3 eggs
1 tsp vanilla
8 Tbsp butter, melted
1 box (16 oz) confectioners sugar
1 tsp cinnamon
1 tsp nutmeg

Preheat oven to 350 degrees. To make the crust, combine the cake mix, egg, and melted butter. Mix well with an electric mixer. Pat mixture into the bottom of a lightly greased 9x13x2-inch baking pan.

For the filling, beat softened cream cheese and pumpkin until smooth. Add eggs, vanilla, and melted butter. Beat until smooth. Add powdered sugar, cinnamon, and nutmeg. Mix well. Spread pumpkin mixture over cake crust and bake for 40 to 50 minutes. Do not over-bake. The center should be a little gooey.

*Mt. Olivet Cemetery was established in 1856. The Southern aristocracy was buried in a separate section of the cemetery that included prominent Nashvillians, former governors of Tennessee, U.S. Senators, and U.S. Congressmen. Each October, there is a walking tour of the cemetery where actors portray individuals from Nashville's past while stationed at their burial sites.*

## COOKIES

**reward cookies.**

*These crunchy cookies were Daddy's favorites! Serve with a dish of fresh fruit or ice cream! Or as a breakfast treat!*

| | |
|---|---|
| 1 C shortening | 1 tsp baking soda |
| 1 C white sugar | 1/2 tsp baking powder |
| 1 C brown sugar, firmly packed | 2 C Rice Krispies |
| 2 large eggs, beaten | 1 C shredded coconut |
| 1 tsp vanilla | 2 C quick oats |
| 2 C all-purpose flour | 1/2 C chopped nuts |

Preheat oven to 375 degrees. Thoroughly cream the first five ingredients. Sift together the dry ingredients, and combine with the first mixture. Mix the remaining ingredients and add this last. Roll into balls the size of a small walnut. Place on a cookie sheet, and flatten with the bottom of a floured glass. Bake for about 7 minutes or until brown. Cool on a rack.

*****

*My father, whom I called Daddy all my life, was one of the younger of thirteen children. His father died from a farming accident when Daddy was ten, and he began working about the age of 14. For a while, he lived with his older brother, Charlie, in Altoona and worked in the railroad yard. Then he worked in the Ford Motor Plant in Pittsburgh. In 1931, Daddy acquired the Bedford County franchise for distributing Sinclair Oil products and retired in 1964.*

*In the 1940s and 1950s, Daddy also owned two school buses. He or the men who worked for him drove students to and from school, the Bedford High School Marching Band to events, and sports teams to their games. In addition, he built a large building on Pitt Street that he leased to Thomas Chevrolet. Daddy also built and owned three gas stations and an apartment building in Bedford.*

*Having only an eighth-grade education, he learned from life, was a very private person, and got along with everyone.*

## COOKIES

### rosemary shortbread cookies.

*I combined several recipes to create this tasty rosemary shortbread cookie. During the holidays, I often bake these and present them as gifts, along with a bag of rosemary pecans. (See Savories Category.)*

2 Tbsp fresh rosemary
1 C butter, at room temperature
2/3 C confectioners sugar
1/8 tsp salt
1 tsp pure vanilla extract
2 C sifted all-purpose flour
2/3 C chopped pecans

Preheat oven to 350 degrees. With scissors, finely cut rosemary leaves. Mix leaves and all remaining ingredients, except pecans. Stir until smooth. Then, stir in the pecans.

Measure dough by teaspoonful. Roll into a small ball, flatten to about 1/4-inch thick with the bottom of a glass, covered in butter and dipped in granulated sugar. Place 2 inches apart on an ungreased cookie sheet.

Bake for about 12 minutes or until cookies are lightly browned. Allow to cool on the cookie sheet for 10 minutes, then remove to cool completely. Store in a tightly covered tin cookie container. Yield: 6 dozen.

*****

*To make dryer sheets, take a small drawstring bag and fill it with dried rosemary sprigs to naturally scent your laundry. Adding dried lavender flowers to this bag enhances the fragrance.*

## COOKIES

### sand tarts.

*This recipe for sand tarts was a family recipe of Jesse Barclay, Director of the Children's Welfare Agency in Bedford. In the early 1930s, when she and Daddy were first married, Mother worked as Jesse's secretary. Hands down, this is our family's favorite Christmas cookie.*

*Mother mastered rolling the cookie dough very thinly, until you could almost see through it. Then, she cut the shapes with a cookie cutter, and we three sisters decorated the tops. Eating the little scraps, containing uncooked egg, was frowned upon, but we did it anyway.*

*When our families spent Thanksgiving in Bedford, our tradition was to bake sand tarts on the day after Thanksgiving. Amazing how quickly we four could turn-out pan after pan of sand tarts!*

1 C butter
1 C margarine
1 1/4 C white sugar
1 1/4 C brown sugar
2 eggs
4 C flour
White of 1 egg

In a large bowl, cream butter, margarine, and sugars. Add eggs and then add flour. Mix well. Cover and place in refrigerator overnight.

Preheat oven to 375 degrees. Remove a ball of dough from the bowl and return the rest to the refrigerator. On a floured surface, using a floured rolling pin, roll the dough into a very thin sheet. Press desired shapes with a cookie cutter (tree, Santa Claus, star, camel). Remove cookie with a spatula and place on cookie sheet. Beat egg white, with a little water, until fluffy.

Decorate the sand tarts by dipping a pastry brush into egg white and painting the cookie surface with the egg wash. Sprinkle green sugar on trees, multicolored sprinkles on Santas, trees and stars, and cinnamon-white sugar mix on camels, stars, and trees. Bake for 8-10 minutes.

## COOKIES

### scotcheroos.

*Laurie Bradley and I met when she transferred to our PEO Chapter E. In the mid-1960s, Laurie found this recipe printed on the Rice Krispies box. Quickly, Scotcheroos became her daughters' first choice of cookie.*

*Courtney Crowder, in the* Des Moines Register, *reported, "A Rice Krispies Treat on steroids, Scotcheroos take the basic concept of the Krispies Treat and candify it by adding peanut butter to the bar and a melted chocolate-and-butterscotch topping."*

1 C sugar
1 C light corn syrup
1 C crunchy peanut butter
5-6 C Rice Krispies
6 oz chocolate chips
6 oz butterscotch chips

In a large pot, bring sugar and corn syrup to a gentle boil. Cook until the sugar dissolves. Add and blend in peanut butter.

Turn off heat and stir in Rice Krispies, amount depends on how gooey you want it. Place in a greased 9x13x2-inch pan.

Melt together chocolate and butterscotch chips and spread on top.

## COOKIES

### sweet potato-nut balls.

*When they were younger, Patsy Weigel's grandchildren enjoyed making these cookies and serving them to guests, garnering bragging rights for their cookie-making expertise!*

*No more cookie baking! Today Patsy's grandchildren's bragging rights come from their own achievements in golf, music, journalism, sports, or chess.*

4-6 cooked sweet potatoes
Salt, pepper, butter to taste
Honey
Chopped pecans
Pretzel sticks (optional)

Preheat oven to 350 degrees. Mash cooked sweet potatoes. Add salt, pepper, and butter to taste. Chill mixture. Shape into 1 1/2-inch balls. Heat honey in a small pan. Use 2 forks to roll balls in honey and then in pecans. Place balls on a greased baking sheet so they are not touching. Bake for 20 minutes. If desired, stick a pretzel stick in the ball for serving.

*****

*What children need most are the essentials
that grandparents provide in abundance.
They give unconditional love, kindness, patience, humor,
comfort, lessons in life. And, most importantly, cookies.*
-Rudy Giuliani

In 1996, friends and I spent the summer barging on France's Canal du Midi. Usually we tied up along the canal in the morning and biked into town. At the open-air market or in the shops, we purchased lunch that might include a freshly roasted chicken, assorted cheeses, fruit, a loaf of French bread, and wine

# sweets

## desserts

**Life is like an ice-cream cone.
You have to lick it one day at a time.**
-Charles M. Schultz

**Wouldst thou both eat thy cake and have it?**
-George Herbert

**Stressed spelled backwards is desserts. Coincidence?
I think not!**
-Unknown

## DESSERTS

### apple cake.

*Shortly after our move to Naples, Florida, in 1985, Elke Schmid and I met at an art opening in the Naples Depot. Back then, Friends of Art, led by Lucille Howe, sponsored three art exhibitions during the season. That year, a highlight was the work of Walter Anderson, a painter of nature scenes, from Ocean Springs, Mississippi.*

*Soon I became the volunteer coordinator, scheduling docents for tours during exhibition hours. In 1989, Friends of Art merged into the Philharmonic Center for the Arts.*

*Through art, Elke and I became good friends. She is a most gracious Naples hostess. Elke's apple cake has become an autumn treat in my home. During the Christmas holidays, it replaces fruitcake.*

| | |
|---|---|
| 1 1/2 C sugar | 2 tsp baking soda |
| 1/2 C oil | 1/2 tsp ground cloves |
| 2 eggs | 1/2 tsp nutmeg |
| 1/4 C rum | 1 C chopped nuts |
| 1/4 C brandy | 1 C golden raisins |
| 2 C all-purpose flour | 4 C Granny Smith apples, peeled and chopped |
| 2 tsp cinnamon | |

Preheat oven to 350 degrees. In a mixing bowl, combine sugar, oil, eggs, rum, and brandy. In another bowl, combine dry ingredients. Combine contents of both bowls, and stir until moistened. Add apples, nuts, and raisins. Stir and pour into a prepared Bundt pan. Bake for 1 hour.

*****

*In order to realize the beauty of man,
we must realize his connection to nature.
-Walter Inglis Anderson*

## DESSERTS

### better than sex cake.

*Frank Yake, my brother-in-law, and his wife, Sharon, are definitely not swingers! However, Frank is never at a loss for providing quirky recipes. This cake was popular around 2004, and the Internet is filled with different variations of this cake, aka Better Than Anything Cake or Almost Better Than Sex Cake. Or – in front of the kids – Better Than You Know What Cake.*

*Of all of Frank's concoctions over the years, this is hands-down a winner. Yes, it is that good!*

1 box yellow cake mix with pudding
1/2 C oil
1/2 C water
4 eggs
1 C sour cream
1 Hershey's candy bar, grated
1 C chocolate chips
1 C butterscotch chips
1/2 C chopped pecans

Preheat oven to 350 degrees. Combine the first 5 ingredients and beat at medium speed for 5 minutes. Add the remaining ingredients, and mix well. Bake in a greased 10-inch Bundt pan for 45 minutes.

*Want a sweeter cake? After removing the cake from the pan, poke holes in the cake with a fork and pour caramel topping over it. Spread whipped cream over the top and sprinkle with chopped Heath Bar chips. Refrigerate before serving. Don't even think about cholesterol or calories! Go for it!*

## DESSERTS

### bourbon-eggnog sauce.

*Patsy Weigel shared the following delicious recipes. Consider the bourbon-eggnog sauce for gifting this holiday season! She says, "I pour it into empty baby-food jars and give it to guests as a Take-Home-Treat."*

1/2 C butter, softened
1 C sugar
1 egg
1 C heavy cream
3/4 oz bourbon

Cream butter and sugar. Add egg and beat well. Add cream and place in a double boiler. Stir constantly over medium heat until thick. Remove from heat and add bourbon. The sauce lasts, almost forever, in the refrigerator.

*Patsy serves her bourbon-eggnog sauce over any sliced cake, rice pudding, or even pancakes. But she usually uses pound cake. (See Desserts Category.) Sometimes, she pours the sauce over her bread pudding.*

### bread pudding.

3 C milk
3 eggs, beaten
1 C sugar
1/2 tsp salt
1 1/2 C bread crumbs
1 tsp vanilla

Preheat oven to 350 degrees. Combine all ingredients and heat. Place mixture in a greased 8x8-inch baking dish. Bake for one hour.

## DESSERTS

### chocolate mousse.

*Over the years, Sue Brown and I have shared several interests: the Cheekwood and WNBA book groups, garden club, and the Salvation Army Auxiliary. In February 2004, Sue prepared this delicious dessert for the luncheon in her home following our Sow 'n Sow garden club business meeting. That day the menu included frozen cherry salad, pork tenderloin, rice with peas, oven-roasted green beans, and Sue's chocolate mousse, served with strawberries.*

1 pkg (8 oz) Baker's semi-sweet chocolate squares
3/4 C white sugar
4 Tbsp cold water
3 egg yolks
3 egg whites
1/2 box vanilla wafers
1 pint heavy whipping cream

Melt chocolate squares in a microwave on high for 2 minutes. Whisk in sugar and water. Microwave again 1 1/2 to 2 minutes on high. Stir well. Set aside to cool.

Beat egg whites stiff, and add beaten egg yolks. Whip cream and fold in egg mixture. Add all together to the chocolate mixture.

Line bottom of a 9x13x2-inch glass dish with crushed (food processed) vanilla wafers. Layer chocolate mixture into pan. Sprinkle a little of crushed vanilla wafers on top of chocolate.

Refrigerate at least several hours. Serves 12-15.

## DESSERTS

### chocolate peanut clusters.

*Jean Howe and I met in the 1999 Cheekwood Docent Class when she was the President-Elect of the Cheekwood Friends of Art. Jean gifted us with these peanut clusters many times. Finally, I begged for the recipe so I could also gift others during the Christmas season.*

6 blocks of chocolate bark
1 can (9 oz) roasted Spanish peanuts, without shells

Melt the chocolate bark very slowly in a saucepan or a skillet. When melted and stirred well, pour in the peanuts, completely coating them. Drop immediately onto waxed paper by the teaspoonfuls. Sets up within a few minutes. Store in an airtight container.

*****

### chocolate-coated strawberries.

*One Valentine's Day, Sherry Covington surprised Gary and me with an awesome package of luscious strawberries! This dessert is really delicious paired with a glass of wine or champagne!*

Strawberries with leaves
Ghirardelli melting chocolate, milk and white

Rinse and dry strawberries, keeping the leaves intact. Melt milk and white chocolate in separate dishes, according to package directions. Hold by leaves, and dip strawberries by hand in either milk or white chocolate. Place on wax paper to harden. Drizzle other chocolate flavor over the strawberry with a fork.

## DESSERTS

### date cake.

*Emma and Charlie Sellers were life-long friends of my parents. Their Christmas tree farm near Imlertown, Pennsylvania, was located on the land that was originally the Fletcher Farm, belonging to my father's family.*

*On our return to Bedford as adults, we sisters spent many memorable Sundays there with our children. Charlie's farm became the location for family reunions and picnics. Charlie always included a white-knuckle jeep ride through the pine trees for us. We bounced over those same hills that my father had skied over in the early 1910s on his way to attend class in the one-room schoolhouse in Imlertown.*

*Emma's cake is delicious served warm from the oven with sweetened whipped cream! Equally delicious with vanilla ice cream!*

2 C chopped dates
2 tsp baking soda
2 C boiling water
1 C butter
2 C sugar
3 eggs
1 tsp vanilla
3 C flour, sifted
1 C chopped English walnuts

Preheat oven to 350 degrees. Sprinkle soda over the dates and cover with boiling water. Mix and cool. Cream the butter, sugar, eggs, and vanilla. Add flour, date mixture, and nuts. Bake in a greased rectangular pan for 35 to 45 minutes. Serve with vanilla ice cream or sweet whipping cream.

# DESSERTS

## derby pie.

*Judy Anderson prepared her version of Derby Pie for a May 2019 dinner party at Suzanne Regen's home. The legendary secret recipe of this classic Southern dessert has chocolate and choice walnuts. Most recipes are similar and contain pecans or walnuts, chocolate chips and bourbon in a custard-like filling poured into a pie crust.*

2 9-inch baked pie shells
1 stick butter, melted and cooled
4 eggs, beaten
1 Tbsp flour
1 tsp vanilla
3/4 C white sugar
1/2 C brown sugar
1 C corn syrup
1 C chocolate chips
1 C pecans
2 Tbsp bourbon, if desired

Preheat oven to 350 degrees. Mix butter, eggs, flour, vanilla, white sugar, and brown sugar together. Add corn syrup, chocolate chips, pecans, and bourbon. Mix and place in two 9-inch pie shells. Bake for 45 minutes. Serve with whipped cream.

*The Kentucky Derby is held at 4pm on the first Saturday in May. This is the first race for the Triple Crown, followed by the Preakness and the Belmont. A horse must win all three races to win the Triple Crown. For several years, our PEO chapter has held a Derby Day Party as a fundraiser. Of course, our hats were spectacular!*

# DESSERTS

## fresh fruit in brandy syrup.

*In September 1962, June Jackson and I met each other on the first day of school. Both of us had been hired to teach English at Springbrook High School in Silver Spring, Maryland. Over the years, June shared her Southern dishes from Monroe, Louisiana. I even learned to make a roux. Her recipe for fresh fruit with brandy is divine!*

1/2 C sugar
1 C water
2 tsp lemon juice
Dash salt
3 Tbsp Triple Sec liquor or Curacao brandy

Simmer sugar, water, juice, and salt for 5 minutes. Add liquor or brandy. Pour over fresh fruits and chill until serving.

*****

## frozen custard – mother's style.

*Patsy Weigel's family serves this dessert during the holidays – a Virginia tradition! And Patsy enjoys serving it at her bridge parties!*

1/2 gallon vanilla ice cream
1/2 C white raisins
1/2 C chopped pecans
3/4 C sherry wine (NO MORE, Patsy says!)

Cut up raisins and soak in sherry overnight. Add raisins and nuts to the ice cream. Pack back in the container and freeze until ready to serve.

# DESSERTS

## german chocolate pie.

My friend, Marilyn Cornish's best dessert of all time is one that her mom baked for Marilyn's birthday every year. She continues to make it for herself on her birthday, and now her daughter requests it for her special day each year. This chocolate pie recipe originated with Marilyn's aunt in Montgomery, Alabama, around 1958.

2 egg whites at room temperature
1/4 tsp cream of tartar
2/3 C sugar
1/2 tsp vanilla
1/4 to 1/2 C chopped pecans

Preheat oven to 250 degrees. Whip egg whites with cream of tartar. Add sugar, 2 tablespoons at a time. Stir in vanilla and pecans. Pour meringue into a greased 9-inch pie plate. Bake for 1 hour.

chocolate pie filling:

1 bar German chocolate
1/2 tsp vanilla
1/2 pint whipping cream

Melt German Chocolate bar with 3 tablespoons of water. (You can do this in the microwave, but a double boiler always works.) Cool. Add vanilla. Whip whipping cream and fold into cooled chocolate. Fill baked meringue and refrigerate several hours before serving. Decorate top with dark chocolate shavings, if you wish.

*I really enjoy meringue crust. If you do, try the Heath Torte and the Ozark Pie. (See Desserts Category.)*

## DESSERTS

### haunted bridge log.

*My cousin, Peggy Lou Reda, was a few years older than I. I envied her, because, as the oldest volunteer at the Bedford Public Library, she was seated at THE desk across from the head librarian who checked-out books. Peggy's job was to check-in returned books and then shelve them. I began my library work by shelving books and later assumed Peggy Lou's desk position. I enjoyed the easy access to my preferred books, initially the Nancy Drew series.*

*During the 1970s, I served a log-shaped, chocolate wafer-whipped cream dessert but lost the recipe. Recently, I discovered it in* The Nancy Drew Cookbook: Clues to Good Cooking *by Carolyn Keene.*

1 pkg Nabisco Famous Chocolate Wafers
1 pint heavy whipping cream
2 Tbsp sugar
2 tsp vanilla flavoring

Whip cream until it forms peaks. Fold in the sugar and vanilla. Stack 3 or 4 wafers at a time, spreading a teaspoon of whipped cream between each. Save one chocolate wafer for later. Place stacks on their sides on a dish to form a log. Cover the log with the rest of the cream.

Crumble the saved wafer and sprinkle on top. Refrigerate at least 3 hours. Cut diagonally at a 45-degree angle. Serves 10.

*Nancy Drew, a mystery series detective, was created by publisher Edward Stratemeyer as the female counterpart to his Hardy Boys series. First published in 1930, the books were ghostwritten by a number of authors and published under the pseudonym Carolyn Keene. Over the decades, Nancy Drew has evolved to comply with changes in culture, fashion, and tastes. In the 1980s, an older and more professional Nancy emerged. By 2013, Nancy was driving a hybrid electric vehicle and using a cell phone as she solved mysteries.*

## DESSERTS

### heath torte.

*Of all the recipes that June Jackson shared with me, this dessert is definitely her finest! A make-ahead dessert and a crowd-pleaser!*

3 egg whites
3/4 C sugar
6 Heath bars

1/2 pint whipping cream
Sugar, to taste

Preheat oven to 270 degrees. Beat egg whites with a pinch of salt until stiff. *Gradually* add sugar and beat until very stiff. Form the meringue in a 9-inch circle on brown paper, using a spoon form an indentation in the middle of the circle. Bake 1 hour and 15 minutes. Cool the shell on a wire rack.

Whip cream until stiff and holds a peak. Crush Heath bars and sprinkle 1/2 inside the cooked shell. Cover this with whipped cream and sprinkle with the remaining Heath bars. Store in the refrigerator. This is best if made the day before.

*****

### hot chocolate sauce.

*Carolyn Harris prepared this sauce for the PEO 2012 Christmas Luncheon. Three ingredients and a few minutes yield a wonderful hot fudge sauce to serve over ice cream. Great gift, as well!*

1 stick butter, soft
1 C chocolate chips (Carolyn prefers Ghirardelli Semi-Sweet Chips.)
1 can sweetened condensed milk

In a medium sauce pan on medium heat, melt the butter. Stir in the chocolate chips. Add the sweetened condensed milk. Stir well to combine. The butter will take a minute to incorporate into the sauce. It will be smooth and silky. Store any leftovers in the refrigerator. Serves 10.

## DESSERTS

### hot cranberry casserole.

*Suzanne Regen always serves luscious desserts! This is definitely a perfect Christmas choice! And its aroma from her oven during dinner is tantalizing! The hot cranberry is delicious with frozen vanilla yogurt!*

3 C peeled and chopped apples
2 C whole cranberries
1 1/2 tsp lemon juice
1 1/2 C granulated sugar
1 1/3 C quick cooking oatmeal
1 C chopped pecans
1/3 C brown sugar
1 stick margarine, melted

Preheat oven to 325 degrees. Spray a 2-quart casserole dish with Pam. In the dish, place apples and cranberries. Sprinkle with lemon juice. Cover with sugar.

Make crumb mix by blending oatmeal, pecans, brown sugar, and margarine until it is moistened. Pour over fruit. Bake uncovered for 1¼ hour.

*For a Christmas centerpiece, place fresh cranberries in the bottom of a clear glass vase. Then, fill the vase with holly branches and fresh white flowers, such as mums, Alstroemeria, or Casablanca lilies.*

## DESSERTS

### individual cheesecakes.

*The PEO Bookies rely on Jan Taylor, a voracious reader, for the latest new books. In February 2013, Jan prepared these delicious cheesecakes for our PEO Book Group discussion.*

2 pkgs (8 oz each) cream cheese, softened
1/2 C sugar
1 tsp vanilla
2 eggs
Vanilla wafers
1 C sour cream
2 Tbsp sugar
1 tsp vanilla
Blueberries and red raspberries

Preheat oven to 325 degrees. Mix cream cheese, 1/2 cup sugar, and vanilla well on medium speed. Add 2 eggs, one at a time. Place one vanilla wafer in the bottom of a cupcake paper. (Use 2 papers each.) Fill 3/4 full. Bake for 20-25 minutes.

Prepare topping by mixing sour cream, 2 tablespoons sugar, and vanilla. Let cheesecakes cool a few minutes, then spoon on the topping. Return to oven for another minute or two. Chill. Before serving, top with blueberries or raspberries. Yield: 12.

*According to cheesecake.com, the writer Athenaeus of Naucraris is credited for writing the first Greek cheesecake recipe in 230 A.D. By this time, the Greeks had been serving cheesecake for over 2,000 years, but this is the oldest known surviving Greek recipe!*

**DESSERTS**

### lemon cake.

*This cake has long been a family favorite. Helen Hess, a former neighbor in Potomac, Maryland, introduced me to this simply wonderful cake. A perfect dessert for a summer luncheon or supper.*

1 box lemon cake mix
1/3 C white sugar
1 C apricot nectar
1/2 C salad oil
3 large eggs
1 C confectioners sugar
Juice of 1 lemon

Preheat oven to 325 degrees. Mix the first 4 ingredients, and beat for two minutes. Add the eggs one at a time. Beat well after each addition. Pour mixture into a greased and floured 10-inch tube pan. Bake for 1 hour.
    Cool on a rack before removing from the pan. Mix confectioners sugar and juice of one lemon to make a glaze. Pour over the top and sides.

*****

*Anytime the perfume of orange and lemon groves wafts in the window; the human body has to feel suffused with a languorous well-being.*
*-Frances Mayes*

# DESSERTS

### miniature fruitcakes.

*You may hate fruitcake, but you definitely will adore these miniature ones! Another of Harriet's scrumptious recipes! These are a perfect addition to an assortment of Christmas cookies.*

1 C Wesson oil
1 1/2 C brown sugar
4 eggs
2 C flour
1 tsp baking powder
1/2 tsp salt
2 tsp cinnamon
2 tsp Allspice
1 tsp cloves
1 C orange juice
1 C (more) flour
1 1/2 C candied cherries, chopped very fine
1 1/2 - 2 C candied pineapple, chopped very fine
1 C raisins, chopped fine
1 C dates, chopped fine
2/3 C chopped nuts

Preheat oven to 275 degrees. Combine oil, sugar, and eggs. Beat for 2 minutes. Combine the flour, baking powder, salt, and spices. Stir into oil mixture alternately with orange juice. Mix other cup of flour with fruit and nuts. Pour batter over fruit and mix well. Place about 2 tablespoons of batter into each miniature muffin tin. Place a pan of water on the rack below the muffin tins. Bake for 20 minutes. Yield: 7 dozen.

**DESSERTS**

### mud pie.

*Billy and I discovered mud pie in Park City, Utah where we skied during spring break in March 1982. Later that spring, he initiated a pie-baking competition at Georgetown Day School. Billy and two friends gathered in our Chevy Chase kitchen and prepared their entries: apple and walnut pie, pecan pie, and mud pie. In the 1990s, Billy continued these competitions in Los Angeles when his company produced* Making the Video *for MTV.*

1 10-inch pie pan
1 box Nabisco Famous Chocolate Wafers
1/2 C melted butter
1 1/2 gallon coffee ice cream
1/2 C cocoa
2/3 C sugar
1/3 C heavy cream
3 Tbsp melted butter
1 tsp vanilla
Whipped cream, sweetened with sugar to taste

Roll wafers into crumbs, and mix with melted butter. Press into a 10-inch pie pan and freeze. Melt ice cream enough to spread into frozen crust and freeze.
    Make a fudge sauce in a double boiler by cooking cocoa, sugar, cream, and butter over low heat. Add vanilla. Cool and pour over ice cream and freeze. Allow to stand at room temperature 5 minutes before serving. Top with whipped cream. Serves 8.

# DESSERTS

## ozark pie.

*Crispy, chewy texture! I have no idea where this recipe originated, but everyone really enjoys it! And, you only need one apple. What a wonderfully cooling, summer-time ending to dinner! Or a breakfast dessert?*

1 egg
3/4 C sugar
1/8 tsp salt
1 1/2 tsp baking powder
1/4 C flour
1/2 C tart apples, pared, cored, and chopped
1/2 C chopped walnuts
1 1/2 quarts vanilla ice cream
3 chocolate-covered Heath bars, frozen

Preheat oven to 350 degrees. Combine the first five ingredients; beat well. Stir in apples and nuts. Pour the mixture into a well-greased 10-inch pie pan. Bake for 25 minutes. Cool completely. (The crust will rise and fall while baking.)
      Soften ice cream slightly and spoon into the cold shell. Sprinkle crushed Heath bars over the ice cream. Freeze. Remove from freezer 15 minutes before serving. Serves 8.

*****

*After the war, my parents frequently went to Pittsburgh to shop. We three girls stayed home with Koontzie. (You may remember her as the Wilted Dandelion Salad Queen.) We couldn't wait for Mother and Daddy to return because they always stopped at Islay's Ice Cream Store for Klondike Bars, chocolate-covered ice-cream bars on a wooden stick. Packed in dry ice, the Bars were frozen solid, even after a three-hour drive.*

# DESSERTS

**pecan tassies.**

*In the 1960s, Peg Alderson taught eighth-grade Home Arts at Mt. Lebanon's Mellon Junior High. Her pecan tassies were often served at faculty bridge parties. I was delighted to rediscover this treat at a Friends of Cheekwood tea in Nashville in the late 1990s.*

*Pecan tassies are a favored Southern cookie, especially at Christmas. They appear to be the cookie version of pecan pie, believed to have been made in New Orleans by French settlers in the early 1700s. In any event, these little tarts are extremely addictive!*

1 pkg (3 oz) cream cheese
1/4 pound butter
1 C all-purpose flour
2 eggs
1 1/2 C brown sugar
2 Tbsp melted butter
1 tsp vanilla
1 C pecans

Preheat oven to 325 degrees. Mix cream cheese, butter, and flour. Place in refrigerator for 1 hour. Cream the eggs, brown sugar, melted butter, and vanilla. Press dough into mini-muffin tins. Place a layer of pecans on the dough. Pour in the filling to 3/4 full, and add another layer of pecans. Bake for 25 minutes or until set.

*****

*Gary and I have enjoyed our involvement at Cheekwood for the last twenty years. As members of Cheekwood's 1929 Club, we donated funds to support the restoration of the mansion as it was in the 1930s. In 2015, with the Bovenders (Barbara and Jack) and the Smalls (Lisa and Stephen), we underwrote the purchase of Bruce Munro's* Bell Chandelier *that hangs in the loggia level of the mansion.*

## DESSERTS

### pistachio cake.

*My friend, Karen Kane's family enjoys this pistachio cake on special occasions, or in the summer months. So very refreshing! Karen's mother acquired this recipe from a fellow teacher in the 1970s. With three young daughters, a husband, and a teaching career, her mother relied on recipes that were fairly easy to prepare – but delicious! Pistachio cake quickly became a family tradition!*

1 box white cake mix
1 pkg pistachio pudding mix
1 C oil
3 eggs
1/2 C chopped pecans
1 C club soda

Preheat oven to 350 degrees. Combine all ingredients and beat for 4 minutes with an electric mixer. Pour into a greased and floured 10-inch tube pan. Bake for 45-50 minutes. Turn out onto a wire rack and cool.

pistachio frosting:

2 envelopes Dream Whip
1 1/2 C cold milk
1 pkg pistachio pudding mix

Combine all ingredients and beat at high speed with electric mixer until fluffy. Spread frosting over the entire cake. Refrigerate the cake, unless serving immediately.

**DESSERTS**

### pot de crème.

*Carol Wattleworth and Susan Vanston are vivacious mother-daughter members of PEO Chapter E. This spring, Susan's triplets graduated from high-school! Hopefully, Susan will have more time to prepare this decadent, luscious dessert for us, that she served at the 2012 PEO Christmas Luncheon in Liz Weller's home!*

1 pkg (12 oz) Ghirardelli Sweet Chips (Susan prefers bittersweet.)
4 Tbsp granulated sugar
2 tsp vanilla
3 tsp Chambord (You can also use Grand Marnier or rum.)
1 tsp salt
1 1/2 C milk (Susan uses 2 cups.)

Heat milk in saucepan over medium high heat until just about to boil. Be careful the milk does not scald. Pour hot milk over rest of ingredients in a blender. Blend 30 seconds max.

Pour into little ramekins and set in fridge to chill for at least an hour. (Susan chills them overnight.)

Top with whipped cream, raspberries, and chocolate shavings, if you wish. Serves 4-6, depending on how full you pour the ramekins.

*If you're making this for a crowd, Susan recommends that you use paper ramekins. The Container Store in Nashville's Green Hills Mall stocks them.*

# DESSERTS

## pound cake - diane.

*In the mid-1970s, June Jackson, Diane Rehm, and I were volunteers on the Culinary Committee of The Hospitality and Information Service (THIS), located in Washington, D.C.*

*In the late 1970s, Diane and I enrolled in a class for women at George Washington University entitled* Returning to the Workplace.

*At the completion of the class, Dianne interviewed at WAMU as a volunteer researcher for a talk show. Six years later, she was anchoring a nationally syndicated radio talk show on WAMU, The Diane Rehm Show. In 1995, PBS offered the show to stations around the country. Remarkably, Diane's final show was in December 2016 after 37 years on the air.*

*Diane and I have lost touch. I wonder if she finds time today to bake her delicious pound cake? And does she invite friends to share a glass of wine and admire the first blooms on the cherry tree in her garden? Someday soon I plan to reread her autobiography,* Finding My Own Voice.

5 eggs
1 2/3 C sugar
2 C flour, sifted
2 sticks butter
1 Tbsp brandy

Preheat oven to 300 degrees. Combine ingredients and beat well. Bake in a greased and floured large loaf pan for 1 1/2 hours.

*****

## the hospitality and information service

*In 1960, Meridian House at 1630 Crescent Place in Northwest Washington, D.C., served as headquarters for a non-profit organization called the Washington International Center.*

*During the early 1970s, one division of the Center was The Information and Hospitality Service (THIS). The purpose of the organization*

# DESSERTS

*the hospitality and information service* (cont.)

was to provide an orientation to Life in the United State for the wives of the embassy staff personnel who had recently arrived in Washington.

Various THIS committees offered cooking classes, excursions to stores like Safeway and Garfinkel's Department Store, tours of Capitol Hill, as well as cocktail parties for couples.

On a summer evening in 1976, the Culinary Committee invited embassy couples to my home in Olney, Maryland. There we volunteers presented a demonstration of preparing food for An American Picnic. A picnic supper by our pool followed.

Volunteering at THIS was exciting, especially for those of us who were relatively new to Washington. June, Diane, and I all enjoyed our volunteer days with THIS.

Once a year, The Benefit Committee of the Meridian House Foundation held a formal ball as a fundraiser. Dinner preceded the ball and was hosted by ambassadors at their embassies. In 1972, I served as Hostess for a dinner at the Embassy of Barbados. As an Embassy Dinner Hostess, I was invited to a tea at Blair House and to a tea in the Diplomatic Reception Rooms at the Department of State. In her thank-you letter to the committee, Betty Lou Ourisman, 1972 Ball Chair, informed us of a $41,000 net profit from the ball - or $246,300 in 2019 dollars.

THIS, founded over 55 years ago as a non-partisan, non-profit organization, works with other governments, the private sector, and the diplomatic community to develop training and cultural programs to help leaders better address global challenges and opportunities.

The organization is still headquartered in the historic Meridian House, designed by John Russell Pope, who also designed the Jefferson Memorial and the West Building of the National Gallery of Art.

## DESSERTS

### pound cake - hannah.

*This family recipe is a special-occasion dessert for my niece, Hannah Ward's family. Hannah's mother began the Pound Cake tradition when Hannah and her brother, Christopher, were very young.*

*Hannah continues this tradition by baking the cake to celebrate the birthdays of her husband Mike, Harriet and Tom's son, and for Caroline and Luke, Hannah's children.*

1 pkg (8 oz) cream cheese
3 sticks butter
1 Tbsp lemon extract
3 C sugar
6 eggs
Pinch salt
3 C flour

Preheat oven to 325 degrees. Beat the cream cheese and butter until fluffy. Add lemon extract and sugar. Stir in a pinch of salt and the flour.

Spoon batter into a greased and floured Bundt pan. Bake for 1 1/2 hours. Cool 10 minutes. Turn over onto a wire rack and remove from pan. Serve thin slices of this very rich cake with ice cream and strawberries.

*Pound cake, which originated in Europe in the first half of the 18th century, initially weighed four pounds. The recipe called for a pound of each of four ingredients — flour, butter, eggs, and sugar! In her book,* **American Cake,** *Anne Byrn writes that "the first mention of pound cake, which came to the U.S. from England, is in a recipe dated 1754 from Wicomico Church, Virginia."*

## DESSERTS

### spring birds' nests.

*In the 2000s, the Strang family - Sam, Perian, Little Sam, Holland, and Pia - were our neighbors. Each Halloween, Perian organized the Howell Street children's "Trick or Treat" visits with the neighbors. A pizza party followed at the Strangs' home. Gary and I always looked forward to welcoming the gang to our home on Halloween. When the Strang children were young, their Easter tradition was to create spring birds' nests for the family dinner.*

1 Tbsp butter to grease muffin tins or non-stick baking spray
6 oz chocolate chips
6 oz butterscotch chips
1 C creamy peanut butter
6 oz of chow mien dried noodles
36 mini candy eggs (like Robins eggs), jelly beans, or Peeps

Grease muffin tin. In the microwave, heat both kinds of chips at 30 second increments, stirring until melted. Add peanut butter and mix well. Carefully add chow mien noodles. Stir with wooden spoon or spatula until they are coated with the peanut butter mixture. Use large spoon and mold mixture into the wells of the muffin tins. Indent the top with the back of the spoon. Chill approximately 1 hour. Use a small butter knife to pop the "nests" out of the tins. Add the colored candy eggs, jelly beans, or Peeps. Yield: 12 nests.

****

*In the 1940s and 1950s, attendance at Sunday school and the following church service were mandatory. Sunday attire required a good dress, stockings, Sunday shoes, gloves, and a hat. Before Easter, we went to Altoona to purchase our Easter hats. Each hat store had long tables, filled with carefully spaced hats perched atop hat stands. Hats on each table were marked at the price of $2.99 or $3.99 and up. Extra adornments of flowers and ribbons raised the price. We visited every hat store and tried on hats for hours before selecting the one that we would have to wear each Sunday until fall.*

## DESSERTS

### tiramisu.

*Gary and I seldom have dessert unless we have company. But Sherry Covington's tiramisu was our downfall when she returned a container of mine – filled with two generous slices of her signature tiramisu! What a friend! Returning a dish –filled with a luscious dessert!*

6 large eggs
1 C sugar
1 1/4 C mascarpone cheese, room temperature
1 3/4 C heavy whipping cream
2 packages (7oz) Italian Lady Fingers
1 C cold espresso
1/2 C Kahlua
1 oz cocoa for dusting

Combine egg yolks and sugar in a double boiler over boiling water. Reduce heat to low and cook for 10 minutes. Stir constantly. Remove from heat.

Whip yolks until thick and lemon colored. Cool briefly. Add mascarpone to yolks and beat until combined.

In a separate bowl, whip cream to stiff peaks with electric mixer. Gently fold whipped cream into mascarpone mixture. Set aside.

Mix expresso with Kahlua. Dip ladyfingers until they are wet – not soaked. Arrange ladyfingers in the bottom of a 9x9-inch dish. Spoon half of the mascarpone cream filling over the ladyfingers. Repeat with another layer of ladyfingers. Add the remaining mascarpone cream. Refrigerate at least four hours – or overnight.

Before serving, dust with cocoa powder. Serves 9.

June 1997. Myra Daniels, Founder, President, and CEO of the Naples Philharmonic Center for the Arts with me at our home in Grand Bay, Naples.

    In her memoir, Secrets of a Rutbuster: Breaking Rules and Selling Dreams, Myra states, "Every private citizen has a public responsibility." Myra was an exceptional mentor. Through my association with her at the Philharmonic Center for the Arts, I expanded my organizational and management skills. I will be forever indebted to her for her astute advice.

In June 1997, Gary and I hosted a celebration of our move into our new Grand Bay home in Pelican Bay, Napes. There, we enjoyed watching the sunrise over the golf-course lakes, swimming in the pool that separated the main house from the cabana (Gary's office), and a secluded koi pond in our enclosed garden. Our daily ritual was to walk through Pelican Bay. One day, we were stopped by a car containing Katherine Graham, publisher of *The Washington Post,* and George Schultz, former Secretary of State. They were hopelessly lost and late for a meeting at the Ritz Carlton Hotel. We readily provided the needed directions and sent them on their way.

# epilogue

You don't have to cook fancy or complicated masterpieces,
just good food from fresh ingredients.
-Julia Child


There is no sincerer love than the love of food.
-George Bernard Shaw


We should look for someone to eat and drink with
before looking for something to eat and drink.
-Epicurus

**EPILOGUE**

Other than writing travel articles for the *Naples Daily News* in the 1990s, I hadn't really done much writing. For years, I compiled recipe books and booklets for others, as well as editing others' books. In 2019, Gary and I co-authored *The Journey of an Inquiring Mind*. Finally, with Gary's urging, coupled with needling by Dianne May, Suzanne Regen, and Julie Schoerke I decided to record my recipes with associated memories, as well as recipes from family and friends.

Compiling these vignettes has become one of the most interesting experiences of my life! Writing one snippet reminded me of one or two other related events that I needed to explore. And in recording a friend's recipe, I relive pleasant memories of our relationship. These recollections, in turn, recalled other past experiences.

Sometimes, I wonder, why we cook today? Grocery stores provide us with prepackaged entrees, appetizers, salads, assorted fruits that are cut and ready to serve, and too numerous desserts. Stores will shop for us and deliver the order to our door. Restaurants, as well, will deliver dinner to the door.

But, to me, there is nothing more satisfying than selecting my own ingredients and preparing a deliciously attractive dish or meal for family and friends. How gratifying to view my beautifully set table and hear appreciative words from my guests!

I'm reminded of a friend who invited me for brunch. She set her table with linens, silver, crystal, and fresh flowers. And, she lovingly prepared her signature dish. Only for me. How very special I felt!

Like Lee Fairbend, I prefer simple recipes and have discovered that most of mine are just that. Many times, I have watched the film, *Julia and Julie*. I marveled how Julie painstakingly prepared each one of Julia Childs' recipes. And, I remember her supreme satisfaction at having prepared complicated ones for dinner parties, to the admiration of her guests. I certainly related to that.

I am resolved to, once again, prepare each of the recipes in this book, transporting myself back in time, to savor the memory that each recipe inspired. And I envision myself, many years from now, rereading the vignettes to recapture my wonderful life's experiences with friends and family members!

# EPILOGUE

During the writing of this book, as you might imagine, in my mind I've been preparing the most spectacular meals from the recipes that I've been recording each day. Actually, this is not quite true. I've depended on Gary to grocery shop, cook now and then, and enjoy last-minute simple dinners.

Last evening, after I had been on the computer for nine hours indexing the recipes, I was exhausted and had no ideas for dinner. Then I recalled that Lisa Manning had told me about her favored spring-time supper: Poached eggs over freshly-picked lettuces from her garden. I had no fresh lettuce in our garden, but some fresh basil did the trick. Quickly, I marinated fresh tomato slices in blood-orange olive oil and champagne-mimosa balsamic vinegar, topped with chopped basil. I scrambled eggs with cheese and placed the eggs on a bed of Boston lettuce leaves, surrounded by the tomatoes. So beautifully rewarding – and so delicious! With a glass of Pinot Grigio, of course.

Ironically, in today's (June 15, 2019) *Wall Street Journal,* there is an article by Bee Wilson entitled:

*True Luxury in Food Doesn't Cost a Fortune:*
*Just because a dish is rare or expensive doesn't mean*
*it's better than the humbler tastes we love.*

Bee Wilson reminded me that "An egg doesn't have to be laid by a quail or a duck to be luxurious. To me there are few greater treats than a perfectly soft-boiled regular hen's egg. The liquid yolk is like riches, even though it only costs pennies." That was last night's supper!

As one recipe led to another, one memory has led to another. Literally, this book has written itself.

My most sincere thanks to each of you who has shared your culinary delights and experiences with me.

Bon appetite!

June 14, 2019

In October 2002, Demetria Kalidimos, former Nashville Channel 5 News Anchor, and I participated in the Fisk University Inauguration Ceremony of President Carolynn Reid-Wallace. In the formal Opening Processional, 70 Delegates of Colleges and Universities proceeded in order of their college's founding. First was William and Mary, founded in 1693. 15 delegates later, Demetria represented Illinois Wesleyan University, founded in 1859. 13 delegates later, I represented Wilson College, founded in 1869. 38 more followed. Quite a colorful processional of delegates, wearing caps, gowns, and hoods from their respective colleges and universities! Again, in 2005, I represented Wilson College at the inauguration of President L. Randolph Lowry III at Lipscomb University.

## INDEX: ALPHABETICAL

**Ap**ple Butter, 184
Apple Cake, 238
Apple Pancake Casserole, 126
Arancini – Rose Murdocca's, 30
Asparagus Rolls, 31

**B**acon Crackers, 32
Bacon-Wrapped Stuffed Dates, 33
Baked Potato Chips, 110
Baked Zucchini Slices, 110
Banana Bread, 56
Banana Wheat Quick Bread, 57
Basil Tomato Tart, 127
Bea's Whipped Mustard Sauce, 157
Becky's Brunch Casserole, 128
Besse's Ham Loaf, 156
Better Than Sex Cake, 239
Billy's Garlic-Smashed Potatoes, 111
BLT Bacon, 154
Blueberry Hill Muffins, 58
BMCC Frozen Tomato Salad, 88
Border Guacamole, 34
Boston Brown Bread, 59
Bourbon-Eggnog Sauce, 240
Brandied Cherries, 185
Bread Pudding, 240
Breakfast Blintzes, 60
Broccoli-Raisin Salad, 89
Broiled Grapefruit, 129
Brown Sugar Muffins, 61
Bulla Tomato Relish, 185
Buttermilk Pancake Balls, 62

**C**aramel Brownies, 212
Casserole Rockefeller, 168-169
Cheese-Cake Bars, 213
Cheese Enchiladas, 130
Cheese Holiday Party Pops, 35
Cheese Wafers – Ambolyn's, 36
Cheese Wafers, 37

Chicken Salad w/ Herb Dressing, 90
Chicken Sniff, 144
Chicken Thighs with Peppers, 145
Chilled Cucumber Dill Soup, 76
Chinese Chicken Salad, 91
Chocolate-Chip Cookies, 214-215
Chocolate-Chip Oatmeal, 216-217
Chocolate-Coated Strawberries, 242
Chocolate Mousse, 241
Chocolate Peanut Clusters, 242
Chopped Chicken Salad, 92
Christmas Cheese Souffle, 131
Christmas Wreaths, 218
Cinnamon Puffs, 63
Concord Grape Butter, 186
Covington Mexican Lasagna, 158
Covington Potato Salad, 93
Cranberry Cordial, 14
Cranberry-Sour Cream Salad, 94
Cream Cheese-Olive Spread, 38
Cream of Crab Soup, 77
Cream of Red Pepper Soup, 78-79
Crepes Provencal, 132
Crisp Oatmeal Cookies, 219
Crunchy Cole Slaw, 94
Cucumber Tea Sandwiches, 39
Curry Rice Salad, 95

**D**andelion Wine, 15
Date Cake, 243,
Date Pinwheels, 220
Derby Pie, 244
Dilly Beans, 187

**E**gg-Hash Brown Casserole, 133

**F**lank Steak Teriyaki, 160
Forgotten Cookies, 221
Fourth of July Salsa, 40

## INDEX: ALPHABETICAL

French Breakfast Muffins, 64
Fresh Fruit in Brandy, 245
Fresh Lemon Squares, 222
Fresh Spinach Dip, 41
Frozen Custard, 245

Garlic Cheese Grits, 112
German Breakfast Cake, 65
German Chocolate Pie, 246
Georgia Peach-Chicken Salad, 96
Gin Cool, 16
Grandma York Oyster Dressing, 170
Greek Salad, 97
Grilled Shrimp, 172

Ham Biscuits, 42
Hartzell Potato Salad, 98
Haunted Bridge Log, 247
Heath Torte, 248
Helen's Brownies, 223
Hello, Dolly! Bars, 224
Hoppin' John, 113
Hot Artichoke Dip, 43
Hot Chocolate Sauce, 248
Hot Cranberry Casserole, 249
Hot Mulled Cider, 17
Hot Mulled Spice Mix, 18
Hot Tea Toddy, 18
Hot Tomato Soup, 80-81

Individual Cheesecakes, 250
Infused Water, 19

Janet's Raspberry Cordial, 19
Judy's Curried Rice, 114
Julie's Poppy Seed Chicken Salad, 99

Kalua, 20

Laurel's Cheese Ball, 44
Lavender and Rosemary Focaccia, 66
Lavender Bundles, 188
Lavender Grilled Salmon, 173
Lavender Iced-Tea Sangria, 21
Lavender Wand, 188
Lemoncello, 23
Lemon Cake, 251
Lemon-Balm Iced Tea, 22
Low Country Tomato Pie, 134
Low-Cal Jam, 192

Marilyn's Sugar Cookies, 225
May Wine Punch, 24
Mellon's Snickerdoodles, 226
Meng Cheese, 44.
Mexican Wedding Cookies, 227
Mini Prosciutto & Cheese Quiche, 45
Miniature Fruitcakes, 252
Mitford Marmalade Muffins, 67
Mom's Coleslaw, 100
Mother's Baked Beans, 115
Mother's Seafood, 174
Mother's Vegetable Soup, 82
Mother's Waffles, 68
Mud Pie, 253
Mushrooms Escargot, 46

Oatmeal Lace Cookies, 228
Orange-Spice Cookies, 229
Ozark Pie, 254

Panko Chicken with Hummus, 146
Pat Nixon's Hot Chicken Salad, 147
Peach and Basil Chicken Breasts, 148
Peach and Tomato Salsa, 101
Peach Chutney, 189
Peach Jam, 190
Pecan Tassies, 255

## INDEX: ALPHABETICAL

Penne with Olives & Tomatoes, 135
Pickled Beets and Eggs, 102
Pickled Franks, 162
Pike Place Salmon, 175
Pimento-Cheese Spread, 47
Pistachio Cake, 256
Pizza Casserole, 163
Pizza Margherita, 69
Pot de Crème, 257
Potato-Corn Chowder, 83
Pound Cake – Diane, 258-259
Pound Cake – Hannah, 260
Pumpkin Bars, 230

Quick, Low-Cal Jam, 192

Real Southern Cornbread, 70
Red Pepper Jelly, 190
Red Raspberry Jam, 191
Reward Cookies, 231
Ricotta & Walnut Stuffed Endive, 48
Rosemary Pecans, 49
Rosemary Shrimp Skewers, 176
Rosemary Shortbread Cookies, 232

Salad a la Parisienne, 103
Sand Tarts, 233
Sauerkraut Cooked in Beer, 116
Savory Chicken and Ham Bake, 149
Scotch Eggs, 50
Scotcheroos, 234
Seafood Casserole, 177
Sequi Inn Baked French Toast, 136
Sesame Chicken, 150
Seven-Layer Salad, 104
Shrimp-Asparagus Pasta Toss, 178
Shrimp-Corn Salsa-Ed Marcoe's, 51
Shrimp-Feta Cheese Casserole, 179
Shrimp -Grits, 180-181

Shrimp Bisque, 84
Shrimp Cream Dipping Sauce, 52
Shrimp Dijon Dipping Sauce, 52
Shrimp Louisiana, 53
Smoked Pheasant Crepes, 142-143
Soupe au Pistou, 85
Sour Cream Coffee Cake, 71
Spaghetti alla Carbonara, 164-165
Spinach and Spaghetti Bake, 137
Spring Bird's Nests, 261
Spring Supper Eggs, 267
Squash Casserole, 117
Strawberry Jam, 191
Sweet Mango Preserves, 193
Sweet Pickle Slices, 194-195
Sweet Potato Casserole, 118
Sweet Potato-Nut Balls, 235
Sweet Refrigerator Pickles, 195
Swiss Cheese Bake, 138
Syrian Pilaf, 119

Tea Punches, 25
The Sagittarius, 26
Tiramisu, 262
Tom's Taco Salad, 105
Tomato-Cheese-Spinach Strata, 139
Tomato Pudding, 120
Tommy's Barbecue Sauce, 151

Vanilla Lemonade, 26

Wild Rice & Cranberry Salad, 106
Wild Rice Casserole, 121
Wilted Lettuce, 107

Yellow Squash Casserole, 122

Zucchini Bread, 72
Zucchini-Potato Casserole, 123

Between 2003 and 2010, I assisted the Cheekwood Education Department by chairing the logistics for the annual Middle Tennessee Scholastic Art Competition. The SAC Team included Kelly McGinnis, Hillary Steinwinder, Chris Gregory, Gary, and me.

## INDEX: CATEGORY

### Aperitifs
Cranberry Cordial, 14
Dandelion Wine, 15
Gin Cool, 16
Hot Mulled Cider, 17
Hot Mulled Spice Mix, 18
Hot Tea Toddy, 18
Infused Water, 19
Janet's Raspberry Cordial, 19
Kalua, 20
Lavender Iced-Tea Sangria, 21
Lemon-Balm Iced Tea, 22
Lemoncello, 23
May Wine Punch, 24
Tea Punches, 25
The Sagittarius, 26
Vanilla Lemonade, 26

### Savories
Arancini – Rose Murdocca's, 30
Asparagus Rolls, 31
Bacon Crackers, 32
Bacon-Wrapped Stuffed Dates, 33
Border Guacamole, 34
Cheese Holiday Party Pops, 35
Cheese Wafers, 36-37
Cream Cheese-Olive Spread, 38
Cucumber Tea Sandwiches, 39
Fourth of July Salsa , 40
Fresh Spinach Dip, 41
Ham Biscuits, 42
Hot Artichoke Dip, 43
Laurel's Cheese Ball, 44
Meng Cheese, 44
Mini Prosciutto Cheese Quiche, 45
Mushrooms Escargot. 46
Pimento-Cheese Spread, 47

### Savories (cont.)
Ricotta & Walnut Stuffed Endive, 48
Rosemary Pecans, 49
Scotch Eggs, 50
Shrimp-Corn Salsa-Ed Marcoe's, 51
Shrimp Cream Dipping Sauce, 52
Shrimp Dijon Dipping Sauce. 52
Shrimp Louisianne, 53

### Breads
Banana Bread, 56
Banana Wheat Quick Bread, 57
Blueberry Hill Muffins, 58
Boston Brown Bread, 59
Breakfast Blintzes, 60
Brown Sugar Muffins, 61
Buttermilk Pancake Balls, 62
Cinnamon Puffs, 63
French Breakfast Muffins, 64
German Breakfast Cake, 65
Lavender & Rosemary Focaccia, 66
Mitford Marmalade Muffins, 67
Mother's Waffles, 68
Pizza Margherita, 69
Real Southern Cornbread, 70
Sour Cream Coffee Cake, 71
Zucchini Bread, 72

### Soups
Chilled Cucumber Dill Soup, 76
Cream of Crab Soup, 77
Cream of Red Pepper Soup, 78-79
Hot Tomato Soup, 80-81
Mother's Vegetable Soup, 82
Potato-Corn Chowder, 83
Shrimp Bisque, 84
Soupe au Pistou, 85

## INDEX: CATEGORY

### Salads
BMCC Frozen Tomato Salad, 88
Broccoli-Raisin Salad, 89
Chicken Salad w/ Herb Dressing, 90
Chinese Chicken Salad, 91
Chopped Chicken Salad, 92
Covington Potato Salad, 93
Cranberry-Sour Cream Salad, 94
Crunchy Cole Slaw, 94
Curry Rice Salad, 95
Georgia Peach-Chicken Salad, 96
Greek Salad, 97
Hartzell Potato Salad, 98
Julie's Poppy-Chicken Salad, 99
Mom's Coleslaw, 100
Peach and Tomato Salsa, 101
Pickled Beets and Eggs, 102
Salad a la Parisienne, 103
Seven-Layer Salad, 104
Tom's Taco Salad, 105
Wild Rice and Cranberry Salad, 106
Wilted Lettuce, 107

### Sides
Baked Potato Chips, 110
Baked Zucchini Slices, 110
Billy's Garlic-Smashed Potatoes, 111
Garlic Cheese Grits, 112
Hoppin' John, 113
Judy's Curried Rice, 114
Mother's Baked Beans, 115
Sauerkraut Cooked in Beer, 116
Squash Casserole, 117
Sweet Potato Casserole, 118
Syrian Pilaf, 119
Tomato Pudding, 120
Wild Rice Casserole, 121
Yellow Squash Casserole, 122

### Brunch
Apple Pancake Casserole, 126
Basil Tomato Tart, 127
Becky's Brunch Casserole, 128
Broiled Grapefruit, 129

Cheese Enchiladas, 130
Christmas Cheese Souffle, 131
Crepes Provencal, 132
Egg and Hash Brown Casserole, 133
Low Country Tomato Pie, 134
Penne with Olives & Tomatoes, 135
Sequi Inn Baked French Toast, 136
Spinach and Spaghetti Bake, 137
Swiss Cheese Bake, 138
Tomato-Cheese-Spinach Strata, 139

### Entrees
#### Pheasant and Chicken
Smoked Pheasant Crepes, 142-143
Chicken Sniff, 144
Chicken Thighs with Peppers, 145
Panko Chicken with Hummus, 146
Pat Nixon's Hot Chicken Salad, 147
Peach- Basil Chicken Breasts, 148
Savory Chicken and Ham Bake, 149
Sesame Chicken, 150
Tommy's Barbecue Sauce, 151

#### Meat
BLT Bacon, 154
Bea's Whipped Mustard Sauce, 157
Besse's Ham Loaf, 156
Covington Mexican Lasagna, 158
Flank Steak Teriyaki, 160
Pickled Franks, 162
Pizza Casserole, 163
Spaghetti alla Carbonara, 164-165

## INDEX: CATEGORY

### Entrees (cont.)
**Seafood**
Casserole Rockefeller, 168-169
Grandma York Oyster Dressing, 170
Grilled Shrimp, 172
Lavender Grilled Salmon, 173
Mother's Seafood, 174
Pike Place Salmon, 175
Rosemary Shrimp Skewers, 176
Seafood Casserole, 177
Shrimp-Asparagus Pasta Toss, 178
Shrimp-Feta Cheese Casserole, 179
Shrimp and Grits, 180-181

### Preserves
Apple Butter, 184
Brandied Cherries, 185
Bulla Tomato Relish, 185
Concord Grape Butter, 186
Dilly Beans, 187
Lavender Bundles, 188
Lavender Wand, 188
Peach Chutney, 189
Peach Jam, 190
Quick, Low-Cal Jam, 192
Red Pepper Jelly, 190
Red Raspberry Jam, 191
Strawberry Jam, 191
Sweet Mango Preserves, 193
Sweet Pickle Slices, 194-195
Sweet Refrigerator Pickles, 195

### Sweets
**Cookies**
Caramel Brownies, 212
Cheese-Cake Bars, 213
Chocolate-Chip Cookies, 214-215

### Sweets
**Cookies** (cont.)
Chocolate-Chip Oatmeal, 216-217
Christmas Wreaths, 218
Crisp Oatmeal Cookies, 219
Date Pinwheels, 220
Forgotten Cookies, 221
Fresh Lemon Squares, 222
Helen's Brownies, 223
Hello, Dolly! Bars, 224
Marilyn's Sugar Cookies, 225
Mellon's Snickerdoodles, 226
Mexican Wedding Cookies, 227
Oatmeal Lace Cookies, 228
Orange-Spice Cookies, 229
Pumpkin Bars, 230
Reward Cookies. 231
Rosemary Shortbread Cookies, 232
Sand Tarts, 233
Scotcheroos, 234
Sweet Potato-Nut Balls, 235

**Desserts**
Apple Cake, 238
Better Than Sex Cake, 239
Bourbon-Eggnog Sauce, 240
Bread Pudding, 240
Chocolate Mousse, 241
Chocolate Peanut Clusters, 242
Chocolate-Coated Strawberries, 242
Date Cake, 243
Derby Pie, 244
Fresh Fruit in Brandy, 245
Frozen Custard, 245
German Chocolate Pie, 246
Haunted Bridge Log, 247
Heath Torte, 248

## INDEX: CATEGORY

## Sweets
**Desserts** (cont.)

Hot Chocolate Sauce, 248
Hot Cranberry Casserole, 249
Individual Cheesecakes, 250
Lemon Cake, 251
Miniature Fruitcakes, 252
Mud Pie, 253
Ozark Pie, 254

Pecan Tassies, 255
Pistachio Cake, 256
Pot de Crème, 257
Pound Cake-Dianne, 258-259
Pound Cake-Hannah, 260
Spring Bird's Nests, 261
Tiramisu, 262

In March 2007, members of the HSN Morning Study Group presented their findings from studying Pelargoniums to the membership. A tasting of recipes containing the herb followed the meeting. Left to right: Sara Plummer, Sandra Frank, me, Toni Foglesong, Arlene Haan, Marguerite Peterseim, Molly Schneider.

March 2009. A champagne toast, with the Athena Award Nominees in the lobby of the Schermerhorn Symphony Center, followed the 2009 Award Ceremony. The Nashville Chapter of the Women's National Book Association (WNBA) selected me as their nominee for the Award. In the photo, I am opposite the 2009 Athena Award Winner, Janet Jernigan (in light suit), CEO of FiftyForward.

joanne fletcher slaughter

September 2008 marked the gala opening of the River Gallery and the Cottonwood Terrace at the Shiawassee Arts Center (SAC) in Owosso, Michigan. Gary and I attended with Connie and Jerry Voight, fellow underwriters of these new building additions. In the River Gallery, SAC has hosted the book launches for our *Cottonwood Series, Sea Stories,* and *The Journey of an Inquiring Mind.* We've enjoyed many luncheons on the Cottonwood Terrace, overlooking Curwood Castle and the Shiawassee River.

## INDEX: RECIPE CONTRIBUTOR

**A**dams, Susan     Lavender and Rosemary Focaccia, 66
Alderson, Peg     Pecan Tassies, 255
Armstrong, Judy     Derby Pie, 244
    French Breakfast Muffins, 64

**B**arron, Laurel     Laurel's Cheese Ball, 44
Berry, Kathy     Tea Punch, 25
Bingamon, Judy     Hot Artichoke Dip, 43
Bradley, Laurie     Scotcheroos, 234
Bracken, Judith     Quick, Low-Cal Jam, 192
Brewer, Piper     Tomato Pudding, 120
Brown, Sue     Chocolate Mousse, 241
Bulla, Josh     Bulla Tomato Relish, 185

**C**aldwell, Ginger     Egg and Hash Brown Casserole, 133
Campbell, Carolyn     Forgotten Cookies, 221
    Pizza Casserole, 163
Cartwright, Mary     Lavender Wand, 188
Chaput, Mary     Shrimp Cream Dipping Sauce, 52
Cole, Joan     Blueberry Hill Muffins, 58
    Dilly Beans, 187
    Swiss Cheese Bake, 138
Coleman, Nancy     Sweet Mango Preserves, 193
Cornish, Marilyn     German Chocolate Pie, 246
Covington, John     Covington Mexican Lasagna, 158-159
Covington, Sherry     Chocolate-Coated Strawberries, 242
    Covington Potato Salad, 93
    Tiramisu, 262

**D**aniels, Myra     Hot Tomato Soup, 80-81
Dermon, Adele     Kalua, 20
Diamond, Denny     Casserole Rockefeller, 168-169
    Cream of Crab Soup – Maryland Style, 77
Dibert, Ralph     Concord Grape Butter, 186
Dively, Mary     Pimento-Cheese Spread, 47
Duncan, Carol     Lemoncello, 23

**E**chols, Judi     Oatmeal Lace Cookies, 228
Edwards, Susan     Brown Sugar Muffins, 61
Exton, Janet     Janet's Raspberry Cordial, 19

## INDEX: RECIPE CONTRIBUTOR

| | |
|---|---|
| **F**airbend, Lee | Chicken Sniff, 144 |
| Fels, Eileen | Mom's Coleslaw, 100 |
| Fletcher, Irene | Apple Butter, 184 |
| | Christmas Wreaths, 218 |
| | Cranberry-Sour Cream Salad, 94 |
| | Dandelion Wine, 15 |
| | Mother's Baked Beans, 115 |
| | Mother's Vegetable Soup, 82 |
| | Mother's Waffles, 68 |
| | Peach Jam, 190 |
| | Pickled Beets and Eggs, 102 |
| | Red Raspberry Jam, 191 |
| | Reward Cookies, 231 |
| | Sand Tarts, 233 |
| | Strawberry Jam, 191 |
| | Sweet Pickle Slices, 194-195 |
| | Wilted Lettuce, 107 |
| Frank, Paul | Real Southern Cornbread, 70 |
| Frank, Sandra | Lemon-Balm Iced Tea, 22 |
| Freeman, Babs | Basil Tomato Tart, 127 |
| | |
| **G**illum, Sara | Lavender Iced-Tea Sangria, 21 |
| Gregory, Chris | Cucumber Tea Sandwiches, 39 |
| | |
| **H**aan, Arlene | Infused Water, 19 |
| Harris, Carolyn | Hot Chocolate Sauce, 248 |
| Hartzell, Kathryn | Hartzell Potato Salad, 98 |
| Hartzog, Sil | Chocolate-Chip Cookies, 214 |
| Henley, Ralph | Bacon-Wrapped Stuffed Dates, 33 |
| Hervey, Ambolyn | Cheese Wafers- Ambolyn's, 36 |
| Hess, Helen | Helen's Brownies, 223 |
| | Lemon Cake, 251 |
| Hodges, Judith | Crisp Oatmeal Cookies, 219 |
| Howard, Dori | Cranberry Cordial, 14 |
| Howe, Jean | Chocolate Peanut Clusters, 242 |
| | |
| **J**ackson, June | Fresh Fruit in Brandy, 245 |
| | Heath Torte, 248 |
| | Shrimp Louisiana, 53 |

## INDEX: RECIPE CONTRIBUTOR

| | |
|---|---|
| Jackson, Tommy | Tommy's Chicken Barbecue Sauce, 151 |
| James, Susan | Asparagus Rolls, 31 |
| | Shrimp-Corn Salsa – Ed Marcoe's, 51 |
| Jones, Pat | Brandied Cherries, 185 |
| Jones, Richard | BLT Bacon, 154 |
| | |
| Kane, Karen | Pistachio Cake, 256 |
| | |
| Lane, Anne | Ham Biscuits, 42 |
| Lassen, Christie | Ricotta and Walnut Stuffed Endive, 48 |
| Legan, Robanne | Tea Punch, 25 |
| Legerton, Judi | Buttermilk Pancake Balls, 62 |
| Lester, Celeste | Garlic Cheese Grits, 112 |
| | Gin Cool, 16 |
| Long, Sybil | Hot Mulled Cider, 17 |
| | Hot Mulled Spice Mix, 18 |
| Lysinger, Besse | Besse's Ham Loaf, 156 |
| | |
| MacLeod, Jane | German Breakfast Cake, 65 |
| Manning, Lisa | Spring Supper Eggs, 267 |
| Marcum, Jane | Smoked Pheasant Crepes, 142-143 |
| Massey, Fran | Hello, Dolly! Bars, 224 |
| | Zucchini Bread, 72 |
| May, Dianne | Apple Pancake Breakfast Casserole, 126 |
| Murdocca, Michelle | Arancini – Rose Murdocca's, 30 |
| Myers, Mary | Orange-Spice Cookies, 229 |
| | |
| Norris, SueAnn | Grandma York's Oyster Dressing, 170 |
| Nuecheterlein, Judy | Judy's Curried Rice, 114 |
| | |
| Perry, Bev | Mitford Orange Marmalade Muffins, 67 |
| Pinkley, Joan | Lavender Grilled Salmon, 173 |
| | Low Country Tomato Pie, 134 |
| Plummer, Sara | Chicken Salad/Lemony Herb Dressing, 90 |
| Powell, Dale | Pumpkin Bars, 230 |
| Prosterman, Bea | Crepes Provencal, 132 |
| Psomadakis, Rita | Chicken Thighs with Banana Peppers, 145 |
| | |
| Rainey, Billy | Billy's Garlic-Smashed Potatoes, 111 |
| | Mud Pie, 253 |

joanne fletcher slaughter

## INDEX: RECIPE CONTRIBUTOR

| | |
|---|---|
| Ramsey, Lisa | Bacon Crackers, 32 |
| Regen, Suzanne | Hot Cranberry Casserole, 249 |
| | Shrimp and Feta Cheese Casserole, 179 |
| | Shrimp and Grits, 180-181 |
| Rehm, Dianne | Pound Cake - Dianne, 258-259 |
| Ruiz, Carla | Mexican Wedding Cookies, 227 |
| | |
| Sanders, Dancy | Greek Salad, 97 |
| Scarborough, Sarah | Hot Tea Toddy, 18 |
| Schmid, Elke | Apple Cake, 238 |
| Schneider, Molly | Chilled Cucumber Dill Soup, 76 |
| | Lavender Bundles, 188 |
| Schoerke, Julie | Chocolate-Chip Oatmeal Cookies. 216-217 |
| Sellers, Emma | Date Cake, 243 |
| Slaughter, Gary | Flank Steak Teriyaki, 160 |
| | Grilled Shrimp, 172 |
| | Penne with Olives, Capers and Tomatoes, 135 |
| | Pickled Franks, 162 |
| | Pizza Margherita, 69 |
| | Tomato-Cheese-Spinach Strata, 139 |
| Slaughter, Joanne | Baked Potato Chips, 110 |
| | Baked Zucchini Slices, 110 |
| | Cheese Holiday Party Pops, 35 |
| | Chopped Chicken Salad, 92 |
| | Christmas Cheese Souffle, 131 |
| | Crunchy Cole Slaw, 94 |
| | Hoppin' John, 113 |
| | Mushrooms Escargot, 46 |
| | Ozark Pie, 254 |
| | Peach and Basil Chicken Breasts, 148 |
| | Peach and Tomato Salsa, 101 |
| | Potato-Corn Chowder, 83 |
| | Red Pepper Jelly, 190 |
| | Rosemary Shortbread Cookies, 232 |
| | Rosemary Shrimp Scampi Skewers, 176 |
| | Salad a la Parisienne, 103 |
| | Sauerkraut Cooked in Beer, 116 |
| | Scotch Eggs, 50 |
| | Shrimp Dijon Dipping Sauce, 52 |
| | Soupe au Pistou, 85 |

## INDEX: RECIPE CONTRIBUTOR

| | |
|---|---|
| Slaughter, Joanne (cont.) | Syrian Pilaf, 119 |
| | Wild Rice and Cranberry Salad, 106 |
| | Wild Rice Casserole, 121 |
| Small, Ginny | Yellow Squash Casserole, 122 |
| Smith, Judi | Sweet Potato Casserole, 118 |
| Sneed, Marie | Cheese Enchiladas, 130 |
| Snyder, Paula | Spaghetti alla Carbonara, 164-165 |
| Stamps, Martha | Squash Casserole, 117 |
| Steinwinder, Hillary | Breakfast Blintzes, 60 |
| Strang, Perian | Spring Bird's Nests, 261 |
| | |
| **T**albot, Jana | Peach Chutney, 189 |
| | Rosemary Pecans, 49 |
| Taylor, Jan | Individual Cheesecakes, 250 |
| Terrell, Helen | Fresh Lemon Squares, 222 |
| Thomas, Addice | Meng Cheese, 44 |
| | |
| **V**an Gundy, Bea | Bea's Whipped Mustard Sauce, 157 |
| Vanston, Susan | Pot de Crème, 257 |
| | |
| **W**ard, Hannah | Pound Cake - Hannah, 260 |
| Ward, Harriet | Banana Bread, 56 |
| | Banana-Wheat Quick Bread, 57 |
| | Broccoli-Raisin Salad, 89 |
| | Cinnamon Puffs, 63 |
| | Curry Rice Salad, 95 |
| | Georgia Peach-Chicken Salad, 96 |
| | Miniature Fruitcakes, 252 |
| | Seafood Casserole, 177 |
| | Shrimp Bisque, 84 |
| | Sesame Chicken, 150 |
| | Spinach and Spaghetti Bake, 137 |
| Ward, Julie | Julie's Poppy-Seed Chicken Salad, 99 |
| Ward, Tom | Tom's Taco Salad, 105 |
| Wattleworth, Carol | Cheese-Cake Bars, 213 |
| Weigel, Patsy | Bourbon-Eggnog Sauce and Bread Pudding, 240 |
| | Frozen Custard, 245 |
| | Mother's Seafood – Tidewater/Mobile Style, 174 |
| | Sweet Potato-Nut Balls, 235 |

## INDEX: RECIPE CONTRIBUTOR

| | |
|---|---|
| Weller, Liz | Becky's Brunch Casserole, 128 |
| | Caramel Brownies, 212 |
| | Mini Prosciutto and Cheese Quiche, 45 |
| Whitmore, Marilyn | Shrimp and Asparagus Pasta Toss, 178 |
| | Marilyn's Sugar Cookies, 225 |
| Williams, Besse | Sour Cream Coffee Cake, 71 |
| Williams, Susan | Chocolate-Chip Cookies, 215 |
| Wilson, Carolyn | Fresh Spinach Dip, 41 |
| Wright, Kathy | The Sagittarius, 26 |
| | |
| Yakamoto, Fumie | Chinese Chicken Salad, 91 |
| Yake, Frank | Better Than Sex Cake, 239 |
| Yake, Sharon | Date Pinwheels, 220 |
| | Sweet Refrigerator Pickles, 195 |
| | Seven-Layer Salad, 104 |

February 2012. Sew 'n Sow Garden Club during our annual business and social meeting. Enthusiastic gardeners, excellent cooks, and thoughtful friends!

June 2013. Cheekwood Docents on the stairs of the Mansion's Wisteria Arbor. Here, Chris Gregory, Docent Coordinator, hosted her annual June *Thank You Reception* for docents and their guests. Chef Steve, her husband, prepared gourmet, al fresco dinners for each celebration.

joanne fletcher slaughter

2013 Christmas Party for Howell Place neighborhood children. The culmination of the gathering was the arrival of Santa Claus (Steve Gregory) who stopped at our home for a delightful conversation with the children.

## INDEX: MAJOR INGREDIENT

**A**pple
  Apple Butter, 184
  Apple Cake, 238
  Apple Pancake Casserole, 126
  Hot Mulled Cider, 17
  Ozark Pie, 254
**A**rtichoke
  Hot Artichoke Dip, 43
**A**sparagus
  Asparagus Rolls, 31
  Shrimp-Asparagus Pasta Toss, 178
**A**vocado
  Border Guacamole, 34

**B**acon
  Bacon Crackers, 32
  Bacon-Wrapped Dates, 33
  BLT Bacon, 154
  Covington Potato Salad, 93
  Grama York Oyster Dressing, 170
  Mother's Baked Beans, 115
  Spaghetti alla Carbonara, 164-165
  Swiss Cheese Bake, 138
**B**anana
  Banana Bread, 56-57
**B**asil
  Basil Tomato Tart
  Gin Cool, 16
  Hot Tomato Soup, 80-81
  Peach-Basil Chicken Breasts, 148
  Peach and Tomato Salsa, 101
  Tomato-Spinach Strata, 139
**B**eans
  Chopped Chicken Salad, 92
  Covington Mexican Lasagna, 158
  Curry Rice Salad, 95
  Dilly Beans, 187
  Mother's Baked Beans, 115
  Soupe au Pistou, 85
  Tom's Taco Salad, 105

**B**eef
  Chicken Sniff, 144
  Covington Mexican Lasagna, 158
  Flank Steak Teriyaki, 160
  Pickled Franks, 162
  Pizza Casserole, 163
**B**eets
  Pickled Beets and Eggs, 102
**B**iscuits
  Cinnamon Puffs, 63
  Ham Biscuits, 42
**B**lueberries
  Fourth of July Salsa, 40
  Blueberry Hill Muffins, 58
**B**read
  Asparagus Rolls, 31
  Becky's Brunch Casserole, 128
  Bread Pudding, 240
  Breakfast Blintzes, 60
  Christmas Cheese Souffle, 131
  Cucumber Tea Sandwiches, 39
  Sequi Inn French Toast, 136
  Swiss Cheese Bake, 138
  Tomato-Spinach Strata, 139
  Tomato Pudding, 120
**B**roccoli
  Broccoli-Raisin Salad, 89
  Wild Rice & Cranberry Salad, 106

**C**abbage
  Crunchy Cole Slaw, 94
  Mom's Coleslaw, 100
  Sauerkraut Cooked in Beer, 116
**C**heese
  Basil Tomato Tart, 127
  Becky's Brunch Casserole, 128
  BMCC Frozen Tomato Salad, 88
  Cheese Enchiladas, 130
  Christmas Cheese Souffle, 131
  Covington Mexican Lasagna, 158

joanne fletcher slaughter

## INDEX: MAJOR INGREDIENT

Cheese (cont.)
  Egg - Hash Brown Casserole, 133
  Garlic Cheese Grits, 112
  Low Country Tomato Pie, 134
  Pat Nixon Hot Chicken Salad, 147
  Ricotta-Walnut Stuffed Endive, 48
  Sesame Chicken, 150
  Shrimp-Asparagus Pasta Toss
  Shrimp and Feta Cheese, 179
  Swiss Cheese Bake, 138
  Tomato-Spinach strata, 139

Cherries
  Brandied Cherries, 185

Chicken
  Chicken Salad/Cream Dressing, 90
  Chicken Thighs with Peppers, 145
  Chinese Chicken Salad, 91
  Georgia Peach Chicken Salad, 96
  Julie's Poppy-Chicken Salad, 99
  Panko Chicken with Hummus, 146
  Pat Nixon Hot Chicken Salad, 147
  Peach-Basil Chicken Breasts 148
  Savory Chicken & Ham Bake, 149
  Sesame Chicken, 150
  Tommy's Barbecue Sauce, 151

Chocolate
  Caramel Brownies, 212
  Chocolate-Chip Cookies, 214-215
  Chocolate Mousse, 241
  Chocolate-Oatmeal Cookies
  Chocolate Peanut Clusters, 242
  Chocolate Strawberries, 242
  Derby Pie, 244
  German Chocolate Pie, 246
  Haunted Log Bridge, 247
  Helen's Brownies, 223
  Hello, Dolly! Bars, 224
  Hot Chocolate Sauce, 248
  Mud Pie, 253
  Pot de Crème, 257

Chocolate (cont.)
  Scotcheroos, 234
  Spring Birds' Nests, 261

Corn
  Peach and Tomato Salsa, 101
  Potato-Corn Chowder, 83
  Shrimp-Corn Salsa, 53

Cornmeal
  Boston Brown Bread, 59
  Real Southern Cornbread, 70

Crab
  Cream of Crab Soup, 77
  Seafood Casserole, 177

Cranberries
  Cranberry Cordial, 14
  Cranberry-Sour Cream Salad, 94
  Hot Cranberry Casserole, 249
  Wild Rice & Cranberry Salad, 106

Cream
  Bea's Whip. Mustard Sauce, 157
  Billy's Garlic Smash Potatoes, 111
  Chocolate Mousse, 241
  Cream of Crab Soup, 77
  Dijon Dipping Sauce, 52
  German Chocolate Pie, 246
  Haunted Bridge Log, 247
  Heath Torte, 248
  Shrimp Cream Dipping Sauce, 52
  Sour Cream Coffee Cake, 71
  Tiramisu, 262

Cream Cheese
  Breakfast Blintzes, 60
  Cheese-Cake Bars, 213
  Cheese Holiday Party Pops, 35
  Cheese Wafers, 36-37
  Cream Cheese-Olive Spread, 38
  Individual Cheesecakes, 250
  Laurel's Cheese Ball, 44
  Meng Cheese, 44

## INDEX: MAJOR INGREDIENT

**C**ucumbers
   Chilled Cucumber Dill Soup, 76
   Cucumber Tea Sandwiches, 39
   Sweet Pickle Slices, 194-195
   Sweet Refrigerator Pickles, 195

**D**ates
   Bacon-Wrapped Stuffed Dates, 33
   Date Cake, 243
   Date Pinwheels, 220

**E**ggs
   Apple Pancake Casserole, 126
   Basil Tomato Tart, 127
   Becky's Brunch Casserole, 128
   Christmas Cheese Souffle, 131
   Egg-Hash-Brown Casserole, 133
   Mini Prosciutto Quiche, 45
   Pickled Beets and Eggs, 102
   Salad a la Parisienne, 103
   Scotch Eggs, 50
   Sequi Inn French Toast, 136
   Spring Supper Eggs, 267
   Tomato-Spinach Strata, 139

**E**ndive
   Ricotta-Walnut Stuffed Endive, 48
   Savory Chicken &Ham Bake, 149

**F**ruit
   Fresh Fruit in Brandy Syrup, 245
   Miniature Fruitcakes, 252

**G**rapefruit
   Broiled Grapefruit, 129

Grapes
   Concord Grape Butter, 186
   Georgia Peach-Chicken Salad, 96

**G**rits
   Garlic-Cheese Grits, 112
   Shrimp and Grits, 180-181

**H**am
   Besse's Ham Loaf, 156
   Crepes Provencal, 132
   Ham Biscuits, 42
   Hoppin' John, 113
   Mother's Baked Beans, 115
   Savory Chicken & Ham Bake, 149
   Sesame Chicken, 150

**H**ummus
   Panko Chicken with Hummus, 145

**I**ce Cream
   Frozen Custard, 245
   Mud Pie, 253
   Ozark Pie, 254

**L**avender
   Lavender Bundles, 188
   Lavender Grilled Salmon, 173
   Lavender Iced-Tea Sangria 21
   Lavender- Rosemary Focaccia
   Lavender Wand, 188

**L**emon
   Fresh Lemon Squares, 222
   Lemon-Balm Iced Tea, 22
   Lemon Cake, 251
   Lemoncello, 23
   Vanilla Lemonade, 26

**L**ettuce
   Chinese Chicken Salad, 91
   Chopped Chicken Salad, 92
   Greek Salad, 97
   Seven-Layer Salad, 104
   Tom's Taco Salad, 105
   Wilted Lettuce, 107

**M**armalade
   Mitford Marmalade Muffins, 67
   Orange-Spice Cookies, 229

## INDEX: MAJOR INGREDIENT

**M**eringue
  Forgotten Cookies, 221
  German Chocolate Pie, 246
  Heath Torte, 248
  Ozark Pie, 254
**M**uffins
  Blueberry Hill Muffins, 58
  Brown Sugar Muffins, 61
  French Breakfast Muffins, 64
  Mitford Marmalade Muffins, 67
**M**ushrooms
  Mushrooms Escargot, 46
  Savory Chicken & Ham Bake, 149
  Shrimp-Asparagus Pasta Toss, 178
  Wild Rice Casserole, 121

**N**oodles
  Chinese Chicken Salad, 91
  Spring Birds' Nests, 261
**N**uts
  Chocolate Peanut Clusters, 242
  Pecan Tassies, 255
  Rosemary Pecans, 49
  Syrian Pilaf, 119
  Wild Rice & Cranberry Salad, 106

**O**atmeal
  Chocolate-Chip Oatmeal, 216-217
  Crisp Oatmeal Cookies, 219
  Hot Cranberry Casserole, 249
  Oatmeal Lace Cookies, 228
  Reward Cookies, 231
**O**lives
  Cream Cheese-Olive Spread, 38
  Greek Salad, 97
  Penne/Olives and Tomatoes, 135
**O**ysters
  Gradma York Oyster Dressing, 170
  Casserole Rockefeller, 168-169

**P**asta
  Julie's Poppy-Chicken Salad, 99
  Penne/Olives and Tomatoes, 135
  Shrimp-Asparagus Pasta Toss, 178
  Soupe au Pistou, 85
  Spaghetti alla Carbonara, 164-165
  Spinach and Spaghetti Bake, 137
  Syrian Pilaf, 119
**P**each
  Georgia Peach Chicken Salad, 96
  Peach-Basil Chicken Breasts, 148
  Peach and Tomato Salsa, 101
  Peach Chutney, 189
  Peach Jam, 190
**P**eas
  Hoppin' John, 113
  Seven Layer Salad, 104
**P**eppers
  Chicken Thighs with Peppers, 145
  Cream of Red Pepper Soup, 78-79
  Red Pepper Jelly, 190
**P**heasant
  Smoked Pheasant Crepes, 142
**P**ickles
  Salad a la Parisienne, 103
  Sweet Pickle Slices, 194-195
  Refrigerator Pickles, 195
**P**ie
  Derby Pie, 244
  German Chocolate Pie, 246
  Low Country Tomato Pie, 134
  Mud Pie, 253
  Ozark Pie, 254
**P**izza Crust
  Lavender-Rosemary Focaccia
  Pizza Margherita, 69
**P**oppy Seed
  Georgia Peach Chicken Salad, 96
  Julie's Poppy Chicken Salad, 99
  Swiss Cheese Bake, 138

preserving memories

**INDEX: MAJOR INGREDIENT**

**P**otato
  Baked Potato Chips, 110
  Billy's Garlic Smash Potatoes, 111
  Covington Potato Salad, 93
  Egg-Hash-Brown Casserole, 133
  Hartzell Potato Salad, 98
  Potato-Corn Chowder, 83
  Salad a la Parisienne, 103
  Zucchini-Potato Casserole, 123

**P**rosciutto
  Mini- Prosciutto Cheese Quiche, 45

**P**umpkin
  Pumpkin Bars, 230

**R**aspberry
  Janet's Raspberry Cordial, 19
  Red Raspberry Jam, 191

**R**ice
  Arancini – Rose Murdocca's, 30
  Curry Rice Salad, 95
  Judy's Curried Rice, 114
  Syrian Pilaf, 119
  Wild Rice & Cranberry Salad, 106
  Wild Rice Casserole, 121

**R**ice Krispies
  Cheese Wafers,37
  Helen's Brownies, 223
  Reward Cookies, 231
  Scotcheroos, 234

**R**osemary
  Lavender-Rosemary Focaccia
  Rosemary Pecans, 49
  Rosemary Shortbr. Cookies, 232
  Rosemary Shrimp Skewers, 176

**S**almon
  Lavender Grilled Salmon, 173
  Pike Place Salmon, 175

**S**ausage
  Becky's Brunch Casserole, 128
  Egg-Hash Brown Casserole, 133
  Grama York Oyster Dressing, 170
  Scotch Eggs, 50

**S**hrimp
  Grilled Shrimp, 172
  Mother's Seafood, 174
  Rosemary Shrimp Skewers, 176
  Seafood Casserole, 177
  Shrimp-Asparagus Pasta Toss, 178
  Shrimp-Corn Salsa, 51
  Shrimp-Feta Cheese, 179
  Shrimp and Grits, 180-181
  Shrimp Bisque, 84
  Shrimp Louisiana, 53

**S**pinach
  Fresh Spinach Dip, 41
  Casserole Rockefeller, 168-169
  Spinach and Spaghetti Bake, 137
  Tomato-Spinach Strata, 139

**S**pirits
  Brandied Cherries, 185
  Cranberry Cordial, 14
  Dandelion Wine, 15
  Derby Pie, 244
  Fresh Fruit in Brandy Syrup, 245
  Gin Cool, 16
  Janet's Raspberry Cordial. 19
  Kalua, 20
  Lavender Iced-Tea Sangria, 21
  Lemoncello, 23
  May Wine Punch, 24
  Pot de Crème, 257
  Pound Cake – Dianne, 258-259
  Pound Cake – Hannah, 260
  The Sagittarius, 26

**S**trawberry
  Chocolate-Coated, 242
  Strawberry Jam, 191

## INDEX: MAJOR INGREDIENT

**S**quash
  Squash Casserole, 117
  Yellow Squash Casserole, 122

**S**weet Potato
  Sweet Potato Casserole, 118
  Sweet Potato-Nut Balls, 235

**T**ea
  Hot Tea Toddy, 18
  Lavender Iced Tea Sangria, 21
  Lemon-Balm Iced Tea, 22
  Tea Punches, 25

**T**omatoes
  Basil Tomato Tart
  BLT Bacon, 154
  BMCC Frozen Tomato Salad, 88
  Bulla Tomato Relish, 185
  Hot Tomato Soup, 80-81
  Low Country Tomato Pie, 134
  Penne/Olives & Tomatoes, 135
  Pizza Margherita, 69
  Tomato-Spinach Strata, 139
  Tom's Taco Salad, 105

**T**ortillas
  Cheese Enchiladas, 130
  Covington Mexican Lasagna, 158

**V**egetables
  Crepes Provencal, 132
  Mother's Vegetable Soup, 82
  Soupe au Pistou, 85

**W**atermelon
  Fourth of July Salsa, 40

**W**ild Rice
  Curry Rice Salad, 95
  Wild Rice & Cranberry Salad, 106
  Wild Rice Casserole, 121

**W**ine
  Dandelion Wine, 15
  Lavender Iced Tea Sangria
  May Wine Punch, 24

**Z**ucchini
  Baked Zucchini Slices, 110
  Crepe Provencal
  Zucchini-Potato Casserole, 123
  Zucchini Bread, 72

July 2013. Members of Nashville PEO Chapter E gathered at my home at 608 Jackson Boulevard for a summer picnic.

In my home office, busily writing vignettes and compiling recipes for my memoir, *preserving memories: recollections and recipes from family and friends*.

## INDEX: COOKBOOKS and RECIPE BOOKLETS
## Compiled and Edited by Joanne Fletcher Slaughter

*Recipyle I.* Compiled and printed for Pyle Junior High School Faculty, Bethesda, MD. 1965.

*Recipyle II.* Compiled and printed for Pyle Junior High School Faculty, Bethesda, MD. 1966.

*Kitchen Privileges: Georgetown Day School Cookbook.* Committee Co-chair. Book printed for Georgetown Day School, Washington DC. 1975.

*Delectables: A Treasury of Favorite Recipes.* Compiled and printed as a fundraiser for Women's Suburban Democratic Club. Montgomery County, Maryland. 1978.

*Favorite Recipes from Sew 'n Sow Garden Club 1976-2006.* Compiled and printed for 30th anniversary of Club.

Recipe Booklets compiled for the HSN Morning Study Group.
*2006 Oregano*     *2008 Calendula*
*2007 Lemon Balm*  *2009 Lavender*
*2007 Pelargonium* *2010 Dill*

Recipe Booklets compiled for Nashville Herb Society's Culinary workshops that I chaired.
*2008 Gifts from the Herb Garden*
*2009 Preserving Summer*

*Recipe Shower for Nancy Zuccaro.* Compiled and printed for docents at the Schermerhorn Symphony Center. January 2007.

*Recipe Booklet* compiled for the Installation Team of *Light: Bruce Munro at Cheekwood.* 2013.

*2013 PEO Gifts from the Herb Garden,* compiled for PEO program.

CPSIA information can be obtained
at www.ICGtesting.com
Printed in the USA
LVHW040107290819
629302LV00002B/2/P